W.H. Barker

Hebrew Lexicon

W.H. Barker

Hebrew Lexicon

ISBN/EAN: 9783337225827

Printed in Europe, USA, Canada, Australia, Japan

Cover: Foto ©Thomas Meinert / pixelio.de

More available books at **www.hansebooks.com**

T O

THE HONOURABLE

A N D

RIGHT REVEREND FATHER IN GOD

J A M E S,

LORD BISHOP OF St. *D A V I D's,*

T H I S

L E X I C O N

IS INSCRIBED

By His LORDSHIP'*s*

Moſt Obedient Humble Servant,

W. H. BARKER.

PREFACE.

THE writings of *Moses* and the *Prophets* come recommended to us with fuch facred folemnity, that fhould excite our moft earneft endeavours to underftand them in the language in which they were firft delivered; to effect this, and make if poffible the Hebrew language a part of fchool inftruction, the author of the following Lexicon, about three years fince, publifhed *a plain Grammar of that language*, and now commits to the Public the following fheets, calculated for the ufe of Schools, as well as for private Students. The knowledge of the original Scriptures are fo pleafant, and their beauties fo many, as far outweigh the fmall labour and time expended in the acquifition of their language. So effentially neceffary is the knowledge of thefe original Scriptures to the Minifters of GOD's Word, that he who is ignorant in this point fhould blufh, whenever he undertakes to explain to his hearers a paffage in the facred Code: It is in vain for him to alledge his fkill and knowledge of the Greek language; the Greek of the New Teftament can never be properly underftood by any one, who does not underftand the language of the Old. As all the Scriptures are a revelation from GOD, though they were delivered part by part, at different times, by different perfons, in different places, and in different ages, through the continued fpace of fifteen hundred years, from *Moses* to St. *John* in *Patmos*; yet they muft be every where confiftent in principles, views, fentiments, and

unifor-

uniformity of ſtyle, elſe the ALMIGHTY would be found to contradict himſelf; ſo then the New Teſtament is only the fulfilling of the Old: now who will venture to affirm that he underſtands the latter half of this revelation, when he is at the ſame time.ſo completely ignorant, that he knows not a word, or even a letter, in which the former was written?

IT was an expreſſion frequent in the mouth of *Melanchton*, that he preferred the knowledge of the Hebrew before all the wealth of a kingdom; and well he might, if he was a ſedulous enquirer after truth and knowledge; as a ſcholar he was acquainted with the language, from which all others have branched out as from a parent-ſtock, and which contained an hiſtory of many ages when other languages were mute, and other hiſtories contained nothing that could be depended upon. Without doubt, this was the unvaried language of our firſt parents, and the general one at the Diſperſion: As new objects occurred, and the Children of Iſrael became acquainted with trade, arts and ſciences, many new words might, nay muſt, have been introduced, and other old ones uſed in a more extended ſenſe, yet the ground work remained the ſame, as is ſufficiently evident from the firſt chapters of *Geneſis*, thus, אדם, *Adam*, had his name from דם, *to be like*, becauſe created in the likeneſs of GOD, *Gen.* I. 26. *Eve*, חוה, *i. e. Life*, was ſo named, becauſe ſhe was to be the mother of all living, *Gen.* 3. 20. *Cain*, קין, *i. e. Gain*, was ſo named by *Eve*, who at his birth ſaid, *I have gained* a man from the LORD; but *Abel*, אבל, *Lamentation*, for he was murdered,

and

and thence proceeded a train of woe and lamentation to his parents, and to the murderer in particular, who from that moment was proclaimed a fugitive and vagabond : No sooner was a Son born, to be *fet* in the place of the murdered *Abel*, than his mother named him *Set*, שת, *Seth*. Thefe and many other particulars might be brought of the language being in part the fame before the deluge, as it was in the time of *Ezra*, who fettled the Code of Hebrew Scripture. As this language has fuch evident marks of the higheft antiquity, for in all probability all others were at firft but dialects of it, the author of the following Lexicon has placed the moft evident derivatives in fuch languages as he was acquainted with at the bottom of the page, with fome mark of reference to the root from whence they are fuppofed to fpring : That they may be derived is fuppofed by the word being there placed, but the manner in which they are formed is not always mentioned, in order that the Student may, if he thinks proper, pafs them by unnoticed, or otherwife exercife his own ingenuity.

THE plan on which this Lexicon has been executed is that of Mr. *Pike*'s, who fo digefted his Work, as to eafe the attempt in fearching for the *Root*, which in the generality of books of this kind might have been fought for in feven or eight different places without fuccefs : All the reader has now to do is to obferve this general Rule, *Reject all affixes and letters acquired in forming, and under the three or two remaining letters, the root required may be found.* Sometimes whe᷍ ᷍ly two radicals remain, the ה
with

with an hyphen has been added in the Lexicon,
to fhew that it is not ftrictly radical: nor is
the ֿ֝, which in other Lexicons has been inferted in many roots of two letters, regarded
in this; neither is the feminine noun put down
unlefs neceffary, and it contained a fenfe different from the mafculine. Let it be remem-
bered alfo, that the *Defectives* in *Pe-nun* and
Pe-iod are ranked under their refpective perma-
nent letters, fo that the reader will find his
trouble much more eafed than when he was
obliged to attend to the old rule for finding the
root, which was this, *Reject all affixes and letters acquired in forming, if lefs than three remain,
add* ' *or* ֹ *to the beginning; or* ֿ֝ *or* ' *to the middle;
or double the fecond radical; or add* ה *or* א *to the
end.*

In the courfe of this work all the Chaldee
words, and fome Hebrew ones, have been fupplied, which Mr. *Pike* either purpofely omitted,
or elfe they efcaped his elaborate diligence. The
quotations that are interfperfed, and refer to the
chapter and verfe of the bible, are tranfcribed
from the above Gentleman, with the fame freedom as he tranfcribed them before from the excellent Concordance of Dr. *Taylor* of *Norwich*:
In a word, the author has taken from every
writer that lay in his way whatever favoured
his purpofe without thinking himfelf in the leaft
accountable: Whenever a paffage in Scripture
required a fenfe different from what was ufually
exhibited, it has been freely adopted, though not
without mentioning at the fame time how it had
been rendered by *others:* The Authors moftly
confulted were *Pike, Parkhurft, Taylor* and

Dr.

Dr. *Gregory Sharpe*, but moft of all the Scriptures themfelves.

THOSE who know how many Books muft be
turned over in a compilement of this fort, will
eafily pardon the inaccuracies that may occur, efpecially when he recollects with *Scaliger* the laborious toil of a Lexicon writer.

Si quem dura manet fententia judicis olim,
    Damnatum ærumnis fuppliciifque caput ;
Hunc neque fabrili laffent ergaftula maffâ,
    Nec rigidas, vexent foffa metalla manus ;
Lexica contexat, *nam cetera, quid moror?* omnes
    Pœnarum facies hic labor unus habet. .

To the Student the author would recommend
the being attentive to every particularity of the
language, as well as the different changes each
word might be fuppofed to undergo from a falfe
pronunciation, as this perhaps has been the fource
of greater variation in the original text than ufually imagined : A Scribe would naturally write
as he pronounced, and thus confound letters of
the fame organ, hence perhaps נשׁוּן, 2 *Sam.* 1. 22.
is written for נסוּן, and שׁוּר for סוּר, *Hof.* 9. 12.
words fuppofed to be thus changed, are noted in
the following work ; and the acute Critic might
find out fome hundreds more than are here noticed, though fome words of this kind are now
fo far confidered as feparate roots, that they have
obtained a feparate place for themfelves in every
Lexicon, thus שׁמך and סמך, שׁעף and סעף, are
confidered as diftinct roots, though evidently
related, if not quite the fame. It is to enable
the reader to judge of thefe interchanges that the
letters

letters in the following fhort Grammar are ran-
ged according to the organ of fpeech, by which
they are fuppofed to be pronounced, and at the
fame time it is hinted what letters not of the
fame organ do alfo interchange. There are fome
particular advantages, as Mr. *Pike* has well obferved, which this language has above all others.
In its alphabet it has but juft fo many letters
as anfwer all the fimple articulations of fpeech.
It has but two or three letters to each primitive
root. It has fixed upon thofe letters for ferviles, which are moft eafily pronounced. It va-
ries the root in the moft brief and expeditious
way by an addition of one or two of the ferviles.
It has no more moods, tenfes, numbers and
genders than are neceffary and nature requires.
Throughout all the derivatives of the fame root
the original idea is ftill preferved, thus גלל־ה, or
גול, *to roll.* When it doubles its laft radical, it
doubles as it were its idea, and גלל, is *to roll over
and over;* but when it doubles both its radicals,
as in גלגל, it fignifies *to roll repeatedly over and
over again,* or *repeatedly roll round and round,*
hence this laft word fignifies *a wheel,* or any
thing in perpetual rotation: Again, when a
root takes א, this letter either increafes or elfe
diminifhes, and inverts the fenfe, thus נבא, to be
hollow, comes from נב־ה, to be *prominent,* the א
inverting the meaning, but דכא, fignifies to *deftroy,* to *fmite fo as to kill,* from דכ־ה, fimply to
fmite down. Many more particulars are mentioned in this Lexicon under each fervile letter,
and more ftill might be obferved, but to notice
every fingularity would lead us into a differta-
tion on the language. As the origin of alpha-
betical

betical writing has been hinted under the letter
א, and the ancient form of the letters frequently
mentioned, the author has prefixed the Samaritan form to the Hebrew, as evidently the oldeſt
we are now acquainted with.   Such as the following ſhort Grammar does not ſatisfy, are referred to a larger one, publiſhed by the ſame
hand, with Biblical examples, at *Carmarthen*, in
1773.

THE following ſheets were laboured with a
good deſign ; may the bleſſing of GOD attend
the uſe of them.

FREE-SCHOOL, CARMARTHEN,
      June 26, 1776.

The following ABBREVIATIONS *frequently occur in
this* LEXICON.

Der. Derivatives.   *It*. Italian.   *W*. Welſh.   *Lat*.
Latin.   *Lit, tr*. Literis tranſpoſitis.   ( ) Radical
meaning, not in the Hebrew. *Maſ*. Maſculine.   *Fem*.
Feminine.   ה-, the ה not ſtrickly radical. *Others*, as
rendered by others, *&c*.

A C O M-

HEBREW LEXICON.

THE form of the Hebrew letters, now in ufe, is modern and different from the ancient charaćters, which are ftill retained in the Samaritan; the rude and uncooth fhapes of thefe plainly indicate, that they were originally the outlines of thofe fymbolic figures formerly made ufe of. Egypt is univerfally allowed to have been the parent of idolatry, which had its rife, in all probability, from the ufe of fymbols in the communication of ideas. Inftead of this uncertain method, fome great genius, confidering the powers of the human voice, abridged fome of the moft remarkable of thefe fymbols, and adapted them to founds; hence the names as well as the rude charaćters of the old Phœnician or Samaritan alphabet, might reprefent the image whence the charaćter had been taken: thus אלף which fignifies an ox, might in the firft rude alphabet have been the abridged fymbol of that animal.

א

is the firft vowel and letter of the Hebrew and almoft every other alphabet, as a numeral it ftands for 1, and with two dots over it א̈ 1000. --- It is alfo a fervile (1.) when *prefixed*, (from אני the 1ft pronoun, it denotes the firft perfon fingular future as אפקד *I will vifit*; (2.) it forms fome verbal nouns as אצבע *a finger*, from צבע *to be oblong*; (3.) *poftfixed* to verbs (perhaps from לא) like the alpha of the Greek, it inverts their meaning, as

B ברא

ברא *to concrete*, from בר *to fecrete*; (4.) from הוא, like the Greek alpha it marks fomething eminent in the idea, or adds emphafis, as חבא *to take fhelter*, from חב *to hide*; (5.) it is paragogic, *i. e.* frequently added to words and fupplies the place of adverbs : א paragogic is annexed to fuch perfons of verbs as end in ו and has there the force of הוא from which it feems borrowed, *Eccl.* 11. 3. יהו inftead of יהי הוא there *that tree* fhall *certainly* be. *Ifai.* 28. 12. אבוא they would not, *though thus fpoken to*.

אב־ה to *fwell* with defire, confent, be willing.   אב· a ftate of fwelling greennefs, *Job* 8. 12. green fruits, *Cant.* 6.·10. a father from his affection; inventor, teacher, leader, pl. maf. אב, אוב, אבות. a conjurer, familiar fpirit, one fwoln or infpired, inflation. אבות bottles, bags made of fkins. אבוי forrow, defirous of relief, *Prov.* 23.29. אביון poor, wanting. אביונה defire, the caper tree which excites both appetite and luft. איב to fwell with hatred, *Exod.* 23. 22. איבה bitter enmity. יאב to long for. אביב אבב verdure, new corn, month of corn (March) when the corn eared.*

אבד (בד) to *perifh*, deftroy. אבדה a thing perifhed. אבדון, אבדן deftruction.

אבחה, אבח terror, or clafhing of fwords, *Ezec.* 21. 15.†

אבטח *Num.* 11. 5. melons. *See* בטח

אבך *Ifai.*9.18.to *evaporate*, mount up, be diffipated. אבל to be defolate; mourn; a particle of forrowful affertion, in truth. אובל, אבל a river. *See* בל

אבן a *ftone* (difpofed in ftrata, fee בן); a ftool, feat of ftone; a weight.‡

* Derivatives from this root are ἥβη, youth , α.ἄει, alas ; πατηρ, pater, father; βουτις, obba, a bottle ; abba, abbot; ἀνεω, to defire ; ἀνυ , grandfather.   † W. afwch.   ‡ Even.

אבל *nevertheless, but, yet: Conj.*

אבנט a belt or girdle (quafi א־בנת *the decent* garb.)*

אבעבע blains. *fee* בעה.

אבם to ftuff, cram with food. אבום ftalled, fatted, a ftall or crib for fattening. מאבסים ftore-
houfes, magazines of provifions, *Jer.* 50..26.†

אבק duft; to wreftle, raife a duft; powder of aromatics, *Cant.* 3. 6.

אביר, אבר ftrong, mighty, valiant; bulls, horfes,
Jer 47. 3. a wing, to wing, *Job* 39. 26.‡

אברך father of bleffings, *Gen.*41.43. R. בא and רך

אגדה, אגד a bunch or bundle, *Exod.* 12. 22. *Ifai.*
58.6. a troop or company, 2 *Sam.* 2.25. a bundle
of rays of light which reach to the earth, *Amos* 9.
6. R. גד.

אגוז a nut, walnut, *Cant.*6.11. R. גז to protect.

אגל a drop, *Job* 38. 28. R. גל to roll.

אגם, אגמן a lake or pool; a caldron, *Job* 41. 20.
an aquatic rufh or reed; a band made of rufh,
or according to others an hook bent like a reed,
Job 41. 2. R. גם to abound.

אגן a bafon, goblet R. גן to protect. Goblets were
covered. ‖

אגף the wing of an army. אגפי auxiliaries, parti-
fans R. גף to adhere.

אגר to collect, gather, carry in corn or fruit. אגרה
אגרא a letter with intelligence collected. אגורת a
fmall coin probably the fame as the גרה 1 *Sam.* 2,
36. R. גר to move §.

אגרטלי bafons, *Ezra* 1.9. R. אגר, and טל what falls.

אד a mift or vapour, *Gen.* 2. 6. *Job* 36. 27. אוד a

---

* Der. bonnet, bind, band, &c.   † Obefus, fat; Apis; Βους, bos,
an ox; and the letters of this root being tranfpofed, or read from left
to right, we have fepe, as præfepe, a ftall for oxen, and fepio, to inclofe.
‡ W. briaw; οβριμος, ftrong; αβρος, fair. lit. tra. robur, ftrength.
‖ Αγγος, αγγειον, a veffel.   § Αγειρω, to gather, αγγαροι, letter carriers;
agger, an heap.

fire-brand emitting fparks, *Ifai.* 7.4. *Amos* 4. 11.
Zech. 3. 2. אורת, ארות n. f. pl. motives; becaufe
of, concerning. איד calamity, dejection. R. יד to
caft forth.*

אדב to wafte, confume, grieve, torment, 1 *Sam.*
2. 33.

אדם to be red, died red, a fardius or ruby; Adam,
man, *fee* דם. אדמה ground, red earth, vegetable
mould. אדמדם, אדמונה very red. †

אדן a bafe or focket. ארני, אדון, אדן, a fuftainer,
lord, mafter, an hinge. A particle of time, then.
R. דן to judge.‡

אדר to be magnificent, pompous, glorious, famous,
&c. אדיר mighty, noble, excellent, &c. *a robe
of honour* adorned with fur. אדרת אדר magnificence, אדרי threfhing floors, *Dan.* 2. 35. אדר
the twelfth month of the Jews (part of Febuary
and March) famous for the event noticed, *Eft.* 9.1.‖

אדרגזריא nobles, prefects, *Dan.* 3.2,3. R. אדר and
גדר decree.

אדרזדא pompoufly, *Ezra* 7.23. R. זד pride.

אדרכן a *Daric,* a coin ftruck by Darius the Mede,
Ezra who revifed the Chronicles might reduce the
money in David's time to what was known in his
own, *Ezra* 8.27. 1 *Chron.* 29.7. value about 1 *l.* 5 *s.* §

אדרמלך Adrammeleck (R. אדר and מלך king)
name of an idol, 2 *Kings* 17. 31.

†   אהה an expreffion of nature in grief, ah! alas.

אהב to love (from אב q.) נאהב lovely, אהב אהבה
love, מאהב a lover.

אהל to fix, eftablifh (from אל to protect), pitch a
tent, a tent. אהלים, אהלות aloes, an aromatic

---

* Οιτος, calamity; ατω, to ruin. lit. tra. ὄαιω, to burn. † αὀαμας,
diamond. ‡ αὀωι:, dominus; Sp. don. ‖ αὀξος:, abundant;
αἴ;, æther. § ὀξαχμη, drachm, dram.

                                                      tree

+ *a clidulud*

tree, with *ſhadowing* branches fit to tent under.*
אורה to ſigh after, chooſe, deſire, long, luſt after,
מאוי אות, תאוה, deſire, luſt, תאות utmoſt bounds;
rather, deſirable productions, *Gen.* 49.26. נאוה de-
ſireable, comely, נאות pleaſant places, paſtures,
habitations. או a particle implying *choice*, or, או ‡
either, whether, if, &c. אוי, אויה an exclama-
tion in diſtreſs, oh! woe! alas! אי a place or
country diſtant from Judea, to find which they
muſt aſk *Where? Gen.* 10.5. *Iſai.* 23.2,6. איה a
ravenous bird of the hawk kind, a merlin, *Job* 28.
7. *Lev.* 11. 44. *Deut.* 14.13. איים Jackalls, *Iſai.*
13: 22.†
אוב אוד, אול, &c. *ſee* אב &c. omitting the ו
אז, אז then, at that time, מאז from there, ſince. †
אזא אזה to heat with fire, *Dan.* 3. 19, 22. ‡
אזב, אזוב *Hyſſop*, *ſee* זב. ‖
אזד eſcape, get away, *Dan.* 2. 5, 8.
אזל to go away, begone, *Deut.* 32. 36. *Prov.* 20.14.
be ſpent, 1 *Sam.* 9.7. fail, *Job* 14. 11. מאוזל going to and fro, *Ezek.* 27. 19. תאזלי for תזלי gad-
deſt thou about, *Jer.* 2. 36.
אזן the ear, to weigh, give ear, conſider, ponder,
Eccleſ. 12. 9. מאוזנים balances, ſcales hanging
like ears. אזן a girdle, weapon, *Deut.* 23. 14.
ſee זן §
אזק a chain or handcuff, *Jer.* 40. 1, 4. R. זק
אזר to gird, bind round; the ancient garments were
long, whence to *gird up the loins* was to prepare
for action, hence it ſignifies military ſtrength
and fortitude. אזור a girdle. ¶

* Der. αυλη, aulæum, hall.   † μαω, to deſire earneſtly; ευ, well;
οιαι, woe! ευ, where; heu, væ, alas; αια, alas. W. dihewyd.   ‡ αζω
to dry, alſo roaſt; αζα, foot; ζεω, to be hot, ſeeth.   ‖ υσσωπος, hy-
ſop.   § ευς, ους, an ear.   ¶ ζειρα σειρα, a chain or cord.

אח־ה to confociate; אח a brother, relation, coufin, country-man. אחות a fifter. אחוה brotherhood, *Zech.* 11. 14. אח an hearth or grate where fuel is heaped to burn, *Jer.* 36. 22, 23. אחו a flag, whence many *brothers* from one ftock, *Job* 8. 11. a meadow, place where flags grow, *Gen.* 41. 2, 18. אָח a natural note of grief, ah! heh! *Ezek.* 6. 11. האח a particle of gladnefs, aha! ahah. אֲחֲלַו O that, from אח and לי to me, 2 *Kings* 5. 2. *Pfal.* 119. 5. אוח, אהים doleful creatures or yells of wild beafts, *Ifai.* 36. 22, 23. אהיה a declaration, from חוה *

אחד from אחת *one*, each, any, firft, once. *v.* יחד

אחז to *take*, feize, lay hold of, poffefs. אחזה poffeffion.†

אֲחֲלִי O that, *v.* אח ‡

אחמתא a veffel, cheft, &c. *Ezra* 6. 2.

אחר, אחרי behind, after, afterwards, another; to come after, tarry, defer, delay, אחור backward, hinder part, the weft, אחרון latter, laft, future, hindermoft, afterward, weftern, אחרנית backward, back again, אחרית laft, latter end, extremity. ‖

אחשדרפנים *Perfian noblemen* who waited near the king, from אחש great, דר to *remain* and פני *in the prefence.*

אחשתרנים *mules* in Perfic, *Efter* 8. 10, 14.

אחת fem. one. *fee* אחד

אט, לאט, לאטי foftly, flowly. אטים conjurers, charmers who in a low manner muttered their charms, *Ifai.* 19. 3.

אטד bramble, thorn, *Judg.* 9. 14, 15. *Pf.* 58. 9.

אטם to fhut, ftop the lips, *Prov.* 17. 28. ears, *Pf.*

---

* Der. ειαμ̄ιη, meadow; hay.   † ιχουσα, poffeffing.   ‡ αξαλι, I wifh.   ‖ other, after; W. gohir. αιριον, morrow.

אֲחֹורַנִּית *backward*   18. 5.

18. 5. applied to windows, narrow, clofed, 1 *Kings* 6. 5. *Ezek.* 40. 16.

אָטוּן fine linen yarn, or tapeftry made of fuch yarn.*

אָטַר to fhut, obftruct, clofe, *Pf.* 69. 15. left-hand-ed, obftructed in the right hand, *Judg.* 3. 15.†

אַי, אֵיה where; whence אִי for אוֹי *Eccl.* 4, 10: 10. 16. אִיִּם Jackalls, אַיָּה a Kite. *fee* אוֹ־ה

אִיב, אֵיד, אֵיךְ, &c. *fee* אַב &c. omitting י

אֵים terrible, אֵימָה terror, אֵימָתָה deadly terror, from אִים and מֵת to die. אֵמְתָנִי terrible, *Dan.* 7. 7.

אַךְ a particle of earneftnefs, furely, neverthelefs, but only, &c.

אֵיךְ, אֵיכָה, אֵיכְכָה how, where? from אִי and כֹּה thee.

אַכְזָר cruel. *fee* כָזַר

אָכַל to eat, feed, devour, confume, אֹכֶל, אוֹכִיל, אוֹכִיל, מַאֲכָל, אָכְלָה meat, food, fuel. מַאֲכֶלֶת a knife or fword.‡

אָכֵן certainly, furely, verily, &c. *fee* כֵּן

אָכַף to crave, or urge. *fee* כַף

אִכָּר an hufbandman. *fee* כָּר ‖

אֵל־ה this root occurs not as a verb; but the radi-cal idea is fuppofed to mean interpofition, hence it is the name of God as an interpofer; alfo to adjure, fwear, curfe; an oath, curfe, *Lam.* 3. 65. אֱלוֹהַּ a title of Chrift who was to be a curfe for us. אֱלֹהִים God, Gods; the divine Trinity mutually *engaged* for our redemption, or Him by whom we fwear and to whofe curfe we are fubjected: *princes, rulers,* judges fworn to protect, and who have power to curfe their fubjects. אֵלֶּה the

---

* Der. οθονη, οθονιον, linen, thread; Αθηνη, Minerva. † ατερ, with-out. ‡ ακολος, bit of bread; κολον, χιλος, food; χολας, κολον, inteftines; ειλος, lip; κωλην, gammon of bacon; κωλην, culina, kitchen; colo, to train; culinder; and with *mem* prefixed, macellum, a market; μακελη, cleaver. ‖ Ager, acre.

large

C

large rump of the eaftern fheep, a part devoted to God and confumed by fire, *Exod.*29.22. *Lev.* 3.9.   אל prefixed to nouns fame as ל *to*, &c. but preceeding verbs future, fame as לא: אל to, at, againft, towards, of, among.   אלול אליל an idol, thing of no value, vain, אלול *Neh.* 6. 15. a month (part of Auguft and September) when nothing remained in the fields.   אללי woe to me, I am come to nought, *Job* 10.15. *Mic.*7.1.   אלי lament, *Joel* 1.8.   אלה, אל pronoun *thefe*.   אלו if, tho', *Eccl.* 6.6. *Eft.*7.4. behold, fee, lo, *Dan.* 2.31.--- אול אולי as a *noun* a defence, *Pf.* 73.4. defenders, 2 *Kings* 24.15. a particle of uncertainty, peradventure, if fo be, &c.   אוילי, אויל a fool acting uncertainly, rafhly; foolifh, mad, *evil*; אולת folly. איל ftrength, defence, power, a mighty one; ftrong cattle with horns for a defence, a ram, ftag, hart, hind; leader; porch or fome principal part of a building.   אלה, אלון, אל a ftrong oak. אילות *Pf.* 22.19. ftrength.   לאל in the power of, *Gen.* 31.29.   אל mighty God.   הואיל יאל to *fix*, refolve upon, attempt, begin, be pleafed with, be content, inflexible.   נואל, נאל to be refolute, obftinate and foolifh, Jer. 50.36. to dote.*

אלגביש great hail-ftones, *Ezek.* 13.11,13: 38.22. *fee* גבש

אלגומים (from אל not, and גם to fill) a wood which will not rot, or imbibe water;

אלמנים (from אל and מג to diffolve) the algum, or almug tree, a fpecies of the cedar, or fome hard wood not fubject to decay, Brafil-wood, 1 *Kings* 10.11, 12.

אלח to rot, be putrid, ftink, *Job* 15.16. *Pf.*14.3. and 53.4. †

* Der. ελλος, a fawn; υλη, alnus, tree; ελαινος, the olive; nil, nihil, nothing; W. clain, ffōl; evil.   † Oleo, to fcent.

אלך

אֵלֶךְ pron. thofe, *Dan.* 3. 12.

אָלַם to tie together, bind; אֵלֶם, אֲלֻמָּה a fheaf.
אָלַם, נֶאֱלַם to be tongue-tied, dumb; אַלְמֹנִי
(from אַל and נִי I) fuch an one, fuch and fuch
not naming perfon or thing, *Ruth* 4. 1. 1 *Sam.*
21. 2. אֵילִם, אוּלָם, אֻלָּם an arch, vault, porch
of materials compacted together. אוּלָם a particle of firmnefs, but, truly. אַלְמָן (from אַל not
and מָנָה a part) forfaken, widdowed, one who
has loft her *part*, or perhaps who moans in filence; אַלְמָנוּת, אַלְמוֹן widowhood.

אֵלָן a grove of oaks, a plain. *fee* אָל*

אֵלֶּן, אֵלֵּין thefe, thofe, *Dan.* 2. 44.

אָלַף to guide, direct, teach; to learn, *Prov.* 22.25.
a duke, director, leader. אַלּוּף difciple, inftruction.
אֶלֶף a thoufand, the chief divifion of an army,
אַלּוּפִים heads of thoufands, *Gen.* 36. אֶלֶף an ox.†

אָלַץ to urge, teaze, moleft, *Judges* 16. 16.‡

אָם to fuftain; אֲמוֹת pofts, pillars, fupporters, *Ifa.*
6. 4. אֵם a mother fupporting her child, a me-
tropolis, 2 *Sam.* 20. 19. *Jer.* 15. 8. the mother of
a way, *i. e.* where two ways meet, *Ezek.* 21. 21.
אָמָה a female flave, *viz.* porter; alfo the arm
which fupports a man in reclining; a cubit, a-
bout 22 inches. אוֹם, לְאוֹם a family or nation
fprung from one mother; אִם conditional particle, if, fuppofing that. אִים terrible, אֵימָה
terror, death, fear; אֵמִים אֵימִים terrors; giants,
Deut. 2. 11. idols, *Jer.* 5. 38. *fee* אַיִּ ||

אָמַל to faint, be weak; אֻמְלַל languifh, be very
feeble. R. מָל.

אָמַן to be firm, ftable, trufty; fupported, eftablifh-

---

* Der. with Beth prefixed, βαλανος an acorn which grows on the oak.
† αλφω find, ιλεφα; elephant. lit. tr. πολυς many, φυλη tribe. ‡ αλυσος
intolerable; and with Mem prefixed, moleftus, moleft. || Arm.
W. amaeth. amo μαμμαια, μαμμη μαμμα mamma, μαια nurfe, οιμη road,
μην truly.

C

ed;

ed; fo be it. האמין believe; אמן faithful. אמונה
fet office, truft, faith, faithfulnefs, truth. אמנות
ftrong pillars, 2 *Kings* 18.16. אמנם אמנם truly,
indeed, in truth; אמת truth. אמן a fofter father,
אמנת a nurfe. אמון a child, a nurfling.*

אמן multitude. *fee* המן

אמץ to fortify, make ftrong, courageous. אמיץ
ftrong, אמצה ftrength. מאמצים forces, *Job* 36.
19. אמץ bay colour, *Zech.* 6. 3, 7.

אמר to branch out, fay, think, refolve, command,
appoint, &c. אמרי, אמיר branch, branches, *Ifai.*
17.6,9. אמר, אמרה a word, faying. מאמר a decree. האמיר to advouch. התאמר to boaft.†

אמש dark, gloomy, gloominefs, *Job* 30. 3. yefter-
night, late in the evening, lately.

אמת truth. *fee* אמן

אנה, אן whither, where. אנה ואנה hither and thither, any whither. עד אנה how long? אנה to
mourn, lament, *Ifai.* 3. 26: 19. 8. to happen as
occafion of forrow, caufe to come, impel, deliver, *Exod.* 21. 13. happen, affault, befal, *Pf.* 91.
12. *Prov.* 12. 21. feek a quarrel, 2 *Kings* 5. 7.
תאניה, אניה *Ifai.* 29. 2. *Lam.* 2. 5. grief, lamentation, moan. תאנה occafion of grief, *Judg.* 14.
4. impetuofity of luft, *Jer.* 2. 24. התאנן to
complain, *Num.* 11. 1. *Lam.* 3. 39. און, אן iniquity caufing moan, vanity, trouble, idolatry;
an idol, *Ifai.* 56. 3. תאנים lies, vanities, *Ezek.*
24. 12. אנים unjuft men, *Prov.* 11. 9. און
impetuous ftrength, activity. אניה, אני a fhip
or navy. אין no, not, without, nothing, nobody.
אנה, אנא I pray thee. אנכי, אני pron. I, me;
plu. נהנו, אנחנו, אנו we, us.‡

* Der. Man, *pro* truly, Amen. † lit. tr. ερμης Mercury, god of
fpeech, ερμηνευω interpret; ramus, branch, rumor. ρημα word. W. ym-
adrodd. ‡ anx, nænia, forrow; na that; ιαυ; a fhip; unus one;
any, aneu without.

אנה to figh, groan; אנחה a figh, grief, groan. אנחנו we miferable.*

אנך to diffolve, melt; lead, a plumb-line, *Amos* 7. 7. אנכי I.

אנס to compel, *Eft.* 1. 8. give trouble, *Dan.* 4.6.†

אנף to breathe thro' the noftrils, be angry; אף noftrils, anger, face. אנפה a furious bird, hawk, *Lev.* 11. 19. *Deut.* 14. 8. אנפי face, countenance, *Dan.* 2. 46: 3. 19.‡

אנק to cry out in anguifh; אנקה a crying out; ferret, lizard, from its doleful cry, *Lev.* 11. 30.

אנש to be fick to death, אנוש incurable; mortal man. נשים women, wives. *fee* נש §

אסוך a pot of oil. *fee* סוך

אסם barn, ftorehoufe, *Deut.* 28. 8. *Prov.* 3. 10. *fee* סם

אסן mifchief, productive of death, *Gen.* 42. 4, *&c.* *fee* סן ¶

אסף to gather, collect, bring in, affemble, gather in, take away; and from סוף to confume; מאסף rereward, *Numbers* 10. 25. אסיף in-gathering. אספות, אספים affemblies. אספסף a collected multitude. ::

אספרנא (from ספר to recount) ftudioufly, exactly. אסר to bind with cords, chains, unite; to bind by a vow, imprifon, to harnefs a chariot, fet an army in array, מוסר, מסרת a bond, אסיר a prifoner. אסר an obligatory decree, *Dan.* 6, 7. 8.‖‖‖

אע, אעא wood, *Ezra* 5. 8. *Dan.* 5. 4.

אף (from אנף) the nofe, noftrils, face; wrath, fury. As a particle, alfo, yea, certainly, plainly;

---

* Der. anxious. W. chwi. wane, wan, want. † W. annos. onus burden. ‡ ανοπαια bird of prey. W. enaid, wyneb. ‖ anguifh, anxious, ango. W. uchenaid. lit. tra. xηυυω cano to found; χαυω yawn or bawl. § αινος miferable. lit. tra. νοσος fick. ¶ σειυω hurt; fin. :: Cπαω draw, νοσφιζω withdraw, νοσφιν apart. ‖‖‖ σειρα.

how

how much more, how much lefs. אפה to bake;
מאפה אופה, אפה, a baker. תפינים pieces baked, *Lev.*6.21. אפה, איפה, א, איף an ephah, a meafure
equal to 7 gallons 2 qts. half pint wine meafure.
איפוא איפה, אפו, אפוא, where, now, here, what
fort, (the א and ה are here paragogic) אפף to
furround with violence.*

אפד to bind clofe or gird a garment, *Exod.* 29. 5.
Lev. 8. 7. אפד, אפוד, אפדה an ephod, a garment belonging to the high prieft. אפדת an
idol's garment, *Ifai.* 30. 22.

אפדן a royal tent, pavilion, *Dan.* 11. 45.†

אופז Uphaz, *Dan.* 10. 5. *Jer.* 10, 9. *fee* פז

אפל, אפלה, מאפל dark, darknefs; מאפליה (the יה
from יהוה being paragogic) grofs darknefs, *Jer.*2.
31. אפילת not grown up, concealed in darknefs,
Exod. 9. 32.‡

אפן, אופן a wheel (from פן) ||

אפס to fail, ceafe to be; end, failing, defect,
nought; ancles, extremities of the feet, *Ezek.*47.
3. only, neverthelefs, except, none befides.

אפע a viper, badly render'd nought, *Ifai.* 41. 24.
fee פע §

אפק to reftrain, conftrain, keep within bounds, to
retain, refrain; force onefelf, 1*Sam.* 13.12. אפיקים
mighty, *i.e.* men retaining courage, *Job* 12. 21.
אפיק a channel, river, ftream; compact, firm,
ftrong; אפיקי ftrong pieces, channels, *Job* 40.18.
גאוה אפיקי מגנים his pride (fcales) is the cavi-
ties of fhields, *Job* 41. 15. ¶

אפתים a kind of tribute, *Ezra* 4. 13. ||||

---

* Der. αὖ, face; שרה לשם to drefs meat; oven; αβαρ cake. W.
pobi; αμφι about. † apto apt. ‡ πιλος, pullus ruffet; pallor
pale. W. Ffael, pabell. || απηνη carriage. § οφι; viper. ¶ πηγνυ
ñgo; pango, fix, πηγη fountain. Fr. empecher. |||| affatim abun-
dantly.

אֵפֶר aſhes, אוֹפִיר.ophir. אִפִּרְיוֹן *פר *fee

אוּן ,אַיִן narrow, *Joſh*. 17. 15. haſty, *Prov*. 21. 5:
29. 20. to preſs, be ſtraitened, haſten.†

אָצַל near, beſides, by; to place near oneſelf, ſelect,
reſerve; אֲצִילִים nobles, ſelect ones, *Ezod*. 24.11.
אַצִּיל an arm-pit; אַצִּילָה a great cubit, *i.e.* reaching to the arm-pit, *Ezek*. 41. 8.‡

אָצַר to ſtore or treaſure up. אוֹצָר a treaſure, trea-
ſury.‖

אַקּוֹ a wild goat, from its cry, *Deut*.15.5. *fee* אָנַק

אוֹר ,אָר to flow, ſhine, light, enlighten; a river,
Amos 8.8. מָאוֹר a light, luminary; מְאוּרָה a den
open to the light, *Iſai*.11.8. אָרָה to pluck, tear
off, crop; eat, devour, *Pſ*. 80. 12. *Cant*. 5. 1.
ſet on fire, or tear off, *Iſai*. 27. 11. אָרֹת herbs,
2 *Kings* 4. 39. *Iſai*. 6. 19. אֲרֻיוֹת ,אֲרָיוֹת ſtalls.
אֲרִי ,אַרְיֵה the tearer, *i. e.* a lion. אֲרִיאֵל ,אַרְאֵל
lion of God, lion-like. אוּרִים Urim and וְתֻמִּים
Thummim, lights and perfections, *Exod*. 28. 30.
perhaps ſhould be rendered ſtones *irradiating* and
perfect; or perhaps *Urim* and *Thummim* might be
put on the breaſt-plate, as *Holineſs to the Lord*
was on the mitre. יְאֹר a river, flood. אָרַר to
curſe, מְאֵרָה curſing. אֲרוּ to ſee, behold, *Dan*.7.2.§

אָרַב to lie in wait, in ambuſh, מַאֲרָב ambuſh-
ments, a den, place of ambuſh, window, hole,
chimney, *Hoſ*. 13.3. אָרֻבוֹת ſpoils taken by ambuſh, *Iſai* 25. 11. אַרְבֶּה a locuſt, graſs-hopper.
fee רב

אָרַג to weave; a weaver, a weaver's ſhuttle, *Job*
7. 6. אַרְגָּז a coffer, 1 *Sam*.6,8,11,15. ¶

רגם *fee* אַרְגָּמָן ,אַרְגְּוָנָא ,אַרְגָּוָן purple. *fee* רגם

* Der. Africa; τεφρα duſt; frio, crumble. † Haſte. ‡ axilla,
arm-pit; Fr. aiſelle; ala, wing. ‖ σωρευω σορος acervus, amaſs; ϑησαυρος
treaſure. § αρα curſe; air, hour, year, heart, hearth, jar. W.
awyr, dwyn. αρω lift up. ¶ εργανη, Minerva; αραχνη, araneus.
Fr. araignee. ſpider.

ארז a Cedar: the radical idea is *firmnefs*, and ftill remains in the Arabic.

ארח to journey; a way, path, manner; a traveller, wayfaring man; ארחות company of travellers, *Ifai.* 21. 13. ארחה provifion for a journey, allowance.*

ארך long, length, to be long, prolonged, tarry. ארוכה health, the prolongation of life.†

ארמן a palace. *fee* רם

ארן, ארון an ark or cheft; an afh, *Ifai.* 44. 14. *fee* רן ‡

ארנבת the *hare*, *Lev.* 11.6. *Deut.* 14.7. from ארה to crop and ניב the produce of the ground.

ארע the fame as ארץ

ארץ the earth, a country, land, ground.‖

ארקא *Jer* 10. 11. the fame as ארץ §

ארש to betroth, efpoufe, ארשת *Pfalm* 21. 2. requeft or betrothing.¶

אש fire. אשה offering made by fire. אשישיה, אשש 2 *Sam.* 6. 19. 1 *Chron.* 16. 3. *Cant.* 2. 5. *Hof.* 3. 1. *Ifai.* 16. 8. a flagon; rather confectionaries prepared by fire. אשישים, אשש *Ifai.* 14. 7. אשיות *Jer.* 50. 15. foundations. איש (*fee* יש) a man, hufband, אשה woman, wife. התאששו to fhew yourfelves men, or be fired at onefelf, *Ifai.* 46. 8. אשון, *fee* ישן. יאש to defpair, give over, *Eccl.* 2. 20. נואש defpair, 1 *Sam.* 27. 1. defperate, fruitlefs, vain, *Job* 6. 26. without hope. ‖‖

אשד a fpring or ftream, *Num.* 21. 15. *Deut.* 4. 49. *fee* שד

אשך the ftones, tefticles, *Lev.* 21. 20. ‡‡

---

* Der. W. cyfarwys. ἐρχομαι go.   † αρκυς net; εςιγω ftretch out; αρκεω arceo keep off.   ‡ ornus, wild afh; ηριον urn.   ‖ εζα earth; lit. tr, Ceres; hard, hurt. W. dacar.   § ωχρα ocre.   ¶ caςις uxores, wives; αρεςον a reft.   ‖‖ afhes; εςια vefta; aflo, roaft; αιlus, heat. ‡‡ χοςχη fcrotum.

אשל

אשל a grove, *Gen.*21.33. tree, 1 *Sam.*22.6: 31.13.
אשלא a rope, cord, or band, made perhaps of
twifted fhrubs.*

אשם liable to punifhment, to trefpafs, be guilty,
make defolate, deftroy, a trefpafs offering, אשמה
guilt, &c.   אשמן defolate place, *Ifai.* 59. 18.
אשימא 2 *Kings* 17. 30. Afhima the expiator, idol
of Hamath. *fee* שם and יישם†

אש, אשון darknefs, blacknefs, *Prov.*7.9. obfcure,
Prov. 20.20. pupil of the eye, *Deut.*32.10. *Pfal.*
17. 8. *Prov.*7.2.

אשף a quiver, cafe for arrows.   אשף *Dan.* 1. 20:
2. 2. an aftrologer.‡

אשפות dung, dunghill, *fee* שפת ||

אשר to proceed, go on, *Prov.* 4. 14: 9. 6. be fuc-
cefsful, happy, bleffed; promote happinefs : the
pron. who, which, that, &c. a conjunction, &c.
אשרי fteps, fuccefses.   אשרה a grove facred to
idol worfhip where men prayed for happinefs.
תאשור fome *thriving* tree, perhaps ever-green,
Ifai. 41. 19: 9. 13.   אשרו relieve, righten, put
for ישרו *Ifai.* 1. 17.

אתה to come near, approach.   את, אות a particle,
the, with, to, from, &c. a pronoun, את, אתה
thou.   את a coulter, ploughfhare, 1 *Sam.*13. 20.
Ifai. 2. 4. אתיות things to come; התיו brought,
*Ifai.*21.14. come, *Jer.*12.9. ית', אתא *Deut.*33.
21. to haften.   איתון an entrance, *Ezek.* 40. 15.
את, אות a fign, mark, enfign, token. יאת to confent, *Gen.*34.15. יאתה fubmiffion, acquiefcence,
Jer. 10. 7.§

את איתן ftrong, hard, ftrength; אתון the Zebra
or female afs, famous in the eaft for fpeed and

---

* Der. affylum, αλσος grove.   † afham--ed. lit. tr.μισος; Fr. me-
chant, guilty.   ‡ σοφος fapiens, wife. || σπατιλη, σπελιθς;, dung.
§ ad, to, at; lit. tr. tu, τυ thou, thee, the.   W. daeth.

                                                    ftrength;

ftrength; אתן ftrength of vegetation, *Gen.* 49.11.
אתנים a month (part of September and October)
1 *Kings* 8.2. אתון a furnace.*

אתנן, אתנה hire, reward. *fee* תן

אתיק, אתנק a gallery. *fee* נתק and תק

אתר a fpy. *fee* תר alfo a place, *Ezek.* 5.15.

ב

בית is the firft confonant and fecond letter of the
Hebrew alphabet, is a labial and fhuts the mouth
which א had opened. This letter has the outlines of an houfe or hollow cave, which is the
meaning of its name :† It is one of the eleven
ferviles, and more frequently occurs in this than
almoft any other language; (1.) when prefixed,
from בה *hollow*, it fignifies *in, into, with, among,
on account of*, Gen. 29.18. Deut. 19.21. againft,
Num.21.7. of, Lev. 6.2. by, Exod. 14.21. after, Num. 28.26. according to, Numb. 14.34.
upon, above, 1 Sam. 8.11. 1 Chron. 5.2. (2.)
prefixed to an infinite, imports the time when a
thing *is done* or *in doing*, as בפקדו when he vifited.
(3.) it alfo expreffes what the grammarians call
the fuperlative degree, as היפה בנשים fair among
women, *i. e.* faireft or very fair.

בא, בוא to come, go, enter; applied to time, come,
advance, *Jud.* 14.18. בטרם יבא חרסה before
the fun advanced, *i. e.* before noon. הביא to
bring in, בוא מובא, מבוא entry, advancing in,
תבואה revenue, produce, fruits, increafe, income.
אבי, הבי, מבי, *fee* בי. יבו is ufed for יבאו ----

* Der. Αιθνη Ætna; αιθω burn; 9ιω, 9ιω it run; autumn.   † Βαιτα in
Tyrian is an houfe, in old Greek it is αιτα, in Latin ædes, in Ægyptian αθ. The habitations of many nations of old were tents covered
with fkins; and βαιτης is ftill a fheep's fkin in the Greek.

נבא to prophefy, נבא a prophet, נבאה a pro-
phetefs, נבואה a prophecy.*

באר to open, declare, make evident, explain; engrave deep, infcribe. *Deut.* 27. 8. an opening, a
well, a pit.†

באש to ftink, putrify, be loathefome: difpleafed,
Dan. 6. 14, 15. a ftink. באשה cockle, a noifome
weed, *Job* 31. 40. באשים wild or four grapes,
Ifai. 5. 2, 4. באושתא abominable, bad, *Ezra* 4.
12.‡

בב, בוב, נבוב hollow, vain, בת, בבת the fight, pupil of the eye which feem hollow. יבב to cry a-
loud, *Judges* 5. 28.‖

בבל Babylon, *q.d.* in confufion. *fee* בלה

בג fpoil or meat, *Ezra* 25.7. meat, *Dan.* 1. 5,&c.
11, 26.§

בגד to deal deceitfully; a cloak, veil, garment;
cloak of diffimulation, perfidy, בגודה treacher-
ous.¶

בד alone, fingle, folitary; flax, (or rather its bark
which thro' all the length of its ftem is feparated
into *fingle* threads) linen, made of flax. plu.
בדים linen garments, alfo ftaves, or branches,
poles or levers. בדא to invent, devife of himfelf, 1 *Kings* 12. 33. *Neh.* 6. 8. בדים lies, liars.‖‖

בדל to feparate, a part, or piece, *Amos* 3. 12. בדיל
tin, a feparating mettle. *Ifai.* 1. 25. בדיליך thy tin
like ones, *i. e.* fuch as feem fhiningly beautiful.**

בדלה Bdellium, pearl, *Gen.* 2. 12. *Num.* 11. 7.
(from בדל and לח fmooth) a fmooth gem feparated from the oyfter.

Der. βαω, βω, βαδω. vado, to go; βαινω, venio, to come; via, a way.
Fr. voye, whence voyage. † φρεαρ a well. ‡ πνος, pus, matter.
Bafe. ‖ Hubbub. βαυζω, baubo, cry out. W. baban, pîb, pipe.
§ Beg. ¶ Baggage, bigod or bigot. ‖‖ Viduus, widow,
bad; βαδδιν linen. ** διεθυω feparate. Beetle.

ברק a breach, crack, fissure, in a building, 2 *Chron.* 34.10. לבדוק for the breach, *i.e.* to repair the breach.*

בדר to scatter, disperse, *Dan.* 4.11: 11.24., (from בזר)

בה hollow, hence בהו emptiness, *Isai.*34.11. empty, void, *Gen.*1.2. *Jer.*4.23. בת a Bath, a liquid measure containing 7 gallons, 2 quarts and half a pint. בת, plu. בתים an hollow den, cavity, house, houshold. בת to lodge, pass the night, *Dan.*6.18. בית, ביתה, מביתה inward, within, home, homeward. בבת *see* בת the sight. בת for ביתן---בנה *see* בנה a palace. בתה desolate waste. תבה an ark, hollow vessel, *see* בת and תבה from this root.†

בהט red marble, porphyry, emerald, some beautiful stone, *Esther* 1.6.

בהל to confound, be troubled, seized with great fear; be precipitate, rash, hasty; בהלה terror, consternation. בהילו haste, hurry, *Ezra* 4.23. תבהלה the same, *Dan.*2.25: 6.19.

בהמה, בהמות inarticulate, hence a beast, brute, as opposed to man; quadruped, as opposed to creeping things; tame cattle, as opposed to wild: בהמות Behemoth, the sea or river horse.

בהן the thumb, great toe.

בהק to shine; a kind of plague, shining spot or pimple, *Lev.*13.39.

בהר, בהיר bright, shining, *Job* 37.21. בהרת shining spot, *Lev.* 13.

בוז, בוב, בוא, *&c. see* בא, *&c.* without the ו

בוז, בזה to spoil, plunder, strip; despise; בז, בזה a spoil, prey. בזיון, בוזה, בוז contempt, con-

---

* Der. Botch. † Boat, boot, booth, tub, tube. Βατος, βατις, liquid measure; bay.

temptible;

temptible; נמבזה vile. בזז plunder repeatedly;
בזא spoil entirely. נבזבה a reward, *Dan.* 2. 6 :
5. 17.*

בזק (to difperfe) a flafh of lightening, *Ezek.*1.14.
בזר to fcatter, *Pfalm* 68. 30. *Dan.* 11.24.
(בה) נבה to bark as a dog, *Ifai.*56.10.
בחל to naufeate, retch, abhor, *Zech.*11.8.†
בחן to try, prove, examine : בחון, בהן an obfer--
vatory, a watch tower, whence we fpy and examine.‡

בחר to choofe. בחור a young man in the vigour
of life, fuch as one would choofe for labour;
בחורות youth. מבחר, בחיר a chofen choice one.
(בט) נבט, הביט to look towards, attend to, confider, have refpect to ; מבט the object of one's
attention, expectation, hope.
בטה to fpeak rafh, foolifhly, בטא to fpeak exceeding rafhly; מבטא what is fo fpoken, *Numb.*
30. 8.‖
בטח to cling, hang clofe on; truft, rely upon; be
confident, fecure, truft, confidence: boldly, fafe-
ly : בטחה, בטחון, מבטה truft, confidence.
אבטחים melons that cling where they can.
בטל to ceafe, leave off, intermit, *Ecclef.*12.3.§
בטן the belly, womb, middle part of a pillar; pif-
tachia nut fhaped like a belly, *Gen.*43.10.¶
בי oh! a particle requefting attention, attend to
me; pity me. מבי bringing. הבי bring, *Ruth*
3. 15. אבי I will bring, 1 *Kings* 21. 29. *Micah*
1.15. here בי is ufed for ביא from בא
בית fee בן, ביר, ביק, בין, &c. without the י
בכ־ה, בוך to perplex, confound, entangle; to utter a perplexed confufed found, to weep, howl,

* Der. Booty.   † Belch.   ‡ Beacon, beckon.   ‖ βαττος.
§ βαταλος effeminate.   ¶ Batten.   W. potten.

moan. בכי, בכות, בכיא weeping. נבכים springs
which wind in perplexed mazes on and under the
earth, *Job* 38. 16.   מבכי winding floods, *Job* 28.
11.   מבוכה perplexity.

בכא mulberry or pear-tree, 2 *Sam.* 5. 23. 1 *Chron.*
14. 14, 15.*

בכר to proceed, be firſt born, בכור, בכירה firſt-
born, בכורה primogeniture, birthright; to inveſt with the rights of primogeniture, firſt fruit;
to bring forth fruit, or delicate fruit. בכורים
firſt fruits. בכור מות untimely death, *Job* 18. 13.
בכרה בכר a dromedary, or young camel, which
is ſwifter than other beaſts, *Iſai.* 60. 6. *Jer.* 2. 23.
בל־ה to mix, mingle, confound; hence בבל Babylon; בלה־ה great trouble, confuſion, terror of
mind. בלה to be worn out with age and uſe.
בלי corruption, abolition, deſtruction, *Iſai.* 38. 17.
בלי, בלוא, בלא, בל particles of negation; not,
no, without. בלעדי, בלתי beſides, without, except. בול the eighth month, part of October
and November, 1 *Kings* 6. 38. בלואים, בלוים
old. מבול deluge, when all was confuſed. תבל
beſtiality, inceſt: the world; the mixed globe of
earth and water. תבלית deſtruction, *Iſai.* 10.
25. (בל for לב the heart, *Dan.* 6. 14.) בלל to
mix greatly. בליל mixt provender. תבלול a
diſorder of the eye from a mixture of the humours, *Lev.* 21. 20. אבל in truth, *q. d.* may I
be confounded. יבל gave mixt provender. בלתי
I ſhall be anointed, *Pſalm* 92. 11. בלא to deſtroy, wear out, *Dan.* 7. 25. בלו a tax, or tribute, *Ezra* 4. 13, 20 : 7. 24. יבל to bring, or
carry from place to place, to preſent. יובל יבל,
אובל, *Dan.* 8. 2, &c. אבל a ſtream, watercourſe,

---

* Der, βακχη, bacca ; berry.

current

current with water carried along. בול, יבול produce of the earth; provender, bud of the vine,
*Hab.*3.17. יובל a protracted blast of the trumpet, *Exod.*19.13. Jubilee, proclaimed by found
of trumpet; the jubilee was every seventh year,
and prefented liberty to flaves, שוכרת היובלים,
Jofh. 6. 3, 12. trumpets of jubilees; קרן היובל
the jubilee horn, *Jofh.* 6. 4. יבלת having a running fore, *Lev.* 27. 22. נבל (run off) to be exhaufted of the natural moifture or fpirits; to fade,
wither, caft off; difgrace; act foolifhly; vile,
worthlefs perfon, a fool. נבלה folly, vilenefs;
carcafe, *i.e.* body fallen to decay. נבל a bottle,
made of a carcafe fkin; fome mufical inftrument
fhaped like a bottle.*

בלג to comfort, encourage, be refrefhed, ftreng-
thened.†

בליעל (from בלי without, and על a yoke) wicked,
mifchievous, *Pfal.* 41. 8. a thing of Belial, punifhment, the wicked one.

בלימה nothing, *Job* 26. 7: from בלי not, and מה
what.

בלם to bind, manage, curb, *Pfalm* 32. 9. ‡
בלם to pluck off, to gather fruit, *Amos* 7. 14 ‖
בלע to fwallow up, devour.§
בלעדי except, without, from בל not, and עד unto.

בלק to lay wafte, ravage, *Ifai.*24.1. *Nah.* 2. 10. ¶
בלתי without, befide. *fee* בל

במה an high place, plu. במות high places, high
ones, 1 *Kings* 12. 31 : 13. 32. 2 *Chron.* 11. 15.

---

* Der. Jubilee, &c. βαλλω caft; ball, bell, boil, bull, bubble, bab-
ble; βωλος glebe; fall; nebulo, vile; νεβελ bottle; navel; ναβλα lute;
νεφελη cloud; παλαι of old; pell-mell.   † Bulk; βληχρος ftrong.
‡ Balm.   ‖ Blaft.   § Belly, and perhaps fwallow; φαλαινα Ba-
læna, Whale.   ¶ Pluck, bleak.

Ezek.

Ezek. 16. 16. יבם to act the hufband's brother, to marry as next of kin, *Gen.* 38. 8. an huf-band's brother, *Deut.* 25. 5,7. יבמת a brother's wife, *Deut.* 25. 7, 9. fifter-in-law, *Ruth* 1.15.* במה wherein, wherewith, why? what? from ב in, and מה what.

בנה to build, difpofe, feparate in parts (בית *fee* מבנה (בת a frame, *Ezek.* 40. 2. בן a fon by whom the family is built; בת for בנת a daugh-ter, plu. בנות daughters; villages, *i. e.* the daughters of cities. תבנית a pattern, model, or plan. בנה to have children, *Gen.* 16.2:30.3. בין to difcern, diftinguifh, underftand, confider, regard, perceive, make to underftand, inftruct, בינה underftanding; תבונה underftanding, dif-cretion, fkill; reafon, *Job* 32.11. בנן *Deut.* 32. 10. to inftruct, perhaps better feparated them, *viz.* from other nations. ביתן a palace, *Efther* 1. 5: 7.7,8. בין, בינים, בינות particles, between, among. אבן a ftone, a perpendicular or plum-met. *fee* אבן †

בנס to rage with anger, *Dan.* 2.12. ‡

אבנט, בנט a belt or girdle.

בס to trample under foot, tread down, defpife; מבוסה a treading down, *Ifai.* 22. 5. תבוסה de-ftruction, 2 *Chron.* 22. 7. §

בסר a four, unripe grape.‖

בע־ה to gufh out; enquire, *Ifai.* 21. 12. *feek for* Obad. 6. *in the* Chaldee *fenfe*; but in the He-brew it fignifies to fwell out, boil, *Ifai.* 30. 13: 44.2. אבעבעות blains, inflamed tumors, *Exod.* 9. 9,10. נבע to flow as water from a fpring;

---

* Der. βωμος; altar; beam.   † Bound (terminate). · W. maen. שוה apprehend.   ‡ Bounce.   § פעש, pes, a foot. Fr. bas, abbaiffer; bafe, abafe.   ‖ βοτρυς grape; four..

throw

throw off, emit, pour out, utter abundantly.
מבוע a fpring or fountain.*
בעט to kick up, *Deut.* 32. 15. 1 *Sam.* 2.29.†
בעל to have or take poffeffion or authority over;
to marry; a mafter, owner, lord, hufband. בעלה
miftrefs. בעל שער hairy, 2 *Kings* 1.8. בעל אף
angry, *Prov.* 22.24. בעל לשון a talker, *Ecclef.*
10. 11. בעלי הצים archers, &c.‡

בער to confume, make bare, clear away, graze,
eat up, kindle, burn; to be or become brutifh,
a brutifh perfon. ביער a brute beaft which
grazes. בערה, תבערה fire or burning, *Exod.*
22. 6. *Numb.* 11. 2.‖

בעת to affright, בעתה terror, בעתים things terrible, terrors.¶

בי, בצה mud, mire; בצאת muddy places. בוץ
fine linen or cotton, the Goffipium or cotton
plant, at this day a native of Smyrna and Pa-
leftine, it might delight in oozy places. ביצים
eggs of birds.‡‡

בצל an onion, from its coats, *Num.* 11. 5. (in A-
rabic to peel)

בצע to break or cut off, complete, finifh; gain,
profit, covetoufnefs, greedy; in this fenfe reference is had to the cutting off pieces of filver
or gold to have the exact weight in their deal-
ings.

בצק to be foft or tender as pafte; dough.**

בצר to fhut up, fortify; with-hold, reftrain, *Gen.*
11,6. *Job* 42. 2. to gather in, or houfe grapes;

---

* Der. Boil. W. Pwnga.   † πατεω to walk; pat for paw.
‡ This root enters into the compofition of feveral Carthaginian names,
as Hannibal, Afdrubal, Maharbal, &c. φαλλος.   ‖ πυξ, φαρος
fire; βραζω boil up; baro dolt; φτρ brute; bare, boor, boar. lit. tr.
burn. W. pori.   ¶ lit. tr. ϑαμϐω affright.   ‡‡ Βυσσο; byffus,
linen.   ** Veffica, bladder.

gold

בצרה gold or treafure fecured, *Job* 22.24: 36.19.
בצרת dearth, drought, when rain is with-held,
Pfalm 10.1.' *Jer.*14.1: 17.8.   בציר the vintage.
מבצר, בצרון a fortrefs, defence.*

בק to make empty, evacuate, depopulate.   בוקה
empty, מבוקה void, *Nahum* 2. 10, 11.   בקק to
make entirely wafte, &c.   בקבק בבקוק a narrow
necked bottle, 1 *Kings* 14. 3. *Jer.* 19. 1, 10.†

בקע to divide, cleave, fplit, rend, tear, rip, burft,
open; break through, hatch; a Bekah, half a
Shekel, *i.e.* a Shekel divided.   בקעה a break between two mountains, a valley.   בקיעים clefts
or breaches.

בקר to feek, fearch, examine; morning; an herd,
horned cattle, oxen, either from their rifing early to feed, or their lowing and fearching after
each other when feparated.   בקרה a feeking,
Ezek. 34.12.   בקרת a fcourging with a thong
of ox hide, *Lev.*19.20.   בוקר an herdfman, *Amos*
7.14.‡

בקש to feek, require, apply to,   בקשה a petition
or requeft.§

בר-ה to fecrete, feparate, felect, choofe; make
clean, clear, bright; to purge, polifh; manifeft,
declare; eat delicately, pick a bit.   a fon, pure,
clean, purity; pure corn or wheat feparated from
the chaff.   ברי, בר cleannefs.   ברית purification, purifier, foap, *Jer.* 2.22. *Mal.* 3. 2.   ברית,
ברת a covenant, to make a covenant, that is to
facrifice a purifying victim, fee *Gen.* 15. 10. 18.
Jer. 34.'18, 19.   ברת a fmall fpace of ground,

---

* Der. Βασσαρευς Bacchus βασσαρις priestefs. Bazar, a market-houfe
among the eastern nations. Burfe, burfar. F. Baftir to build and
baftion.   † Bucket. Vacuus, vacant, vacuum, &c.   ‡ Quæro,
inquire; vacca, pecora, cattle, whence πικερος butter.   § Pofco, to
require.

Gen.

Gen. 35. 16: 48. 7. 2 *Kings* 5. 19. בְּרוֹתִים for בְּרוֹשִׁים fir-wood, made of fir, *Cant.* 1. 17. בוֹר, בַּר and sometimes בִּיר and בְּאֵר a pit, well for sepa-ration of water; a dungeon, ciftern, grave, בֵּירָה, בִּיר a palace. בְּרִיה, בְּרוּת meat, dainty, a dainty bit. בִּירָנִיוֹת caftles.--בְּרַר to feparate thorough-ly, eminently felect, &c. בְּרָא to concrete, form anew by concretion; to create; eat; choofe, *Ez.* 21.19. 1 *Sam.* 17. 8. a field, pafture, *Dan.* 2. 38. בְּרִיאָה a new thing, *Num.* 16. 30. בְּרִיא fat, to make fat; to difpatch or clear away, *Ezek.* 23. 47. cut down, *Jofh.* 17. 15, 18. בְּרֻבְּרִים the moft choice of fatted fowls or cattle, 1 *Kings* 4. 23.*
ברד to hail, hail; grifled, fpotted like hail, *Gen.* 31. 10, 12. *Zech.* 6. 3, 6.†
בַּרְזֶל iron, from בַּר and זָל to flow; *q. d.* the fon of heat or the furnace.‡
בְּרַח to flee from; run acrofs like a bar; בְּרִיה crofs bar. מִבְרָחִים fugitives; בָּרַח crooked, piercing, *Job* 26. 13. *Ifai.* 27. 1.‡‡
בֶּרֶךְ the knee, to kneel; the pofture of receiving a bleffing from a man, or afcribing it to God; to blefs. בְּרָכָה a bleffing; a pool of water, *i. e.* a bleffing in thofe hot countries; to blefs, *i. e.* bid adieu to, bid farewel, difregard, tranflated to blafpheme and curfe, 1 *Kings* 21. 10, 13. *Job* 1. 5, 11: 2. 5, 9. but better rendered to blefs.||
ברם, בְּרוּמִים gorgeous apparel, *Ezek.* 27. 24.
ברם neverthelefs, but, truly, *Ezra* 5. 13. *Dan.* 2. 28.¶

---

* Der. Purus, pure ; puer, bairn, barn, a child; παρθενος virgin : Bar prefixed to names, as Bartholomew, i. e. fon of Ptolemy ; πρασσω to make; βοξα food ; voro, devour. βαραθρον dungeon, βαρις bier; birth, burrow, barrow, brat, bright; far, farina, barley, bread; beer, broth, barn. W. bara, prain, pûr, mêr. † παρδος pardus, leopard. ‡ Bafaltes, a kind of marble tough as Iron. ‡‡ Bar, barrier. W. barr, bêr. || Precor, to pray ; βρακκαι breeches. ¶ Verum, but.

ברק to lighten; lightening, a flafh; a gliftering weapon; ברקת a carbuncle, a precious ftone that fhines like lightening, *Exod*.28.17: 39.10. *Ezek.* 28.13. ברקן a thorn, or prickly brier, *Jude* 8. 7, 16.*

ברש, ברוש a fir-tree or Cedar, ברושים things made of fir, 2 *Sam*. 6. 5. *Nahum* 2. 4.†

ברת *fee* ברי־ה

בש, בוש to be afhamed, abafhed, confounded, difappointed; בשנה, בשה, בושה fhame, confu- fion. מבשים the fecrets, *Deut.* 25. 11. בשש to delay, but better rendered, exceedingly abafh- ed, *Exod*.32.1. *Jud*.5.28. יבש to dry, be dried up, withered; dry. יבשת, יבשה dry land.‡

בשל to ripen, as fruit by the fun's heat, *Joel* 3.18. *Gen*. 40. 10. to drefs with fire, roaft or boil; מבשלות boiling places, *Ezek*. 46.23.||

בשם (Syriac to be fweet) fweet odours, fpice.¶

בשם to trample upon, tread down, *Amos* 5. 11. fame as בסם

בשר (Arabic to fpring, fhoot out) flefh, *i.e.* ex- tended mufcular fubftance; glad tidings, fhoot- ing forth; glad tidings to the Philiftines tho' bad to Ifrael, 1 *Sam*.4.17. בשורה tidings; re- ward for tidings, 2 *Sam*.4. 10.‡‡

בת *(fee* בה) a Bath, meafure; hollow of the eye; a daughter, houfe; in, within, &c. בתה defo- late, *Ifai*. 5.6: 7.19. בתין from בנה to build, which fee.

בתל, בתולה (Arabic to feclude) a virgin, mar- riageable woman, בתולים virginity, the figns of virginity.||||

* Der. βριαχος head of a fpear, βρηκτς fharp point; frico, to rub. βρακατα brocoli. Lit. tr. κεραυνος thunder, and carbo, burning coal, carbuncle. † Brufh. ‡ Vitium, vice, bafe. Abafh, bafhful, and with Lamed inferted, blufh. || Veffel. ¶ Balfam. ‡‡ Σαρξ flefh. ||| βατιλη, ππταλη, puella, girl. F. puelle.

בתק to run through, ſtab, *Ezek.*16.40.
בתר divide afunder. בתרי parts divided. בותר,
באתר *Dan.* 7. 6, 7. after.*

ג

גמיל, more properly גמל, the 3d letter and 2d
confonant in the Hebrew alphabet. This letter
is fuppofed to have had its name as well as form
originally from the Camel whofe name it bears:
In the Samaritan there is ſtill fome fign of the
bunch upon its back. This letter is a palatine,
and as a numeral ſtands for 3.
גא־ה to be elated, lifted up; to lift, roufe, raife
up onefelf; triumph : grow as a plant, *Job* 10.
16. pride, proud. גאון riſing, fwelling, as of
waters, majeſty, excellency, highnefs, pride,
haughtinefs. גאות, גאוה, and גוה (with א dropt)
the fame as גאון. גאינים proud ones, *Pfalm*123.
4. גי, גיא, גיא (the א being dropt) a valley.†
גאל to redeem; a kinfman (in whom by the law
of Mofes the right of redemption was vefted, he
could revenge a murder, redeem a mortgaged eftate, marry the widow of a relation, &c.) to act
the kinfman. גואל an avenger, redeemer, kinfman. גאלה redemption ; right, *Ruth* 4.6. kindred, *Ezek.*11.15. alfo to defile, pollute, reject as
polluted (avengers pollute themfelves). גאלים
defilings, *Neh.* 13.29.‡
גב־ה to be convex, gibbous, prominent, raife up;
high, fwelling, proud, lofty, exalted : a vaulted
or arched chamber, fuch as proftitutes dwelt in.

---

* Der. Batter.   † γαιω proud, and with Mem prefixed, mag-
nus, much, mickle ; γαυρος magnificence ; gay, joy. W. cefn. got,
Goth.   ‡ γαλως glos.

28   גבר   גבח

*Ezek.*16.23,31. height; higher part of an altar,
*Ezek.*43.13. fmall heap or ridge of earth, *Job*
13.12. a back, *Pfalm* 119. 3. *Dan.* 7. 6. boffes
or parts projecting, *Job* 15.26. nave of a wheel,
1 *Kings* 7.33. rings of a wheel, *Ezek.*1.18. eye-
brows, *Lev.*21.20. גוב plu. גבים a fpecies of
locuft or beetle from its gibbous form ; ridges of
earth thrown up, 2 *Kings* 3. 16. vault-beams,
1*Kings*6.9. גבא, גב cavity, pit, *Dan.*6.16:7.12.
marches, *Ezek.* 47. 11.ᴠ גבהות lofty, loftinefs,
Ifai. 2. 11, 17. גבן crook-backed, *Lev.* 21. 20.
גבנה or גבינה cheefe, *Job* 10.10. גבנן abound-
ing hills ; הר גבננים mountain of hillocks, *Pfal.*
48. 16, 17.---יגב, יגבים fields ploughed into fur-
rows, *Jer.* 39. 10. hufbandmen, ploughmen, 2
Kings 25. 12. *Jer.*52.16.---נגב (parched) fouth,
נגבה fouthward.*

גבח forehead, bald, *Lev.* 13.41,42,43,45.
גבל, גבול to bound, terminate; abound, border,
coaft. מגבלה, גבלה end, extremity. גבלים Gib-
lites, a people of Syria near mount Lebanon, not
ftone fquares, 1 *Kings* 5.18.†
גבן, גבינה cheefe. גבן, גבנן gibbous, *fee* גב
גבע (from גבא and גב) hillock, rifing ground.
גביע bowl, cup. מגביעות mitres of the priefts. ‡
גבעל bolled, *Exod.* 9. 31. (from גב gibbous and
עלה afcend.)
גבר to excel, be ftrong, prevail; ftrong. a man, *i.e.*
ftronger than woman or child. גבור ftrong, mighty, valiant. גביר lord, mafter; גבירה, גברת queen,
lady, miftrefs. גבורה maftery, might, mighty
act, ftrength. ‖

Der. γυπη a cave. Gibbus, gibbous, &c. It. gobo, crook-back.
W. cyfodi. Lit. tr. back. κυβαξ locuft. Ital. cavaletta.   † Gab-
ble ; gable end of an houfe.   ‡ W. Cwppan, κυβιος cup; gobblet.
‖ Vir, man ; vires, ftrength ; guberno, govern. W. cawr, gwr.

גבש

גבש, נביש pearl, cryſtal, or ſome precious ſtone reſembling hail, *Job* 28.18.

גג (Arab. expand) the flat top of an altar or houſe. גוד, גד to aſſemble, penetrate, invade in troops, overcome. גד Coriander, of a penetrating quality, *Exod.* 16.31. *Num.* 11.7. a troop, army, band. גדות trenches for water, *Joſh.* 3.15: 4.18. 1 *Chron.* 12.15. *Iſai.* 8.7. גד name of an idol. גדי, גדה a kid. גדה to hew down, *Dan.* 4.11,20. גיד a ſinew. אגדה a company; a ſtream of light; a bundle. גדוד, גדי troop of invading ſoldiers, a furrow, *Pſ.* 65.10. גדרות cuts, cuttings, *Jer.* 48.37. התגודד to cut oneſelf.----נגד before, over againſt. הגיד to lay before, ſhew, tell, declare. נגיד a leader, prince, captain, ruler. נגידים princely, excellent, *Prov.* 8.7. נגד to ruſh forth rapidly, *Dan.* 7.10.*

גדבר, גדבריא for נזבריא treaſurer, *Dan.* 3.23.

גדל to increaſe, grow, be great; educate, nouriſh, make great. גדול, גדל great, greatneſs. גדולה greatneſs, dignity, majeſty. גדלים fringes, *Deut.* 22.12. wreaths, 1 *Kings* 7.17. the ornaments of dignity. מגדל a tower, temple, caſtle.†

גדע to cut aſunder, cut down, cut off.

גדף to reproach, revile, blaſpheme. גדופה a taunt, *Ezek.* 5.15. גדופים reproaches.

גדר to fence in, incloſe, hedge, wall. גדרה, גדרת a fold, fence, hedge, wall. גדרים fence-makers, maſons, 2 *Kings* 12.12.‡

גרש (to gather, heap) גריש heap of corn, *Ex.* 22.6. *Judg.* 15.5. *Job* 5.26. a tomb, *i.e.* heap of earth, *Job* 21.32.‖

* Der. Kid, Gad, Goat, God, Good. W Bagad, Mynegi. † Δαυλις thick. ‡ Garden. W. Gardd, Magwyr. ‖ W. Dâs.

גה to repair, heal, reſtore to its former ſtate. גה גבול repair the boundary, *Ezek*.47.13. נהה to heal completely, *Hoſ.* 5.13. medicine or cure itſelf, *Prov.*17.22. --- יגה to afflict, grieve, vex. יגון, תוגה affliction, grief. --- נגה to ſhine, be bright, glitter; ſplendor.*

גהר to fall proſtrate, kneel with head bent to the knees, 1 *Kings* 18.42. 2 *Kings* 4.34,5.†

גויה (to form into a maſs) גו, גויה a body, carcaſe; ſociety or body of men. גוא, גוה, גו the body or midſt of any thing, *Dan.*3.6. --- גוי a multitude, nation, people. גוים nations.--- גוה for גאה pride.‡ גוב, גוו, גול *ſee* גב &c. *omitting the* ו

גו, גוו to take off, ſhear ſheep, ſhave, *Job* 1.20. mow, hew ſtone. גו, גזה a fleece. גזית hewn ſtone.||

גזבר a treaſurer, from גנו treaſure, and בר ſecrete, *Ezra* 1.8.

גזל to plunder, ravage, take by force. גול, גזלה violence. גוזל young of pigeons and eagles, taken from the dam, *Gen.*5.9: *Deut.*32.11. §

גזם the palmer worm, a kind of locuſt, *Amos* 4. 9. *Joel* 1.4: 2.25. ¶

גזע (Arab. to cut,) a trunk of a tree, *Job* 14.8. *Iſai.*11.1: 40.24.

גזר to divide, cut off, decide, decree: cut, poliſh, a poliſh, *Lam.*4.7. גזרה a retired ſeparate place. מגזרה an ax, 2 *Sam.*12.31. גזר a ſoothſayer, who divides the ſacrifice to inſpect it, *Dan.*2.27,&c.||||

גזח, גזח or גיח to break, burſt forth, *Job* 38. 8. come forth, bring forth, *Judg.*20.33. *Pſ.*22.9. *Ezek.*22.2. to labour, to bring forth, *Miċ.*4.10.

---

* Der. Aκιω heal. Υγιης, Υγιαιω cure. Aγωρ afflicted. Aγωνια ſorrow.　† Γυρος, Gyrus.　‡ Γυιον member. Eγγυη ſponſio.　|| Gaſh.　§ Guzzle. W. Yſglyf.　¶ Sp. Gazanhote, catterpiller.　|||| Sarrio, to harrow.

burſt

burft over, *Job* 40.18.---נגח to butt or gore with horns: butting, apt to butt, *Exod.*21.29,36.*

גחל, גחלת a live coal; burning coal. †

גחן, נחון נחן (to thruft forward from גח) the belly of reptiles, *Gen.*3.14. *Lev.*11.42.

גי for גיא a valley *fee* (גוי a nation *fee* (גוה)‡ גיד, גיל &c. *fee* גד, גל &c. without the י

גל־ה to roll; an heap rolled together; a bowl, pommel, to roll as water: גלים waves. גלות fprings. גלה to roll away, remove, go into captivity. גלות, גולה tranfportation, captivity. גלה גלא to roll back, uncover, open, reveal. גליון *Ifai.*8.1. and מגלה a roll or volume. גלינים tranfparent garments, gauze; badly rendered glaffes, *Ifai.*3.23. גול or גיל to dance round, exult, jump for joy; rejoice. גיל, גילה joy, rejoicing. גיל, כגילים, *Dan.*1.10. of your fort, *i.e.* according to your term, revolution, continuance. אגל a round dew drop. מגל a fickle, from its motion. גלל to roll over and over, a round ftone, *Ezra* 5.8: 6.4. גלל, גללים dung, ordure, rolled through the guts. גלולים idols; revolvers. גלילים circles, rings, *Cant.*5.14. *Efth.*1.6. doors, 1*Kings*6. 34. גלילה the border, coaft, circuit of a country. גלגל to roll round and round; a wheel, or fomewhat turned round; the rolling atmofphere, *Pf.* 77.19. the heart, the organ of circulation, *Ecclef.*12.6. גלגלת the fkull. מגלגל a volume. בגלגל becaufe of, by means of, by his bringing about. ‖

* Der. Γοαω groan; Κιω, Cieo, go; Knock. † Coal. ‡ Γεα, Γαια earth. ‖ Αγαλλω exult; Ικελος, Κικελο; alike. Γυαλα phial. Κυλιω, Κυλινδω, Κυκλεω to roll. Γλωη, rolling eye. Γλοιος filthy. Well, Wheel, Welkin, Glee, While, Gale. W. Gagl, Cylch, Goleu, Gweled, Gwledd. Lit. tr. Λακκος, lacus, lake.

גלב barber, fhaver, *Ezek*.5.1.§

גלד (to condénfe, cruft over : bark) a fkin, hide, *Job* 16.15.*

גלח to fhave the head, beard, &c.

גלם (from גל) to wrap, roll up; a fœtus or embryo in the womb, *Pf.* 139. 16.   גלום a cloak, loofe garment wrapt round one.†

גלמד, גלמוד (from גלם and מד a garment) involved, furrounded, wrapt up; according to others, folitary, defolate, *Job* 3.7: 15.34: 30.3. *Ifai*.49.21.‡

גלע to involve, interfere, meddle, *Prov*.17.14: 18. 1: 20.3.

גם (Arab. and Syr. to abound) imperatively, add; alfo, moreover, yea, though.   בשגם *Gen*. 6. 3. in that alfo, from ב, אשר and גם   אגם a pond, pool, collection of water; papyrus, aquatic reed; אגמן a cauldron: a large rufh; band made of rufh. גמא to fup up, *Hab*.1.9. גמא to drink, fwallow, *Gen*.24.17. *Job* 39.24. a rufh, the papyrus, a reed which fups up as it were the water where it grows, *Exod*.2.3. *Job* 8.11. *Ifai*.18.2.‖

גמד (to contract) the fift; a cubit, about 15 inches, *i.e.* the fhort cubit, *Judg*.3.16.   גמדים *Ezek*.27. 11. inhabitants of Syria about Tripoly, formerly called the elbow of Phœnicia.

גמל to requite, recompence, deal kindly with or otherwife; to wean, *i.e.* drop from the breaft, deal hardly with: a camel, which is revengeful to a proverb: to yield, fhed its flowers or fruits to the earth; ripe, *Num*.17.18. *Ifai*.18.5.   גמול a reward, re-

§ Der. Glaber, fmooth; Glib. Calvere, bald.   * Gelidus, cold ; Gold, from its denfity; Clod, Cloud, Clad.   † Gluma, chaff, Glomus, ball of thread; Clew. Glomero; Gloom, Whelm, Globe. W. Clamp.   ‡ Chlamys, a cloak.   ‖ Κωμη a fort of cup. Κυμα vave.

compence,

compence, benefit.   גְּטוֹלָה, תַּגְטוֹל recompence.**

גֵמִין (to dig) נוֹמִין a pit, *Ecclef.*10.8.*
גָמַר to complete, perform, perfect, *Pf.*57.2: 138.8:.
to finifh, confume, fail, ceafe, *Pf.*7.9: 12.1: 77.8.
גָמִיר confummate, perfect, *Ezra* 7.12.
גַן to protect, defend, fhield; גַן, גַנָּה a fenced garden. מַגַן a fhield. טַגָנָה obftinacy. מַגַנַת לֵב
*Lam.*3.65. a fhielded, *i. e.* hardened heart. גָנַן
to protect entirely.   אַגָן a goblet with a cover.---
נָגַן to fmite, to ftrike, play on a ftringed mufical
inftrument. מַנְגִּינָה, נְגִינַה a ftroke, affliction;
a ftroke, mufic, tune, fong, ftringed inftrument.
מְנַגֵּן a minftrel, performer.†
גָנַב to fteal, fteal away, withdraw; fpeak privately,
Job 4.12. a thief, גְנֵבָה theft.‡
גָנַן (to lay up) גְנָזִין treafuries, repofitories, chefts,
*Efth.*3.9: 4.7. *Ezek.*27.24. גַנְזַיָּא treafures, *Ezra*
5.17: 6.1. גְנַז treafure, *Ezra* 7.20.
גַנְזַךְ a treafury, 1 *Chron.*28.11.
גֵעֹה to low like an ox, 1 *Sam.*6.12. *Job* 6.5. גָוַע
to be in the groans of death, expire, die.---יָגַע to
labour, be weary. יָגֵעַ labour, weary. יְגִיעָה wearinefs. --- נָגַע touch, reach, touch with force,
fmite; ftrike, plague; come, draw nigh, a ftroke,
ftripe, fore, plague.||
גָעַל to reject, caft out, caft away vilely, loathe;
refufe to gender, *Job* 21.10. loathing, *Ezek.*16.5.§
גָעַר to reftrain, reprefs, check, reprove, rebuke.
מַגְעָרָה, גְּרָעָה a reproof.¶

.** Der. Αμελγω Mulgeo, Milk. Μηλον fruit, cattle; Καμιλος Camel; Camlet. W. Cwpl. Cyflog.   * Καμασσς; pit.   † Γανος
garden. Μηγαν great; Μαγιν a fhield. A Can.   ‡ To Nab, Knab.
|| Γοαω roar; Μηκαομαι Mugio, low; Μογεω, Μογος labour; Μογις fcarce.
Cow.   § Goal.   ¶ Jurgari, to reprimand.

גֵשַׁשׁ

נעש to move with violence, tofs, fhake, ftagger, be difturbed as a fhip in a ftorm; be difturbed in mind.*

גּיף ,גּף to adhere, fhut, *Neh.*7.3. inclofe, join together. גוף, גּופה an united mafs, the body, *Ex.* 21.3,4. 1*Chron.*10.12. גּפּין wings, which inclofe the body, *Dan.*7.4,6. גּף a pinnacle of a building, *Prov.*9.3. גּפּן the vine which clings with its tendrils. גּפּן שׂדה the wild vine; the colocynthis or bitter apple.---נּגף to fmite, dafh againft; to ftumble, hurt. מגּפה ,נגף a ftroke, flaughter, plague.

גּפר the Cyprefs or turpentine tree, *Gen.*6.4. fulphur or bitumen.†

גּור, גר־ה to move, drive forward, put in motion, ftir up ftrife, contend; a whelp of any wild creature: to remove; fojourn; ruminate, chew the cud; a cud: a Gerah (called alfo אגורה) a filver coin value not quite three half-pence; a ftranger; inhabitant, *Job* 28.4. to fear as a ftranger; to gather together, affemble. מגּרה a faw from its motion. תּגּרה a blow or conflict, *Pfal.* 39.10. מגּור pilgrimage, dwelling. גרות habitation, *Jer.* 41.17. מגורה,מגּור terror, fear. מגּורה a barn, *Hag.* 2.19. מגּרות barns, *Joel* 1.17. גּרר to move with violence; be a meer fojourner; to faw; מגּררות 1 *Kings* 7.9. fawed. גרגר (to feparate) גּרגּרים berries which grow feparate, *Ifai.* 17.6. גּרגּרות throat, the cartilages of the wind pipe, *Prov.* 1.9: 3.2, 22: 6.21. גּרן threfhing floor. גּרון the throat. גּיר chalk, *Ifai.* 27.9. --- יגּר to fhrink, draw back with fear, be afraid: an heap,

---

* Der. Quaffo, tremble; Gufh, Guft. Sax. Gaft, whence Ghoft, aghaft, &c.   † Κυπρος, Cupreffus, Cyprefs.

Gen.

Gen. 31. 47. --- נגר to fpread, diffufe, fpread, ftretch out, drain off, trickle down, pour out, flow away, fpill.**

גרב (to be leprous) a fcab, fcurf, fcurvy, *Lev.*21. 20: 22.22. *Deut.*28.27.*

גרד to fcrape, *Job* 2.8.†

גרן to cut, cut off, *Pf.*31.23.   גרזן an ax, hatchet, *Deut.*19.5: 20.19. 1 *Kings* 6.7. *Ifai.*10.15. ‡

אגרטל (גרטל) a bafon.   *fee* אגרטל

גורל a lot, that which is determined by lot; an inheritance, portion. ‖

גרם to make bare, corrode, *Ezek.* 23. 34. pick bare, pick a bone; to gnaw, break, *Numb.* 24. 8. *Zeph.* 3. 3. a large bone, *Job* 40. 13. *Prov.* 17. 22: 25. 15. bony, ftrong, *Gen.* 49. 14. the bare top, or fteps without a throne, 2 *Kings* 9. 13. §

גרן threfhing floor, and גרון throat. *fee under* גר

גרס to break, crufh; wear to pieces; wheat beaten out, *Pf.* 119. 20. *Lam.* 3. 16.¶

גרע to diminifh, fubftract, *Numb.* 36. 3, 4. keep back, *Numb.* 9. 7. withdraw, *Job* 36. 7. reftrain, *Job* 15. 4, 8.   מגרעות narrowed refts, 1 *Kings* 6. 6.††

גרף to wrap, fweep, or roll together, *Judg.*5.21. אגרף the fift clenched, *Exod.* 21. 18. *Ifai.* 58. 4. מגרפת clods, earth wrapt together, *Joel* 1. 17.‡‡

** Der. Γαργαρεων throat; Γαργαριζω Gargarifma, Gargle. Γηρις contention; Fr. Guerre, It. Gara, War. Ταυρος arrogant. Κειρω faw. Γραω chew the cud. A Cur, Curro, Current, incur, &c. Grain, Granary, Corn. W. Gôr. Ymogor.   * Grub, Scrub, Scurf. Lit. tr. porrigo. † Radere, Grate, Scratch. W. Crach, Crafu.   ‡ Graze, with a weapon.   ‖ Κληροω, Κληρος a lot, hence clerk, clergy, &c.   § W. Grym. Grim.   ¶ Crufh.   †† W. Gwahardd.   ‡‡ Γριφος a fifhing net: Garb, Wrap, Gripe, Grope, Grapple, Graff or Graft. W. Craff.

גרש

גרש to drive or caſt out, put away, divorce; to
put forth, bud, ſpring, hence tender, green, in
full verdure, *Lev.* 2. 14, 16. If in this place
written for גרס it is then, corn trodden out.
מגרש ſuburbs, without the city.*

גש (to touch, feel, ſearch) גוש filth clinging to
the fleſh, *Job* 7. 5. גשש to feel for, grope for,
Iſai. 59. 10. --- נגש to come near, approach; be
cloſe together, *Job* 41. 16. to ſqueeze, oppreſs,
exact. גש ſtand back, *Gen.* 19. 19. נשה give
place, *Iſai.* 49. 20. meaning ſqueeze cloſe to
ſome other perſon. נגש, נוגש an exacter, taſk-
maſter, tax-gatherer. הנשו brought or put into, 2 *Sam.* 3. 34.†

גשם (to preſs hard upon) to rain; a violent heavy ſhower, rain: a body, ſubſtance, *Dan.* 3.
27. & al. This word ſeems to belong to נש

גת a wine prefs. נתית Gittith, a word of uncertain meaning, perhaps wine-preſſes, alluding
to the wine-preſſes of God's wrath, *Compare*
*Iſai.*63.1---3. *Rev.*19.15. *Pſ.*8. title, 81. title,
and 84. title.

ד

דלת is the fourth letter of the Hebrew alphabet,
it has the name, and perhaps the form, of a
door.

דא־ה to fly ſwiftly, *Deut.* 28. 49. *Pſal.* 18. 11.
Jer. 48. 40. 49. 22. a kite, or vulture, *Lev.* 11.
14. דא Chald. this, that, *Dan.* 5. 6. and elſe-
where.‡

---

* Der. Ceres; Grafs. W. Gyrru.   † W. Agos.   ‡ A Daw.
W. Edn, Hedeg, Hediad.

דאב to faint, languiſh with hunger, thirſt, &c.
be ſorrowful, *Pſal.*88.10. *Jer.*31.12,25. דאבה,
דאבון terror, ſorrow, *Job* 41.13,22. *Deut.*28.65.
דב־ה * *fee* מדיבת

דאג to be troubled; anxious, in fear; דאגה agitation; trouble, uneaſineſs, carefulneſs, fear.---
דאג *Neh.*13.16. fame as דג a fiſh. †

דאן for דן to judge. דאנין judging, *Dan.*7.25.
דאר to dwell. דארין inhabiting, inhabiters,*Dan.*
2.11, &c.

דב־ה to tremble, quake. מדבת cauſing a tremor, *Lev.*26.16. דבה murmuring, muttering,
from the motion of the lips. דוב or דב a bear,
quaſi the growler. דבב to cauſe to tremble or
quiver much: others; to prate, *Cant.*7.9. דבא
ſtrength, *Deut.*33.25.---נרב to incite, be liberal,
bountiful; התנדב to offer willingly. נריב a
ruler, prince; noble, liberal, willing. נדבתי
my dignity, my ſoul, my princely ſpirit, *Job* 30.
15. התנדבה, נדבה a free-will offering. נדיבות
liberalities, liberal things, *Iſai.* 32.8.‡

דבה as a noun maſc. plu. דבחין for זבחים ſacri-
fices, *Ezra* 6.3. מדבחא an altar, *Ezra* 7.17.
דבך walls, a row, *Ezra* 6.4.
דבל (Arabic to dry) דבלה a cake of dried figs.§
דבק to cleave to, ſtick cloſe, purſue, join, overtake, a joint in armour, joint, fodering, *Iſai.*
41.7.
דבר to drive, lead, carry, bring out, to carry off,
deſtroy, ſubdue; produce ones ſentiments, ex-
preſs, talk, promiſe, &c. מדברה, מדבר, דבר
a word, ſubject, matter, thing. דבר peſtilence,
which carries men off. דברת affair, buſineſs.

---

* Der. Debilis, debility.   † κεδεω to be concerned.   ‡ Donavit, gave. W. Pendefig.   § παλαθη, cake of figs.

דביר

דביר oracle, Holy of Holies whence God fpake. על דבר, על דברת, על דברתי upon the matter, an account of. כדברים after their manner, *Ifai.* 5.17. מדבר a wildernefs, remote from converfation. דברים, דבורה a bee, bees who are led out by a captain, *Deut.*1.44. *Jud.*14.10. *Pf.*118.12. הדבר a fold where fheep are led to feed, *Micah* 2.12. דברות floats driven along by paddles, 1 *Kings* 5. 9.*

דבש honey; דבשת honeyed, *i.e.* the bunch of a camel which when galled was anointed with honey.†

דג־ה to multiply, increafe exceedingly as fifh, *Gen.* 48.16. a fifh; to catch fifh, a fifh, *Jer.* 16. 16. דיגים fifhermen, *Ifai.* 19.8. דאג, דגה, דוג fifh. דגן corn from its increafe, דגון Dagon, god of the Philiftines; his lower parts were thofe of a fifh.‡

דגל to fet up a banner or ftandard, *Pfal.*20.9. an enfign or banner. דגול an enfign, or ftandard bearer, *Cant.*5.10. נדגלות bannered, marching with banners, *Cant.*6.4,9. §

דג־ה דגן *fee*

דגר to brood over, fit on eggs or chickens; to gather them, to brood over, *Ifai.*24.15. *Jer.*17.11. דד to urge, thruft forward, *Pfal.* 42. 5. אדדם I urged them to go. אדדה a prolongation, *Ifai.* 38.15. in both places rendered to walk. דוד a pot, cauldron, or veffel of a protuberant form; a bafket, *Jer.*24.2. דדים the breafts of a woman; loves, pleafures of love. דוד, דד a lover, one beloved, an uncle, דדה an aunt.

* Der. Far, fari, to fpeak; verbum, word. Lit. tr. drive. † Dapes. dainty, hence τιθαιβωσσω or τιθαιβωσσω to make honey. ‡ δίτι, δικτυον a net; dagutus, a dolphin. § Hidalgo. Sp. noble.

דרא

דרא a baſket.   דודים Mandrakes, fruit of the Mandragora; Dioſcorides ſays it was uſed in philters or love potions. ידיד well-beloved; ידדות lovely, object of love. * ----- ידה, יד plu. ידים to project, ſhoot, caſt forth, caſt down; any inſtrument or means of action whatever, an hand, paw, ability, mercy, power, dominion, affiſtance, endeavour, contrivance, border, extremity, ſide, tract. ידות tenons, ſtays, props, axes, axle-trees, parts, portions, ledges. הודה to give the hand in token of homage; to confeſs, praiſe, give thanks. תודה thankſgiving, confeffion, praiſe, thank-offering. תודת companies who give thanks, *Neh.*12.31,40. הידות a Jew, *i. e.* a confeffor or worſhipper of God. מתיהדים become Jews, *Eſth.*8.17. יהודית the language of the Jews.---אוד motives. אודות or על אדות on account of. אוד a torch. אד a vapour, dejection, &c. ſee אד in א † ----- נדיה, נוד to move, be moved, to wander, be affected in mind with joy or grief, to nod the head; condole, bemoan, ſhake, remove; put far away as evil and unclean; ſeparation, unclean, uncleanneſs. נד a vagabond, *Gen.*4.12. נידה removal, wandering, *Job* 16.5. *Lam.*1.8. מנוד a ſhaking, *Pſal.* 44.14.---מנדה from מד an appointed tax or tribute, *Ezra* 4.13: 7.24. מדד meaſured, *Job*7.4. from מד, according to others, begone. נדד to move ſwiftly, flee, haſten, fly, *Iſai.*10.14. to depart ſwiftly, as a dream; to wander repeatedly, &c.   נדדים toffings to and fro, *Job* 7. 4. ‡

---

* Der. τιττα daddy, τηθη aunt, τιθυω nurſe; teat. Dad. W. Dilen, Tâd.   † Οδη ode; ιδιος ones own; αδω, αειδω praiſe.   ‡ Nod. ονεω move.

דהב

דהב for זהב gold, *Dan.* 2. 23. מדהבה golden,
*Iſai.*14.4.

דהם to be aſtoniſhed, ſtupified, *Jer.*14.9.*

דהר to bound, gallop, prance as a horſe, *Jud.* 5.
22. *Nah.*3.2. תדהר the pine or yew, ſome tree
famous for its elaſticity, *Iſai.*41.19: 50.13.†

דהון inſtruments of muſic, *Dan.*6.18,19.

דו־ה to languiſh, be faint; languiſhing. דוי languor, ſickneſs. דוה the female periodic ſickneſs. דות, מדוי, מדוה diſeaſe, ſickneſs, languor.
מדוי--- garments, *ſee* מד ‡

דוב, דוג, &c. *ſee* דב־ה &c. without the ו

דח־ה to puſh away, drive, thruſt forth; דוח,
הדוח to diſpel, caſt out, *Jer.* 51.34. purge out,
Iſai. 4. 4: waſh out, 2 *Chron.*4.6. *Ezek.*40.38.
נדחים out caſts, דחי, סדחה falling, ruin. דחן
millet which thruſts forth a quantity of grains,
*Ezek.*4.9.---נדח to impel, force, thruſt, caſt out,
baniſh; make a ſtroke; incite, move : מדוחים
cauſes of baniſhment, *Lam.*2.14.§

דחל for זחל to fear, *Dan.*5.19. to affright, *Dan.*
4.2. דהיל terrible, frightful, *Dan.*2.31.

דחן *ſee* in דה־ה

דחף to haſten, hurry, preſs on, precipitate, 2 *Chro.*
26.2. *Eſth.*3.15: 6.12. דחופים haſtened, *Eſth.*
3.10: 8.14. מדחפית precipices, *Pſal.*140.11.

דחק to thruſt, diſtreſs, preſs upon, *Jud.* 2. 18.
Joel 28.

ד״י ſufficiency, enough, ability. דיך what is ſufficient for thee; *Prov.* 25.16. בריך at thy ſelf-
ſufficiency, *Job* 12. 3. מדי (full time ſince)
when, whenever, ſince, from, ever ſince. שדי
for אשר יד all-ſufficient. ר״י in Chaldee, who,

* Der. δημος, δημα, δειμαινω, δεος, timeo, metus. † Deer. τηχω,
tero. ‡ δυαω, δυη, infirmity. § Need. διωχω, διω, expel.

which,

which; that; of, anſwering to the genitive caſe.*
די־ה (to die, tinge) the black vulture, *Deut.* 14.13.
Iſai. 34.15. דיו ink, *Jer.* 36.18. This root ſeems
to be the ſame as the next above.†

דכ־ה to ſmite, cruſh, break to pieces, oppreſs, be
contrite, broken; to crouch, *Pſal.* 10.20. דך
cruſhed, oppreſſed. מדכה a mortar. דכים
waves, breakers, *Pſal.* 113.3.---דך Chaldee this,
that, *Ezra* 4.13. דכן the ſame, *Dan.* 2.31: 7.20.--
דכא to deſtroy by breaking, afflict exceedingly.‡
דכף, דוכיפת the Upupa or Houp, about the ſize
of a Lapwing, *Lev.* 11.19. *Deut.* 14.18.

דכר the ſame as זכר to remember, דכרונה a memorial, *Ezra* 6.2. plu. דכרניא memorials, *Ezra*
4.15. דכרין rams, *Ezra* 6.17,9: 7.17.§

דל־ה to draw out, as water, to exhauſt, be exhauſted, dried up, fail, impoveriſhed, draw up,
Exod. 2.16,19. *Pſal.* 30.1. *Prov.* 20.5. contracted,
drawn up, *Prov.* 26.7. דל poor, lean. דלה
pining ſickneſs, *Iſai.* 38.12. דלי a bucket. דליות
branches drawing up ſap. דלת hair, drawing its
nouriſhment from the head, *Cant.* 7.5. דל a
door, ſee דלת ----דלל to be entirely exhauſted,
&c.‖

דלג to leap, bound, as a ſtag.
דלח to trouble, diſturb waters or make them muddy, *Ezek.* 32.2,13.¶
דלף to drop down, diſtill, *Job* 16.20. a dropping,
Prov. 19.13: 27.15. to waſte away, decay, *Pſal.*
119.28. *Eccleſ.* 10.18.‖‖
דלק to preſs upon, purſue eagerly and hotly; to

---

* Der. αδψν ſufficient. Δις Jupiter. δα particle of augmentation.
† Die. W. du.   ‡ Dock, decay.   § Recorder.   ‖ δυλος,
ſervant; ταλας, διλος miſerable; doleo, to grieve. Dull, deal, dally,
delay. W. deilen, eiddil, tlawd.   ¶ θολεω, θολοω, to diſturb.
‖‖ δελφυς, αδελφοι uterini fratres. drop, drip, dribble.

kindle, light up, burn; דלקת a fever, *Deut.*28.
22. דלקים purſuers, perſecutors, *Pſal.*7.14.*
דלת (to ſtop up) a door, gate: leaf of a door, *Ez.*
41.24. leaf of a book, *Jer.*36.23. lid of a cheſt,
2 *Kings* 12.9. דל a door, *Pſal.*141.3.

דמ־ה to liken, compare, be like, form a likeneſs
or idea, to think; to be ſtill, quiet, at reſt, דום
wait quietly; juice, blood; murder, crime: דמם
to make entirely quiet; דומיה, דומה, דמי, רממה,
ſilence, ſtill. דמי a cutting off, *Iſai.* 38. 10.
דמות ſimilitude, likeneſs. אדם man, becauſe
created in the likeneſs of God. אדמה mould,
vegitable earth.†

דמן dung for manuring land, מדמנה a dunghill,
*Iſai.*25.10.

דמע to weep; דמעה tears: דמע liquor which
drops from the preſs, wine, oil, *Exod.*22.29.‡

דן, דון, הדין to judge, ſtrive, plead in a diſpute,
contend; דין a judge, judgment, plea, cauſe.
מדין the ſame. מדין, מדון ſtrife, contention.
מדינה a province, a diſtrict under a judge. אדון
ruler, lord; אדני my lord. אדנים ſockets, hinges.
נדן a ſheath, ſcabbard, 1*Chron.*21.27. נדנה
Chaldee, body, *Dan.* 17. 15. דנה Chald. this,
*Ezra*4.11. אדין then.§

דנג (to be ſoft) דונג wax, *Pſal.*22.15: 68.3: 97.5.
*Mich.*1.4.‖

דע knowledge,---ידע to know, feel, acknowledge,
take care of, perceive, &c. מדע, דעת, דעה knowledge. מדעה kindred. ידעני a cunning man,
wizard, conjurer. מודע, מירע acquaintance,

* Der. θαλυκρο:, θαλυω burn, λυχνος link. diligo, diligent. W.
dilyd. † αιμα blood; διμας body; τημνω demno; δαμαω tame.
dumb, dim, dam. W. damneg, mûd. Lit. tr. mute. ‡ Moan.
§ Din, dun, Dan, doom, deem, think. W. dyna, ynad, dyn, noddyn.
‖ Dung. dank.

friend.

friend. מדוע wherefore, why ; from מה what,
&c. דע knowledge.*

דעך to extinguiſh, conſume, put out : conſumed,
Job 6.17.†

דפי ſlander, *Pſal.* 50. 20.---נדף to diſſipate, drive
away, diſperſe, as the wind does ſmoke or chaff.‡

דפק to beat, drive by beating, *Gen.*33.13. knock
at a door, *Judg.*19.22. *Cant.* 5.2.

דוץ, דץ exult, leap for joy, become joyful, *Job*41.
13.§

דק to beat or be beaten thin and ſmall; bruiſe; ſmall,
thin : a dwarf or thin perſon, *Exod.* 21. 20. a
thin curtain, *Iſai.*4.22. דיק a battery, fort.‖

דקר to ſtab, pierce, מדקרות ſtabs, piercings, *Prov.*
12.18.¶

דור, דר to go round, go about; dwell, *Pſal.* 84.
11. *Dan.*4.9,19. round about, *Iſai.*29.3. a ball,
*Iſai.*22.18. round heap for fire, *Iſai.* 30.33. the
period of human life; a generation of men, an
age. מדור habitation, dwelling, *Dan.*2.11, *&c.*
דארין inhabiters, inhabiting, *Dan.* 2. 38, *&c.*
דרור, דרר freedom, liberty, a ſwallow flying
round, *Pſal.*84.4. *Prov.*26.2. מר דרור myrrh
flowing round, *i. e.* freely, *Exod.*30.23. מדורה
round pile for fire, a pyre, *Iſai.* 30. 33. *Ezek.*
24.9. הדורים crooked, round about ways, *Iſai.*
42.2. דרדר a thiſtle ſet round with prickles,
*Gen.*3.18. *Hoſea* 10. 8.‡‡

דראון, דרא contempt, abhorrence, *Iſai.* 64. 24.
*Dan.*12.2.

דרב (be ſharp) ארבן a goad, 1 *Sam.*13.21. *Eccleſ.*
12.11.††

---

* Der. ειδω video, behold ; δαιω know : idea. W. hynod. nodi-
tyngu. † τηχω conſume. ‡ Dab, daub. § Dance. ‖ Dike.
δικω. ¶ W. Dagr, dagger. Lit. tr. dirk. ‡‡ Duro, duration,
endure; dart. W. delor. †† δρεπανον ſickle.

44   דתא   דרג

דרג (to afcend) a fteep place, precipice, *Cant*.2.14.
*Ezek.*38.20.*

דרך to tread, walk, proceed; prefs grapes, threfh
corn, &c. by trampling; ftring, bend a bow by
treading on it; a way, path, cuftom, manner.
מדרך treading, *Deut*.2.5.†

דרכמן a drachm or dram, a Perfic gold coin value
twenty-five fhillings.‡

דרם, דרום דרום the fouth, perhaps from דר and רם
high.

דרע Chaldee, for זרע the arm, *Dan*.2.32. אדרע
Ezra 4.23. the fame.§

דרש to feek, require, enquire. מדרש a record,
where paft tranfactions are to be fought for,
2 *Chron*.13.22.

דש, דוש to tread out corn, threfh, beat to pieces,
tear, rend as with threfhing, מדישת, דיש a
threfhing. דשא a tender bud (juft breaking
forth) herb, grafs: to bud forth, fpring, *Gen*.1.
11. *Joel* 2. 22.||

דשן to confume, deftroy by fire; oil, fat, *i.e.* in-
flamable; to be fat, be made fat, *Pfal*. 23. 5.
afhes, of things confumed by fire; to clear from
the afhes, clear the afhes away, *Exod*.27.3. *Num*.
4.13. to accept, turn to afhes, *Pfal*.20.3. דישון
the Pygarg, an animal like a deer, of an afhen
colour.¶

דת to appoint, fet, place; אשדת fire was placed,
Deut. 33. 2. an appointment, ftatute, decree,
Ezra 7. 14, &c.

דתא (fame as דשא) tender bud, *Dan*.4.12,15,20,
20, or 23.

---

* Der. Gradus, fteps. † τρεχω run, track, trace; dirigo, direct.
W. rhedeg. ‡ ἐραχμη § Drew, throw. || Dafh, dull.
¶ desurv fation.

דתבר

דתבר counfellors, officers, from דת and בר to felect, *Dan.* 3.2,3.

הִי

הא is the fifth letter in the Hebrew alphabet, it
is both a vowel and a fervile; the modern form
of it is made up of the ד with a fmall ftroke
under the left fide. The name and ancient form
are accounted for feveral ways. Boderian thinks,
as the name (הא behold!) implies demonftration,
that the figure of it was taken *a demonstrantis gestu*.
Another derives its form from a fmall red worm.
Mr. Baxter has a fingular conjecture, he fuppofes
it might have reprefented the Ifis of the Ægyptians; the letter indeed imitates the female voice,
and is ufed in feminine terminations.---As a numeral it ftands for 5. As a fervile, ה Prefixed
(from הא behold!) is (1.) emphatic, *the, this*;
(2.) is alfo vocative or pathetic, as השמים *O heavens!* (3.) afks a queftion, or exprefses a doubt,
what? what not? whether? (4.) forms the conjugation הפעיל and its paffive הפעל, the former
with י inferted before the laft radical; (5.) before ת it forms the conjugation התפעל---Poft-
fixed (from היא fhe) (6.) it forms nouns feminine, as אשה woman; (7.) the third perfon fingular preter feminine, as פקדה fhe vifited; (8.)
to a verb or noun *her*, as פקדה he vifited her,
ידה her hand; (9.) to words of time or place,
to, towards; (10.) fometimes to a noun *his*, as
Gen. 12. 18. אהלה his tent; but in this fenfe I
believe it will be found to be (11.) Paragogic,
where it points out fomething eminent in the
idea, and is (1.) added to a verb, as חלצה deliver
thou,

thou, *for thou art able to deliver*, Pfal. 6. 4, &c.
נשכבה בבשתנו we lie down, *alas!* in our fhame,
Jer. 3. 25. it is (2.) added to a noun, ישועתה
certain falvation, or fpeedy deliverance; (3.) to
a particle איכה *alas!* how? *by what woeful calamity?* (4.) to a pronominal affix ולא יענוכה
they will not anfwer *thy repeated cries, Jer.* 7. 27.
הא a demonftrative particle, behold! fee! lo! hah!
Gen. 47. 23. *Ezek.* 16. 43. *Dan.* 3. 25. even, *Dan.*
2. 43.---הוא a pronoun, he, fhe, it. היא fhe, it.
הוה fame as היא *Job* 37. 6. *Ecclef.* 11. 3.
האה hahah, aha, ah.
הב give, bring, go to now, come on, *fupply what
is wanting.* יהב to give, &c. a gift, a burden,
fupply, *Pfal.* 55. 22. הבהב frequent offerings,
Hofea 8. 17.*
הבל to become vain, vile; vanity; a vain idol.†
הבן Ebony, the wood Ebeny, *Ezek.* 27. 15.‡
הבר an aftrologer who views the heavens, *Ifai.* 47.
13. fome take the word here to be a verb, שמים
הברו let the heavens be clear. *Compare* Ifai. 52.
11. *Jer.* 51. 11: 10. 2.
הגה to bring, carry forth, remove out of the way,
2 *Sam.* 20. 13. *Prov.* 25. 4, 5. *Ifai.* 27. 8. to bring
forth words, to utter; a found, *Job* 37. 2. a tale,
Pfal. 90. 9. to bring forth, or purpofe in the mind;
to mufe, ftudy, imagine, mutter, meditate. הגיג
הגיון, הגות intenfe meditation: folemn found,
Pfal. 92. 3. to moan as a dove, *Ifai.* 38. 14. *Jer.*
48. 31. *Ifai.* 59. 11. to growl as a lion, *Ifai.* 31. 4.||
הגן, הגינה, *Ezek.* 42. 12. it is varioufly rendered:
directly, ftrait forward; elegant, fit; right.
הדה הרדה to fend or dart forth, *Ifai.* 11. 8. הד, הוד,

---

* Der. Give, gift.   † Fabula, fable; vilis, vile.   † ἔβε·
ηγεω·· mediteτε.

the

the darting or flaſhing of light; glory, majeſty, honour, comelineſs; any good quality; ſtrength, vigour. *Dan.*10.8. echo, noiſe, ſhouting. הדד, הידד very loud ſhouting, acclaim, acclamation. הדברו rulers, leaders, *Dan.*3.27. from דבר to lead.

הדן to tread down, *Job* 40.12. *ſee* דך

הדכ, הדום a footſtool, ſtand, or reſt, (from דם)
הדם to cut to pieces. הדמין pieces, *Dan.* 2.5:
3.29.

הדר the myrtle tree.*

הדן to thruſt, puſh; expel, caſt out.†

הדו to adorn, deck; honour, reverence; ornament; honour, glory, ſplendor, beauty, majeſty, when הוד and הדר are joined, the firſt ſeems to mean the glory itſelf, the latter the beauty of that glory. הדור a winding way, *ſee* דר ‡

הו ah! alas! alack-a-day! *Ezek.*30.2. אהה ah, alas!

ה oh! oh! woe! alas! *Amos* 5.6.

הוה to be, exiſt: calamity, miſery; iniquity, wickedneſs; to deviſe miſchief, *Pſal.*62.3. יהוה Jehovah, he that is.---הון ſubſtance, riches.||---
הוא to be, *Job* 37.6. *Eccleſ.*11.3. He that exiſts, one of the divine names: a pronoun he, ſhe, it.¶

הו an interjection of exclaiming, ah me! ah! alas! הוי to ſleep, be ſleepy; ſleepy, drouſy, *Iſai.* 56. 10. **

הה to begin, החלה a beginning.

ו a particle of lamentation, hey! ho! *Ezek.*2.10. written אי *Eccleſ.* 4.10.

הי fame as הוה to be, exiſt, become. היא pro-

---

* Der. Ηδυς ſweet; hedera, ivy.   † εδαφος the ground, εδαφιζω
ʊ puſh to the ground.   ‡ W. hardd. || Juno, goddeſs of riches.
● ιαω Jehovah.   ** εζομαι to fit; eaſe, eaſy.

noun he, fhe, it, *Gen.*14.2.   אֶהְיֶה I am, or will be, *Exod.* 3. 14.   יה Jah the Lord, the effence.   נה־ה-- to lament, bewail.   נִי, נְהִי lamentation, plaint. נִהְיָה become, be done, accompliſhed (to faint, *Dan.*8.27) lamentation, *Mic.*2.4. but perhaps the third perſon maſc. præt. of נִפְעַל *

הֵיךְ how? 1 *Chron.*13 12. *Dan.*10.17. fame as אֵיךְ

הֵךְ to go, the fame as הֲלַךְ *Ezra* 5.5: 6.5: 7.13.

הֵכָל (to be fpacious) a temple; a fpacious houfe or palace.†

הִכּוּ to know again, recollect,   הִכָּרַת ſhew, appearance, mien, look.   מַכָּר acquaintance, perſon known.

הֵל to ſhine, irradiate.   תְּהִלָּה praife, glory.----הָלַל to praife repeatedly, make to ſhine, praife one felf, boaſt, be puffed up, be mad with conceit; be mad, fooliſh, rage: הֵילֵל irradiator, Lucifer, *Iſai.* 14. 12.   נַהֲלֹלִים ſhrubs of the fun-flower kind, the emblems of irradiation, *Iſai.* 7. 19. מְהַלֵּל הָלוּל, praife.   הוֹלֵלוּת, מְהֹלְלָה madnefs, תְּהִלָּה folly, *Job* 4. 18. (יָהֵל *Iſai.* 13. 20. for יַאֲהֵל ſhall pitch the tent) הָלְאָ to caſt at a diftance, caſt off, *Mic.* 4. 7.   הָלְאָה at a diſtance of time or place, beyond, further, yonder, formerly, hitherto, henceforth, forward.‡

הַלָּז, הַלָּזֶה, הַלָּזוּ a pronoun, this, that, compounded of ה which, לְ to, and זֶה this.

הָלַךְ local motion, to go, proceed, walk, travel; to increafe continually.----יָלַךְ the fame.   הֶלֶךְ tribute paid to the kings of Perfia, *Ezra* 4. 13, &c. הִתְהַלֵּךְ to walk to and fro, behave ones felf. מַהֲלַךְ a journey, walk.   הֲלִיכָה, הֵלִיךְ a ſtep, going.   תַּהֲלֻכֹת, הֲלִיכָה הֲלִיכוֹת companies of travellers.||

---

* Der. ονοω nænia, lament.   † καλια ικκλησιχ ecclefia, church W. eglwys.   ‡ Laus, laud; ηλιος fun; τηλε yonder; ηλεος, ηλαιω fooliſh; hail, hollow, holy, fool, folly. W. dylluan, haul, ioli, mawl. || Walk.

הלם to fmite, ftrike, ftrike as with an hammer, break. הלמות hammer. *Judg.* 6.26. מהלמות ftrokes. הלם, הלום here, hither, thither, the fpot laft ftricken with the foot, &c. יהלם theᴼ diamond from its almoft invincible hardnefs.*

המה to trouble, difturb, put into confufion, or tumult, difcomfit, vex, break, deftroy; be troubled, &c. rage, roar. מהומה vexation, trouble, deftruction. הם, המה pronoun, they, them, denoting multitude. המיה, המית tumultuous noife, concourfe. הים, הום to difturb, make a noife. המון abundance, multitude, tumult, noife. המן to multiply, *Ezek.*5.7. תהום a chaos, *Gen.* 1.2. plu. תהמות, abyfs of waters fubject to tumultuous motion. המם to difturb exceedingly, put in violent commotion.†

המל, המולה loud tumultuous noife or fpeech, *Ez.* 1.24. tumult, *Jer.*11.16.

המן *fee in* המה

המס, המסים Founder's fire, melting fire, fire of meltings, *Ifai.*64.2.

המר (Arab. to fall down) המרות pits, pitfalls, *Pfal.*140.10.‡

הנה to be ready, prefent one's felf, *Deut.* 1.41. הן, הנה particle denoting prefence, fee, lo, behold! pronoun of the third perfon, them, thefe, thofe. הנה hither, thither, הנה והנה here and there, hither and thither. הין an Hin, a liquid meafure of about five wine quarts, ufed in *prefenting* liquids in facrifice. הון *fee in* הוה הון (תהינו ye were for, *Deut.*1.41. from היה to be)

הס to be filent; make filent, ftill; filence, filently.‖

* Der. αλοαω finite. Lit.tr. μυλλω molo, μυλοω induro; αλμος a mortar; malleus, a mallet; helm, helmet. † Hum, 'em, them. ‡ αμαρα pit. ‖ Hufh.

הפך to turn, change; fubvert, overturn; contrary, diverfe. *Ezek.*16.34. מהפכה, הפכה overthrow. תהפכות perverfenefs, diftortion. מהפכת a fort of ftocks in which the limbs were diftorted into uneafy poftures, 2 *Chron.*16.10. *Jer.*20.2,3: 29. 26.---הפכפך to be continually crooked and varying, froward, *Prov.*21.8.*

הצן fome warlike chariot, perhaps armed with fcythes, *Ezek.* 23. 24.

הר־ה to be eminent, high, rife in height; to be big with child, conceive in the womb, a woman with child; to conceive in the mind, team with, *Job* 15. 35. *Ifai.* 59. 4. הרר, הר a mountain, הרן, חריון pregnancy, conception, יהר, יהיר lofty, proud, *Prov.* 21. 21. *Hab.* 2. 5.†

הרג to kill, flay, הרג, הרגה flaughter.

הרם, הרמון (for ארמון) a palace, *Amos* 4. 3. *fee* רם

הרס to break, demolifh, break down, deftroy; deftruction : הריסות *the fame.*‡

התל to mock, play upon, illude: מהתלות deceits, *Ifai.* 30. 10.‖

התת to lie in wait, devife mifchief, or affault, *Pfal.* 62. 3.

ו

וו is the fixth letter and the third vowel in the Hebrew alphabet, but before another vowel becomes a confonant, and is founded like *b* or *v* : it has the form and name of *an hook*, from whence it might borrow its connective fignifi

* Der. φευγω fugio : Havock.   † ειρος mountain; ουρ wife, whore.   ‡ Harrafs, harfh, crufh, crafh, craze.   ‖ τλαω, ϑηλος trifle. Wittol. W. twyllo.

cation.

cation. As a numeral it ſtands for 6. It is alſo
a Servile. *Prefixed*, (1.) a connective particle,
and; alſo; with, together with; or; but,
but yet. It is exegetical, even, to wit; becauſe. It is relative, therefore; that, to the
end that; when, if. It is uſed in compa-
riſon, as, ſo; although; then; after a negative particle, nor, neither. (2.) Denotes ſucceſſion, if prefixed to a verb future, the action
muſt be underſtood to be future to the time *of*
which the writer is ſpeaking, not *in* which he is
ſpeaking. (3.) *Inſerted* after the firſt radical, it
forms the participle active as פוֹקֵד viſiting, hence
alſo nouns implying a preſent action סוֹחֵר a merchant, one who *is* a trader. (4.) Inſerted after
the ſecond radical, the participle paſſive, as פקוד
viſited, hence alſo nouns, which imply an action
paſt, as אלוּף a diſciple, one that hath been
taught. (5.) *Poſtfixed* (from הוּא) to a noun *his*,
to a verb *him*. (6.) It forms the third perf. plu.
of verbs; in the imperative, ſecond perſon plural.
It is (7.) Paragogic, where it connects the ſenſe
with ſomething preceding, and is added 1ſt. to a
verb, *Deut.* 21. 10. ונתנו and delivered *thoſe*,
i.e. enemies before-mentioned; 2dly, to a noun,
Ezek. 1. 8. וידו and the hands *of thoſe animals*
before-mentioned, *Pſ.* 50. 10. כל היתו יער every
beaſt of the foreſt, or all the beaſts collectively;
hence alſo it forms collective nouns, and ſome
others of a paſſive ſignification, as עָנו humble,
meek; 3dly, to pronominal affixes and particles,
ילְעַג לָמו he ſhall make a mock of *thoſe* wretches,
Pſ. 2. 4. חמת למו the poiſon of *thoſe* impious
perſons, *Pſ.* 58. 5. כְּמוֹ פֶן as the *poiſon* of the

adder, &c. *is their poison.* כמו אבן as *deep* as a ſtone *deſcends*; יחדו all *unitedly* together, *Jer.* 5. 5. 4*thly,* it is added to a noun in regimine, בנו *that impious* ſon of Belial, *Num.* 24. 3.

וו (to connect, link together) ווים hooks.

והב ſuppoſed to be the name of a place near the river Arnon, *Num.* 21. 14. the Vulgate renders it, *and what he did,* which would be good ſenſe, if it could be made out.

ולד a child for ילד, *which ſee.*

†

זין the 7th letter, and 4th conſonant, in the He-brew alphabet. The ſhape of this letter in the old Phœnician alphabet, ſeems taken from a ſhav-ing knife or plane, to which inſtrument it there bears ſome reſemblance; the noiſe of the cooper's ſhaving inſtrument ſeems to be the ſound of this letter. ξᾰΝς is a ſhaving knife, or plane, in the Greek ſtill, and Σανς a plank or board. This letter is a ſibilant; as a numeral it ſtands for 7.

זאב (to be fierce) a wolf, ſhe leopard or panther.*

זאע from עז to tremble, *Dan.* 5. 19 : 6. 26.-----זאת *ſee* זו־ה

זב, זוב to flow, ſtream, run out; waſte, pine away, *Lam.* 4. 9. an iſſue or flux. זב he that hath an iſſue. זבת flowing. זבוב, זבב a fly, from its unſettledneſs, *Eccl.* 10. 1. *Iſai.* 7. 18. זבוב בעל Baalzebub, the idol of Ekron, 2 *Kings* 1. 2, &c.

זבד to portion a woman, endow; a dowry, *Gen.* 30. 20.

זבח to ſlay, ſlaughter, ſacrifice; a ſacrifice. זבחה a ſacrifice, *Hoſ.* 4. 19. מזבה an altar.†

* Der. Sævus; crucl.   † σφαζω ſlay.

זבל

זבל dwell, cohabit with; זבלה, זבול an habitation.*

זבן (to buy, redeem) to gain, protract, *Dan.*2.8.

זג (to join) the ſkin or huſk of the grape, *Numb.* 6.4.†

זור, זד to ſwell, boil; ſwell with pride, be proud, elated, haughty; proud, preſumptuous. זדון pride. זידון tumid ſwelling, *Pſ.*124.5.---- נזד to boil or ſod, *Gen.*25.29. נזיד pottage, broth.‡

זה and נזה ſee under זוה

זהב (to be reſplendent) fair weather, bright ſunſhine, *Job* 37.22. yellow ſhining oil, *Zech.*4.12. gold. *ſee* צהב

זהם to defile, loathe, nauſeate, *Job* 33.20.‖

זהר to ſhine with reflected light, *Dan.*12.3. brightneſs, reflected ſplendor, *Dan.* 12. 3. *Ezek.* 8. 2.

זהר, הזהיר to enlighten, inſtruct, teach, warn, admoniſh; take heed, be cautious. זהירין cautious, heedful, *Ezra*4.22.

זות (Syr. to ſwell) זויה the projecting corner of a building, *Zech.*9.15. corner ſtone, *Pſal.*144.12. מזוי pantries, made in corners, *Pſalm* 144. 13. זון to feed. מזון meat, *ſee* זנ־ה. זה, זו, זאת this, thus, here, hither. זו the month Zif, *ſee* in זי. --- נזה to ſprinkle, this word always drops its נ in the Hebrew, but the Chaldee retains it.

זוב, זור, *&c. ſee* זב, זר, *&c.* without the ו

זו, זוז (to move) זיז a moving animal, rendered beaſt and wild beaſt, *Pſal.*50.11: 80.30. ſplendor, motion, *Iſai.* 66.11. מזוזה a door poſt on which a door is moved.

זח to be lifted up, ſeparated, looſed, *Ex.*28.28: 39.21.

---

* Der. Πολις city. Dwell. † ζευγνυω jungo, join; and with He emphatic Huſk. ‡ Σοιθης, ↓οιθης full of pride. Sod, Sodden, Seethe. ‖ ζημια hurt.

זהל to contract, cringe, crawl; be fhy, fkulk, *Job* 32.6. זחלים reptiles, ferpents, worms, *Deut.*32. 24. *Mic.*7.17.*

זיו, זיק, &c. *fee* זו, זק without the י
זי (to be bright, &c.) זיו brightnefs, fplendor, *Dan.* 2.31. beauty, grace, *Dan.*5.6,9,&c. זיו the month Zif (the month of beauty) 1*Kings*6.1,27. זית the olive, tree and fruit; an olive yard, the tree was perhaps named from the fplendor of its oil.†

זכ־ה to be clear, pure; purify: pure, clean. זכוכית chryftal, *Job* 28.17.‡

זכר to remember, call to mind, record, mention; memorial: a male, who preferves the memory of his family. זכור male fex. זכרון a memorial.

זל, זול to fcatter, lavifh, be prodigal, *Ifai.*46.6. be vile, contemptible, *Jer.*15.19. *Lam.*1.11. תזלי gaddeft thou about, makeft thou thyfelf vile, *fee* אזל. זלות vilenefies, *Pfal.* 12. 8. הזיל defpife. זולל a prodigal glutton. זלזל a luxuriant branch, *Ifai.*18.5.---נזל to flow, diftill, drop, pour, melt. נוזלים floods, ftream. מזלות planets, fluxes of reflected light, 2*Kings* 23.5.||

מזלג, זלג a fork or flefh hook.

זלעפה (from זל to fcatter and עף agitation) a violent ftorm, *Pfal.*11.6. זלעפות רעב tempefts of famine, *Lam.*5.10. terror, horror, *Pf.*119.53.§

זולתי, זולת, זלת befides, except, fave, only.

זמ־ה, יזם to imagine, think, plot, devife; mifchievous, wicked imagination, a lewd device. מזמה the fame.---נזם a jewel for the ear or nofe. זמם to plot, devife, &c. ftedfaftly.¶

זמן to appoint, conftitute; prepare, *Dan.* 2.9. an appointed time.**

* Der. Σιλατης. Snail. Skulk.   † Sait and Sais, Minerva fo named. oleæque Minerva inventrix. Sp. Azete, oil.   ‡ Διχη, Διχαιας juft. || Ζαυλο; debauchee. W. Salw.   § Ζαφιλης, Λαιλαψ tempeft.   ¶ Seem. ** Summon.

זמר to prune, lop off uſeleſs branches: to ſing or compoſe a ſong, where ſuperfluous words are cut off; to ſing praiſes. מזמור, זמירה, זמרה a ſong, melody, pſalm. זמיר a ſinging, *Cant.*2.12. מזמרת things much praiſed, choice things, choice fruits, *Gen.*43.11. זמורה, זמיר a branch. זמר the Chamois, an animal that browſes the leaves and tender branches of trees. מזמרות pruning hooks, ſnuffers.

זנ־ה (to gird round, incircle) זנות zones, girdles, 1 *Kings* 22.38. אזן a girdle, belt, or weapon, *Deut.* 23.13. זנ־ה to play the whore, commit fornication. זונה, זנה a whore, an harlot. תזנות, זנות whoredom, זנונים repeated whoredoms, *Hoſ.* 1.2. זן to feed, nouriſh, *Dan.* 4.9.—־יזן to feed. מזון food, meat; fed, pampered, *Jer.* 5.8. זן a kind of ſpices.

זנב to cut off the tail, attack the rear, ſmite the hindmoſt, *Deut.* 25.18. *Joſ.* 10.19. a tail.*

זנח to caſt off, remove to a diſtance, in *Iſai.* 19.6. the א is added in הפעיל according to the Chaldee form.†

זנק to leap forth, leap up, *Deut.* 33.2.

זוע, זע־ה to move, *Eſth.* 5.9. ſhake, tremble, *Eccl.* 12.3. זועה vexation, *Iſai.* 28.9. זעוה removal: trouble, 2 *Chron.* 29.8. זעת ſweat excited by motion, *Gen.* 3.19. זעזע to put in violent agitation, *Hab.* 2.7. יזע cauſing ſweat, *Ezek.* 44.18.‡

זעך to ſhorten, cut ſhort, abridge, extinguiſh, *Job* 17.1.‖

זעם furious indignation; to have indignation againſt, defy, abhor, abominate.

זעף to rage, be in a fury, fret, be outrageous:

---

* Der. To Snap, Snub.   † Sneak, Snack, Snatch.   ‡ Sway, Swig, Swag, Sweat.   ‖ Seco to cut.

wrath,

wrath, indignation, rage, anger.   זעפים fad in countenance, *Gen.* 40. 6.   betraying uneafinefs, *Dan.* 1. 10.

זעק to cry aloud, to call together, affemble.   זעקה a cry.

זער (to be fmall) זעיר a little, *Job* 36. 2. *Ifai.* 28. 10, 13.   מזער a little while, *Ifai.* 10. 25: 29. 17. fmall, *Ifai.* 16. 14. few, *Ifai.* 24. 6.

זפת fome kind of bitumen or pitch, *Exod.* 2. 3. *Ifai.* 34. 9.*

זק to ftrain off, fine, refufe, purify, feparate from impurities: applied to drops of water ftrained off for rain, *Job* 36. 27.   זקים chains, fetters made of refined iron.   אזקים the fame, *Jer.* 40. 1, 4. זיק, זיקות fparks, *Ifai.* 50. 11.   זקים fire-brands, *Pro.* 26. 18. perhaps it fhould be זקים חצים pure, bright arrows, *i.e.* fharpened.---נזק to injure, damage; damage, lofs, *Efth.* 7. 4.   זקק to refine thoroughly.†

זקן old, to be or grow old; beard, the fign of old age.   זקנה old age.   זקנים the aged elders.‡

זקף to fet upright, erect, *Pf.* 145. 14: 146. 8. *Ezra* 6. 11.

זור זר־ה to difperfe, fcatter, winnow, fan; to prefs out, fqueeze, crufh; prefs matter out of a fore, *Ifai.* 1. 6. *Jer.* 30. 13. to fneeze, *i.e.* difperfeth air, 2*Kings* 4. 35.   מזור wound or fore, *Ifai.* 1. 6. *Jer.* 30. 13. זר to gird, 2*Sam.* 22. 40. compafs, *Pf.* 139. 3. the border encompaffing the top of the ark, table and altar of incenfe. (זרזיר the greyhound, girt in the loins, *Prov.* 30. 31. *fee* צור) זר a ftranger.   מזרה a fan.   מזרים north or fcattering winds. מזרית Mazzaroth, *Job* 38. 32. --- נזר to feparate,

---

* Der. Πιτυς, πιττα, πισσα pitch.   † Ζακχος. It. Cecca, the mint; Scaccarium exchequer.   ‡ Σακος, κωνς Chin; Senex, Senectus. Senefco, Senior, Senate, &c.

feparate

feparate one felf; feparation; a crown, diadem, the badge of diftinction. מנזרים crowned men, *Nah.* 17. נזיר a Nazarite. נזר hair of feparation, in allufion to the Nazarites, *Jer.* 7. 29. undreffed vine, *Lev.* 25.5. *i. e.* left unpruned in fabbatical year. זרא rejected, loathfome, naufeous, *Num.* 11.20.*

זרב to wax warm, melt with the fun's heat, *Job* 6. 17.†

זרזיף (from זר fcatter, and זף overflow) that which waters, rain, *Pf.* 72.6.

זרח to fpring up, arife, rifing; מזרח fun rifing, the eaft. מזרח a native tree never tranfplanted, *Pf.* 37.35. a native, home born perfon.†

זרם to pour forth, pour over; overwhelm, over-flow; a ftorm, tempeft, inundation, torrent. זרמה a copious flux, *Ezek.* 23.20.

זרע to dilate, expand; feed; to fow. הזריע to feed or yield, *Gen.* 1.11,12. conceive feed, *Lev.* 12.2. נזרע the fame, *Num.* 5.28. זרעים pulfe, *Dan.* 1: 16. זרע arm, fhoulder, *Num.* 6. 19. *Deut.* 18. 3. power, ftrength, *Pf.* 71.18: 79.11. *Ezek.* 22.6.‡

זרק to fprinkle, difperfe. מזרק a veffel ufed in fprinkling, a bafon, bowl.‖

זרת (from זרה to fpread abroad) a fpan; the length from the end of the thumb to the end of the lit-tle finger expanded: the larger fpan was half a cubit, almoft 11 inches, the leffer fpan a third of a cubit, 7 inches 1-qr.

זית an olive, *fee* in זי

---

* Der. Sore, Sorrow. W. Diftrewi.   † Sorbeo, Abforb, Surf. ‡ Re-in-furgo, In-furgent. Search.   ‖ Σπειρω Sero, Sow.   § Spar-go, Sprinkle.

ח

חית the eighth letter and fifth confonant in the
Hebrew alphabet; the firſt rude draught of this
letter might have been taken from fome Quadruped, the name implying as much.   This letter is
an afpirate ; as a numeral it ſtands for 8.

חב־ה to hide, lie hid; the bofom, *i.e.* a fecret place,
Job 31. 33.   חביון an hiding, *Hab.* 3. 4.   חבה,
מחבת ,חבת a pan or veffel with a cover.   חוב a
debtor, who fecretes himfelf, *Ezek.* 18.7. to for-
feit, be indebted, *Dan.* 1. 10.   חבב to cover intirely, *Deut.* 33. 3.   אף חבב עמים wrath enve-
loped the nations.   חבא to hide or fecrete.*

חבט to threſh out, ſhake down, beat off corn or
fruits.†

חבל (to bind, tie, connect) a line, cord, rope,
band, binder; a tract of land meafured by a rope:
a maſt of a ſhip; from the ropes faſtened, *Prov.*
23.34. a failor, mariner, one who handles ropes;
a company.   חבל נבאים a ſtring of prophets,
1*Sam.*10.5. a girding pain; to be in pains of labour, bring forth, travail with; to be bound by
a debt; a pledge; to give or take a pledge; to be
under obligation to puniſhment; be ruined; to
deſtroy; deſtruction, *Micah* 2.10. to offend, render one's felf obnoxious, *Job* 34.31. to deal cor-
ruptly, *Neh.*1.7. be corrupt, *Job* 17.1.· תחבלות
well connected counfels, good advice. ---- חבל
(Chald. from הבל) to defpoil, deſtroy, corrupt;
hurt, fpoiling.   חבלא damage.   חבולה harm,
wickednefs, crime.‡

---

* Der. Cave, Cabinet.   † Batuo to Batter. Fr. Abbatre.
‡ Κυβελη Cybele, mother of the gods. Οφειλω to owe. Pilot. Cable-
Rope. Cobel or boat. Καπηλη ſteerage. Πηδαλιον a paddle. Καπηλς a
merchant. Κοβαλευω, Κοβαλος; crafty. Αβαλαι alas! Κολαφος; Colaphus
a ſlap on the face. Κυβαλις an ax.

חבצלת the white lilly, Narciſſus, or perhaps a
roſe bud juſt opening (from חב to hide, and צל
ſhade, *Iſai.*35.1. *Cant.*2.1.)

חבק to embrace, infold, *Gen.*29.13: 33.4. a fold-
ing of the hands, *Prov.*6.10: 24.33.

חבר to join together, conſociate, couple, heap up,
tack together, *Job* 16.4. a companion, company.
מברה, חברה a coupling. התחברות league or
junction, *Dan.*11.23. חבורה a bruiſe or wound,
where blood and humours are collected. חברבר
the ſpots of a leopard, *Jer.*13.23. חבר to charm,
חובר a charmer. חברים inchantments by which
ſerpents and noxious animals were ſuppoſed to
be brought together.*

חבש to bind up or on; to ſaddle, gird; govern,
heal diſorders in government, *Job* 34.17. †

מחבת, חבת *ſee* in חב־ה

חוג, חגה *Job* 27.10. to ſurround, encompaſs, encircle; dance round in circles, celebrate a feaſt
with ſuch dancings; reel to and fro, *Pſal.*107.27.
חוג a feaſt. a circle, compaſs, ſphere, globe, *Pro.*
8.27. *Iſai.*40.22. *Job* 22.14. מחוגה the compaſs,
*Iſai.*44.13. --- חגג to dance repeatedly in circles.
הגא commotion, terror, ſtaggering. חגה, חגוים
clefts of a rock, *Cant.*2.14. *Jer.*49.16. *Obad.*3.‡
חגב (to hide) locuſt or gras-hopper, which ſometimes are in ſuch ſwarms as darken the ground.
חגר to gird on armour, ſackcloth, &c. to arm; to
reſtrain, *Pſ.*76.10. but more properly to reſerve.
חגור, חגורה a girdle or cincture, *Gen.*3.7. מהגרת
a girding, *Iſai.*3.21. ‖

חד־ה to penetrate, be ſharp, make ſharp; to be ea-

* Der. Par, Pair, Peer.   † Εβισκος, Ιβισκος Hibiſcus, marſh-mal-
lows.   ‡ Αγος, Αγιος, Αγιζω holy. Gigue or Gig. Hug. Hag.
‖ Gird, Girt, Girdle.

ger,

ger, fierce as wolves, *Hab.*1.8. to be penetrated or affected with joy, *Exod.*18.9. *Pfal.*21.6. חרוה joy, gladnefs, 1*Chro.*16.27. *Neh.*8.10. the breaft, feat of joy, *Dan.*2.32. חידה a riddle, proverb, parable, problem, *&c.* which penetrates the mind. הוד to propofe a riddle, *&c.* ---- יחד to unite. יחד, יחדו together, altogether at once; alike, likewife, like as. יחיד only, fingle, folitary, darling. חד, חדא one.*

הדל to ceafe, decline, forbear, fail; rejected, *Ifai.* 53.5. unoccupied, *Judg.*5.6. frail, tranfient, *Pf.* 39.4. tranfitory world, *Ifai.*38.11.†

חדק a bramble or thorn, *Prov.*15.19. *Mic.*7.4.

הדר (*Syr.* inclofe, referve) an inner retired chamber; inmoft parts: the fouth, *Job* 37.9. within, *Deut.*32.25.

חדש to renew; new, new moon; month. ‡

חדת new, *Ezra* 6.2. for חדש.

חו־ה to fhew, declare. אחות a declaration, *Job* 13.17. חוא to fhew, *Dan.*2.4,24.----הות towns, *fee* חיה ||

חוב, חוד, חוג, *&c. fee* חד, חב, *&c.* without the ו

חז־ה to fee, perceive, behold, comprehend; provide, look out, *Exod.*18.21. חזה, חזוה a feer or prophet. מחזה, חזות, חזיון, חזון a vifion or prophetic fight. חזות vifible, remarkable, *Dan.*8. 5,8. חזין, חזן lightening, *Job*28.26:38.25. *Zech.* 10.1. מחזה light or window, 1*Kings*7,4,5. חזה the breaft of an animal. מחוז, חוז the utmoft vifible limit, *Pf.*107.30. חזה, חזות a bargain, final agreement, *Ifai.*28.15,18. חזא to fee, *Ezra* 4.14.§

---

* Der. Cudo, incido, cut; Ηδω, Ηδομαι, Ηδος, pleafure, Αδω, Αυδω, to fing; Edge, Hide, Hood. W. Gweddw.   † Τιλος, end: Idle, Addle. W. Gadael, Hadl, Hoedl.   ‡ Adafia, Ειδω, Idus, Ides. || Οιω, Shew.   § Οσσομαι, fee.

חזק to be or make ftrong or firm; take ftrong hold of; ftrengthen, repair, harden; encourage, be courageous, &c. חזקה ftrength, mighty, ftrong.*
חזר (Chald. to wallow, roll) חזיר a boar or fwine.†
חח a thorn, hook, or clafp; bramble, thiftle; a thicket, 1 Sam. 13. 6. to clafp, hook: bracelets, Exod. 35. 22. fetters, chains, Ezek. 19.4,9.‡
חט, חוט a line, thread, a cord, Eccl. 4.12. a fillet, Jer. 52. 21. a line, 1 Kings 7. 15. to make good a lofs, Gen. 31.39. to join, Ezra 4. 12.-----חטה wheat, fee חנט ---- חטא to err or deviate from the line, mifs the mark, Jud. 20. 16. to fin, ex-piate fin, cleanfe, purify : a fin, fin-offering. הטאה the fame. מהטו for מהטא from finning, Gen. 20.6.§

חטב to hew, cut, carve wood.‖
חטם refrain, curb, reftrain, Ifai. 48.9.¶
חטף to feize, catch fuddenly, Judg. 21.21. Pf. 10.9.
חטר a rod, twig, Prov. 14.3. Ifai. 11.1.
חי־ה, חיי to live, preferve, fave, nourifh, quicken, revive, recover. חיה an animal, living creature, beaft; troop of foragers. 2 Sam. 23. 11,13. family or congregation, preferved by one common head, Pf. 68.10 : 74.19. multitude, perhaps beafts, Pf. 74. 19. חיה, חיים, חיות life, lives. חית קנה beaft of the reeds. Pf. 68.31. the Hipopotamos, i. e. a favage people. חות towns, where men live. מחיה fuftenance to preferve life.‖‖
חיל, חין, &c. fee חל, חן without the '
הכ־ה to gape in expectation of, to wait or tarry for; an hook which fifh gape at. חך the palate or roof of the mouth.‡‡

* Der. ισχυς ftrong. † χοιρος. ‡ Hook ; υγκινον uneus. § αταω hurt; hit. ‖ Stab. ¶ Tame, θυμος; anger. ‖‖ Vivo, live; hut. ‡‡ W. Ceg.

חכלל,

חכלל, חכלילי fparkling in the eyes with drinking wine, *Gen*.49.12. חכלילות rednefs, *Prov*.23.29. חכם to be wife, act wifely, make wife, be fkilful. הכמה wifdom.

חל־ה to perforate; to wound, ftab, pierce; defile, profane, an hollow trench, a ditch, 2 *Sam*. 20. 15. 1*Kings* 21.23. *Ifai*.21.6. חיל, חול, חלה to travail with child, to tremble, be in great pain. הנ'ה to be fick, wounded, grieved, and with פנים to put on a doleful face, to fupplicate, intreat, befeech. חיל, חילה, pains, pangs, forrow. מחלי, מחלה, חלי ficknefs, pain, difeafe. חלות infirmity, *Pf*. 73. 10. מחלת Mahaleth, *Pf*. 53. title, perhaps meaning ficknefs. חלי, חלה a bracelet.*Prov*.25.12. *Hof*.2.13. fome perforated ornament. חלה a cake perforated, perhaps fuch as the Jews now make. חלון a window, lattice. מחלות caves, *Ifai*. 2. 19. חול to dance round in hollow circles. מחול, מחלה a dance. מחללות, dancers, *Judges* 21.23. מחלת dancing, exultation, *Cant*.6.13. החל to begin, penetrate or enter on an affair. תחלה a beginning. נחל a valley, a cavity, low ground, a river torrent that hollows out a bed.---חלל to wound much, kill. מחלל flaying, *Ezek*. 28. 9. הליל, חלל a pipe, or flute, player on an inftrument. *Pf*.87.7. הלל to profane much; common, unholy, profane. חלילה, חללה a word of abhorrence, far be it! God forbid! חולל, חלל to bring forth, bear, form.---חלא a jewel, *Cant*.7.1. fome perforated ornament. הלאה foam, froth, *Ezek*. 24. 6. to be difeafed, 2 *Chron*. 16. 12. תחלואים fick perfons, *Jer*.23.19. תחלוא difeafe. חלחלה very great pain.---יחל to wait, abide, expect, hope, remain. תוחלה hope, expectation.

חיל

חיל perſevering ſtrength, activity, valour, virtue, worth, riches, forces, army, wealth, hoſt, band, company, rampart, bulwarks, &c. any thing which can abide the trial.   חול ſand which abides in one place.---נחל to inherit, cauſe to inherit. נחלה an inheritance, heritage, poſſeſſion.   נחל a valley, &c. ſee above.*

חלב fat, milk, fat oily ſubſtance, the moſt nutritious part of wheat.   חלבנה gum Galbanum, *Exod.*30.34.†

חלד (to creep on infenſibly, Syr.) the weaſel of a thieviſh inſidious nature; time, the age of man, *Job* 11.17. *Pſ.*35.9. tranſitory, *Pſ.*89.48. this tranſitory world, *Pſ.*17.14:99.2.‡

חלט to catch at, 1*Kings*20.33.‖

חלך, חלכא the weak, poor, unable to reſiſt, *Pſ.* 10.8: 10.14.

חלם to be firm, to be ſtrong, be in health, *Job* 39.4.   החלים recover health, *Iſai.*38.16.   חלם to dream, a dream.   ריר חלמית the white of an egg, rather the ſlaver, *i.e.* the idle talk of a dreamer.   אחלמה an amethyſt, *Exod.* 28.19: 29.12.§

חלמיש from חלם firm and יש ſubſtance, a flint.

חלף to change, a change, courſe, turn; to paſs away, paſs on, alter, exchange, renew. To paſs, or ſtrike through, *Judges* 5.26. *Job*.20.24. ſpring up afreſh, *i.e.* be renewed, *Job* 14.7. *Pſ.* 90.6. for, in exchange for, *Num.* 18.21, 31. הלוף paſſage or deſtruction, *Prov.*31.8. מחלפים ſacrificing knives, *Ezra*1.9. מחלפות locks of hair which are frequently renewed, *Judges* 16.13,19.¶

* Der. μολυνω wound; ολλυω kill, αλλομαι dance, αυλος; aulædus, flute. Fr. chalumeau. Κοιλα; cave, κωλυω forbid. ληχω, λαγχανω inherit. αλυω ſorry, χηλοω pray. Νειλος; the Nile: hole, hollow, hull, hell, ail, kill. W.gwylio. † Galba, ελφος butter, χαλβανη. W.llaeth. ‡ Eld, Elder, Alderman. glide. ‖ Hold. § Almus; calm. ¶ Cleave,cleft; Caliph.

חלץ to loose, free, difengage as a fhoe, *Deut.* 25.
9, 10. a ftone from a building, ·*Lev.* 14. 40, 43.
to let loofe, let down, *Lam.* 4. 3. to free from
danger, deliver; to expedite, free or be freed from
incumbrance : to be ready, prepared.   החליץ to
make pliant, flexible, *Ifai.* 58. 11.   חליצה fpoil,
Judg. 14. 19. armour, 2 *Sam.* 2. 21. more properly
a loofe robe.   חלצים the loins free from ribs and
more flexible than the upper vertibræ.   מהלצות
loofe garments, *Ifai.* 3. 21. *Zech.* 3. 4.*

חלק to divide, part, diftribute; part, portion: to
fmooth or polifh, *Ifai.* 41. 7. as is the furface of
a thing accurately divided ; to be fmooth, fpeak
fmoothly, flatter.   מחלקה, חלקה, חלק piece, par-
cel, portion, courfe, divifion.   חלקה fmooth parts,
Gen. 27. 16.   חלקות flatteries, flippery places.
חלקלק, plu. חלקלקות great flipperineffes, *Pf.* 35.
6. adulations, great flatteries, *Dan.* 11. 21, 34.
flippery ways, *Jer.* 23. 12. †

חלש to weaken, overthrow, difcomfit, *Exod.* 17. 13.
Ifai. 14. 12. weak, *Joel* 3. 10. to wafte, confume,
diffolve, *Job* 14. 10.   חלושה defeat, overthrow,
Exod. 32. 18. ‡

חם to be hot, warm; to heat, warm.   חם, חמה
heat.   חמה the folar flame, heat of the fun, *Job*
30. 28. *Cant.* 6. 10. *Ifai.* 24. 33 : 30. 26.   חמת an
earthen veffel hardened by heat.   חמי father-in-
law, חמות mother-in-law.   חמן an idol of the
fun.   חום brown, as if fcorched by the fun, *Gen.*
30. 32, 33, 35, 40.   חמה, חומה a wall, of burnt
materials.   חמה wrath, fury.   חמת inflammatory poifon; ftrong inflaming liquor. *Hab.* 2. 15.

---

* Der. Laxo ; lax, relax.   † αικαλλω, κολακευω flatter : calx,
chalk; calculus, a fmall ftone; calculate.   W. achles.   ‡ Laffus,
laffitude ; lazy.

חמה

חמה *Job* 29.6. and חמא, חמאה butter, made by the milk being heated in the churn. חמא *Dan.*3.13,19: 11.44. wrath, fury. --- יחם to be hot, luftful; conceive *

חמד to defire, covet, חמד, חמוד to be defired, delightful, precious, מחמד, חמדה defire, a defireable thing, נחמד pleafant, to be defired.†

חמט (to proftrate) a lizard, tortoife, or fnail, *Lev.* 11.30.

חמל to pity, compaffionate, fpare, חמלה pity, *Gen.* 19.16. *Ifai.*63.9. מחמל compaffion, *Ezek.*24.21.‡

חמן *fee* חם

חמס to offer violence, ravifh, take away by violence, imagine wrongfully. *Job* 21.27. violence, injury, wrong. תמס the night hawk, a rapacious bird, *Lev.*11.16. *Deut.*14.15.

חמץ to ferment, four, leaven, leavened bread; vinegar; to be in a ferment or fury, be grieved, *Pf.* 73.21. a cruel, exafperated man, *Pf.*71.4. חמוץ one oppreffed by others fury, *Ifai.*1.17. ftained or fprinkled as with fermented wine, *Ifai.* 63.1. מחמץ leavened. ||

חמק to turn afide, withdraw, decline, go about, *Cant.*5.6. *Jer.*31.22. חמוקים joints of the thigh bone (acetabula) where they turn, *Cant.*7.1.§

חמר to trouble, put in a turbid motion, be troubled, *Pf.*56.4. mire, clay, flime, mortar, *i.e.* bitumen, a turbid effervefcence of the earth; to daub with it, bemire, *Exod.*3.2. liquor that has undergone fermentation, wine, *Deut.*32.14. *Ifai.*27.2. *Pf.* 75.8. חמר, חמור the he afs of a turbulent nature. יחמור the antilope, an animal fierce, or

---

* Der. Wemb, womb. χωμα rampart. Caminus, chimney; Hummums (hot baths). † Mohamed, i. e. *defire of all nations.* ‡ αιμυλος, clement, clemency. || ζυμα leaven. § Hammock.

the Bubulus, or fierce wild ox, *Deut.*14.5. 1 *Kings*
4.23. חמרמר to be violently troubled, *Lam.*1.20:
2.11. very muddy, foul, or fwollen with inward
agitation.   המר, חמרא, *Ezra* 6.9. *Dan.*5.1,&c.
חמר an heap of things mixed together; an Homer, the largeſt dry meaſure, equal to ten Baths
or Ephahs, or about 75 gallons, 5 pints, wine
meaſure.

חמש, חמשה five, to take a fifth part, *Gen.*41.34.
חמשים fifty, חמישי fifth. חמישית armed, equip-
ped, proved; foldiers were girt under the ſmall
ribs, others becauſe they marched five in a rank.
החמש the fifth rib, 2*Sam.*2.23: 3.27: 4.6: 20.10.
the belly under the five ſmall ribs.

חמת a pitcher, heat, wrath, &c. *fee* חם

חנ־ה to fix, remain, fettle, abide, *Num.*31.19. fix
the tent, encamp, dare, *Iſai.*29.1. המנה a camp,
an army, hoſt, company. תחנה encamping,
2 *Kings* 6. 8. חניות cells, cabins, *Jer.* 37. 16.
חנית ſpear or javelin. חנרה, חנן to fix one's af-
fections, be gracious, kind, merciful, and favourable to any. התחנן to ſupplicate favour.
חן grace, favour. חנינה favour. תחנון, תחנה
ſupplication. חנם for nought, without coſt,
freely, gratis, without cauſe, in vain. חנון gracious. הין the grace and comelineſs of his ſtruc-
ture, *Job.*41.12.*

חנמל (from חנה to fix, and מל cut off, deſtroy) ice,
intenſe froſt, or large hail-ſtones which deſtroys
vegetables, *Pſ.*78.47.

חנט to ſweeten, begin to ripen, fruit bloſſoms,
Cant. 2. 13. embalm bodies, *i. e.* ſweeten them,

* Der. Hen, female of birds, *Mat.* xxiii. 37. ακοντιον contus, a
ſpear.

Gen. 50. 2, 3, 26.   הטה (for חטוה) חטים wheat from its fweetnefs.*

חנך to initiate, hanfel, train up, dedicate, חנכה dedication.   חניכים trained, initiated ones, *Gen.* 14.14.†

חנף to pollute, defile, be polluted; a polluted wicked wretch.   חנף חנפה profanenefs, *Jer.* 23. 15. *Ifai.*32.6.‡

חנק to ftrangle, fuffocate, *Nah.*2.12. hang onefelf, 17.23.   מחנק fuffocation, *Job* 7.15.§

הסה to protect, fhelter, cover; take refuge; truft, or hope in.   מחסה a refuge.   חסות truft, *Ifai.* 30.3.   חום to fpare; pity, *i.e.* cover the eye, or wink at. ‖

חסד exceffive; in a good fenfe, exceeding kindnefs, mercy or goodnefs: alfo, enormous wickednefs, *Lev.*20.17. to be eminently deftructive, *Prov.*14. 34. to regard as an extraordinary villain, *Prov.* 25. 10.   חסיד exceedingly kind, good, holy. חסידה a ftork from its exceeding goodnefs to its parents.   התחסד to fhew ones felf merciful, 2*Sam.*22.26. *Pf.*18.25.¶

חסל to confume, eat, *Deut.*28.38.   חסיל locuft or caterpillar worm that deftroys corn.**

חסם to ftop, fhut up, *Ezek.*39.11. muzzle,*Deut.* 25.4.   מחסום a muzzle, bridle, *Pf.*39.2.††

חסן to be ftrong, fecure, well guarded, *Ifai.*23.18. ftrength, *Ifai.*33.6. *Jer.*20.5. treafure,*Prov.*15. 6. *Ezek.*22.5.   חסן, חסון, חסין *Pf.*89.8. *Ifai.*1. 31. *Amos* 2.9.   חסנא ftrength, *Dan.*2.37. to poffefs, keep, *Dan.*7.18,22.

---

* Der. Wheat, W. ŷd.   † καινος new, Εγκαινια enccœnia   ‡ Knave, knife.   § Αγχω hang, Συναγχη Quincy.   ‖ Houfe.   ¶ Κυδος affront.   ** Chifel; Weevil; Wheafel.   †† Κημος, Camus, muzzle.

חסף (to pound, mix) potters earth, clay, *Dan.* 2. 33, 34, 41.

חספס, מחספס (from חסף and פס bit) fmall as if pounded, *Exod.* 16.14.

חסר to want, lack, abate; מחסור poverty, want. חסרון what is wanting, *Eccl.* 1.15.

חפ־ה to cover, overlay. חף clean, protected by innocence, *Job* 33.9. חוף an haven, harbour. חפה a fecret clofet, chamber, alcove, *Pf.* 19. 5. *Joel* 2. 6. חפף to fhelter entirely, *Deut.* 33. 12. חפא act fecretly, 2 *Kiugs* 17.9. חפן the hand as fhut or clinched, the fift. --- יחף (uncover) un- fhod, barefoot, 2 *Sam.* 15.30. *Ifai.* 20.2, 3,4. *Jer.* 2.25.*

חפן to hafte, hurry through fear, hafte; חפזון hur- ry.‡

חפץ to defire, delight in, love, have pleafure in; defire, delight, will, pleafure, purpofe: to erect and move at pleafure, *Job* 40. 17.

חפר to fink, delve, dig, fearch for; to fink the countenance, *i. e.* be afhamed. חפרפר, plural חפרפרות moles which delve in the earth, *Ifai.* 2. 20.

חפש to free from incumbrance; be free; ftrip, fearch by ftripping; התחפש to ftrip off the ufual garb, difguife ones felf, *Job* 30.18. חפשי free, at liberty, חפשית feparation, liberty. חפשה free- dom.

חצ־ה to difunite, divide or part. חץ, חצץ an ar- row, dart, which cuts what it hits. חצץ gravel, *Prov.* 20.17. grit, gravel, *Lam.* 3.16. חוץ a ftreet, feparating houfes; a field, *Job* 5.10. *Prov.* 8.16. an highway, *Amos* v.16. חיץ a wall or fence, *Ezek.*

---

* Der, Σκιπω cover; hope; haven. W. Hafn.   † Αψ, αιψα fright. κουφος light.

13.10. מחושה without, מחוץ, חצון, חוצה, חוץ,
outward, abroad, חיצונה outward, utter, without. מחצית מצה, חצות, חצי, half, middle,
midſt. חוץ ממני more than I, i. e. beſides me.
חץ a ſwift forcible arrow; מחצצים archers.*

חצב to cut, cut out, hew; engrave, *Job* 19. 24.
cut, divide, *Pſ.* 29. 7. cut in pieces, *Iſai.* 51. 9.
חצבים maſons, hewers: מחצב hewing.

חצן (graſp of both the arms) boſom, arms, lap,
*Neh.*5.13. *Pſ.*129.7. *Iſai.* 49.22.

חצף to urge, be ſtrong, urgent, *Dan.*2.15: 3.22.

חצר (to ſurround) a court, wall, village. חציר
graſs, herb, hay; leeks, *Num.* 11. 5. חצצר to
found the trumpet. חצצרה a trumpet. בעל
חצור a place ſo named in 2*Sam.* 13.23. in honour
of Baal the god of herbage.

חק־ה to delineate, mark, trace out, preſcribe
bounds; print, *Job* 19. 23. a ſtatute, ordinance,
decree, regulation, &c. preſcribed portion; ſet
time, *Job* 14.13. bounds, 26. 10. a taſk, *Exod.*
5.14. to pourtray, carve, 1*Kings* 6. 35. *Ezek.* 8.
10: 23. 14. חיק incloſure, boſom; lap, *Prov.*
16.33. midſt, 1*Kings*22.35. התחקה ſet a print,
Job 13.27. חקק to mark out eminently and con-
ſpicuouſly : to decree, determine, appoint, regulate. חקקי thoughts, *Judges* 5. 15. rather read
חקרי as in the next verſe. מחקק a lawgiver, alſo
ſtaff, enſign of legiſlative authority, *Gen.* 49.10.
*Num.*21.18.†

חקר to ſearch out, explore; a ſearching. מחקרים
receſſes hard to be found out, *Pſ.* 95. 4.‡

חר־ה to be intenſely hot, as when the fire looks
white: to be kindled, be warm, wroth, grieved.

---

* Dcr. Ιος, υσσος haſta, ſpear ; cage, hedge. W. faeth. † ειχω,
ηχων graving. Hack, haggle. ‡ Quæro, enquire.

הֶחֱדָרָה earneſtly, *Neh.*3.20. הר, נחר to be burnt,
(angry) *Cant.* 1.6. הִתְחָר to fret, *Pſ.*37.1,7,8.
*Prov.*24.10. הרי, חרון heat, wrath. חור to be
white, pale. חר, חור an hole ſtopping the intenſe rays of light. חרים, חורים nobles arrayed
in white. חרי net works, *Iſai.*19.9. הרר to be
quite parched, חררים places parched, *Jer.*17.6.
חרא, הראים, הרים dung, excrements, *Iſai.* 36.
12. 2*Kings*6.25: 18.27. מחראות places for dung,
draught houſes, 2*Kings* 10.27. הרחר to kindle
repeatedly, *Prov.*26.21. fever, burning, *Deut.*28.
22. --- יחר for אחר 2 *Sam.* 20.5.*

חרב to waſte, drain off, dry up; draught, dryneſs,
heat: deſtroy, make deſolate: a ſword, inſtrument
of deſolation; knife, *Ezek.* 5.1,2. 1*Kings* 18. 28.
Joſh. 5.2,3. tool, *Exod.*20.25. mattock, 2*Chron.*
34.6. ax, *Ezek.* 26. 9. חרבה dry land, הרבון
draught, *Pſ.*32.4.†

חרג to ſhudder, or quake with fear, *Pſ.*18.45.‡

הרגל (from חרג to ſhake, and רגל the foot) ſome
nimble inſect, graſs-hopper or locuſt, *Lev.*9.22.

חרד nearly the ſame as חרג to tremble, be afraid;
palpitate: to fright away: be careful, diligent,
2*Kings* 5.23. חרדה care, fear, trembling.§

חרז, חרוז (to put in order) necklace of pearls,
*Cant.*1.10.

חרט a bag, 2*Kings* 2. 15. יצר בחרט *Exod.* 32. 4.
ſhould be rendered he *bound in a bag,* comp. *Judg.*
8.24,25. הריטים bags uſed in womens dreſs:
others criſpin pins, *Iſai.* 3. 22. חרט *Iſai.* 8. 1.
Chaldee for הרת a pen or graving tool.   חרטם

---

* Der. Εϱις, ira, ire: uro, ardeo, aridus, arder: hearth, wrath,
wroth: hoary. † Καϱφω dry up. Rapier. Herb, herbage. Fer-
beo, ferveo, fervent. ‡ Ριγος frigus, cold. with ſ prefixed, ſhrug.
§ Horrid.

a con-a conjurer (from חרט or חרת to engrave) who dealt in talifmans.||

חרך to fecure, inclofe in nets, *Prov.* 12.27. others roaft: lattice work. חָרַך Chaldee (from הרה) to burn, finge, *Dan.* 3.27.*

חרול, חרל bramble, briar, *Job* 30.7. *Prov.*24.31. *Zeph.*2.9.

חרם total feparation; to feparate, devote, deftroy; maimed, loft a limb, *Lev.* 21. 18. devoted, accurfed, dedicated thing: a curfe, utter deftruction: a net to feparate and deftroy fifh.†

הרמש from חרם and מש to remove or draw back, a fickle, *Deut.*16.9: 23.25.‡

חרס a burning inflamed ulcer, *Deut.* 28. 27. the fun, folar orb, *Judg.* 8. 13: 14. 18. *Job* 9. 7. שער הרסות gate of burning, *Jer.*19.2. the gate which led to the valley of Hinom.¶

הרף to ftrip, diveft; difgrace, reproach, defy; defpife, hazard, *Judg.* 5. 18. the winter, that uncloaths the earth: the cold, *Prov.*20.4. to winter, *Ifai.* 18. 6. חרפה reproach. חרפי youth, *Job* 29.4. rather days of plenty, of *Autumn* the ftripping time, when fruits abound.||||

חרץ to cut fhort, fmall; to cut fhort, determine, decree, bring to a point; to fharpen onefelf, beftir, 2 *Sam.*5.24. beftir the tongue, fnarl, *Exod.* 11.7. *Jofh.*10.21. חרוץ maimed, pierced, *Lev.* 22.22. decifion, *Joel* 3. 19. what is fharp pointed, *Job* 41.30. *Ifai.*41.15. fharp, active, diligent: inftrument with fharp teeth; threfhing inftrument, *Ifai.* 28. 27. *Amos* 1. 3. חריץ the fame,

2 *Sam.*

2 *Sam.* 12. 31. 1 *Chron.* 20. 3. חרוץ a perforated wall or ditch, *Dan.* 9. 25. native gold in fmall maffes. חריץ fmall cakes of curd; cheefe, 1 *Sam.* 17.18. חרצן grape ftone fharp pointed. ---חרץ Chald. for חלץ the loins, *Dan.*5.6.*

חרצב (from חרץ to cut, and צב to fwell) a band, girding, pangs, *Pf.*73.4. *Ifai.*58.6.

חרצן (from חרץ *which fee*, and צן fharp) grape ftone, kernel.

חרק to grind the teeth.†

חרש (filent thought) to pay attention, to work as carpenters, fmiths, *&c.* do, to contrive, devife fecretly; to plow; engrave: a workman, mechanic; artift, fmith, carpenter, engraver: materials for the artift, wood, potters ware, a potfherd: to be deaf or dumb as one in thought: filently, fecretly, *Jofh.* 2. 1. חרשים, חרשה, works, fortifications, 2*Sam.*23.15,16,18. 2 *Chron.* 27.4. חרשת cutting, carving, *Exod.*31.5. חריש ground for tillage, 1 *Sam.* 8. 11. plowing time, *Gen.* 14. 6. *Exod.* 34. 21. מחרשה ploughfhare, 1 *Sam.* 13. 20, 21. חרישית filent, ftill, fuffocating, *Jon.*4.8.‡

חרות, חרת engraven, *Exod.* 32. 16. perhaps for חרוש ‖

חש־ה to hafte: haften; be hurried, confounded: to be ftill, filent, hufh, to forbear acting, *Judg.* 18.9. 1 *Kings* 22.3. חיש foon, fpeedily, *Pf.*90.10. חשים ready, *Num.* 32. 17. חשש chaff violently hurried by the wind, *Ifai.*5.24: 33.11.---יחש to compute. התיחש a genealogy; to be reckoned by genealogy.¶

* Der. Ορίχω, θξος cut. χρυσος gold; careus, cafeus, cheefe. Harrow; harfh; harrafs; threfh. † Crack, creek, noife. ‡ Αξοσcω, αξοω aro, plough: ars, art. foreft. Κεραμος urceus, Κξωσσος crock, crockery, creufe: creuit. ‖ χαξαττω engrave. character, charta. chart. charter, cartel. write; wright. ¶ Hufh; hafte. W.ach.

חשב to add thing to thing, devices, to devife, think,
imagine, accompt, devife, impute, reckon, &c.
embroider, *Exod.*31.4: 35.32. embroidery, in-
wrought work. חשבון account, reafon, *Ecclef.*
7.25,27. a device, *Ecclef.*9.10. חשבנות inven-
tions, *Ecclef.* 7. 29. engines, 2 *Chron.* 26. 15.
מחשבה a thought, device, purpofe, invention,
curious work.

חשח to need, *Dan.*3.16. חשהן neceffary, *Ezra* 6.9:
7.20.*

חשך to impede, keep back, refrain, reftrain, fpare,
withhold: to be dark, darkened, darken; darknefs, the light impeded. השכח, מחשך darknefs.
חשכים mean, obfcure, *Prov.*22.29.†

חשל to wear out, away, *Dan.*2.40. נחשל feeble,
wearied, *Deut.*25.18.

חשמל (from חש and מל deftroy) fire in its moft
intenfe brightnefs, *Ezek.* 1. 4, 27: 8.2. rendered
amber.

חשמן (from חש and שמן abundant) eagerly, in
great hafte. *Pf.*68.32. rendered prince.‡

חשן (from חסן) the high prieft's breaft plate.

חשף to uncover, make bare, difcover; take away,
*Ifai.*30.14. draw out, *Hag.*2.16. חשיפים fhorn
flocks, 1 *Kings* 20.27.‖

חשק to connect, faften, fillet; to defire to be connected, fix one's love upon, defire, delight: defire, delight. השוק a fillet; fpokes or felloes of
a wheel, 1 *Kings* 7.33.

חשר (to gather, collect) חשרת condenfation, 2 *Sam.*
22.12. חשרים naves of wheels, where the fpokes
are collected, 1 *Kings* 7.33.

---

* Der. lit. tr. neceffe, need. afk.   † Σκια, Σκοτος fufcus, dark.
σχιω reftrain. hufk, hufky.   ‡ Αισυμνητης legate.   ‖ Sheep,
lit. tr. fcoop.

I   חתה

חתﬡה to break in pieces, *Pf.* 52. 5. be broken in pieces, difmayed, afraid, difcouraged; to diffolve by fire, burn : to take a piece of fire and put it elfewhere, *Prov.*6.27: 25.22. *Ifai.*30.14. מחתה a cenfer, fire-pan, fnuff-diſh. חתית, חתה, חת, fear, terror, מחתה terror, difmay, deftruction, ruin. התחתים fears, *Ecclef.*12. 5. --- יחת fhal' come down, *Jer.*21.13. יהתו they go down, *Job* 21.13. תחת entereth, *Prov.*17.10. thefe from נחת *

חתך to determine, finiſh, decree, *Dan.*9.24.

חתל to fwathe, fwaddle, *Ezek.* 16. 4. התול a fwathe, roller, *Ezek.*30.21. חתלה a fwaddling band, *Job* 38. 9.†

חתם to ftop, *Lev.*15.3. feal up, *Job* 37.7. mark, *Job* 24.16. חתם, חתמת a feal or fignet.

חתן to contract affinity by marriage; a relation by marriage; a father or fon-in-law, bridegroom, hufband. חתנת mother-in-law, *Deut.*27.23. ef-poufals, marriage, contract, *Cant.*3.11.‡

חתף to take by violence, *Job* 9.12. a robber, *Prov.* 23.28.

חתר to dig through, plough; to row hard, *Jonah* 1.13. *i. e.* dig the waves. מחתרת a digging through, *Exod.*22.2. a fearch, *Jer.*2.34. ‖

ט

טית the ninth letter, and fixth confonant, in the Hebrew alphabet. The form of this letter is nearly the fame in the Samaritan as in the mo-dern Hebrew; from the curve in its form, it is fuppofed to have been the fymbol of a fcroll, or

---

* Der. ταω take. Αιδεω, οττεια difcourage.   † Τυλω, τυλιττω wind, round. Wattle, and with f prefixed, fwaddle.   ‡ Γεττω. Goody. ‖ Ορυττω dig. Εριτης rower, Εςεττω row.

fomething

ſomething rolled up. The power of this letter is the ſame as the Greek ϑ, which is derived from it. It is a radical, except when uſed for its tenuis ת in the Etpol of verbs beginning with צ, as נצטדק for נתצדק the ט and צ being tranſpoſed. This letter is an aſperate dental, and as a numeral ſtands for 9.

טא, טאטא to ſweep, *Iſai.*14.23. מטאטא a broom, *Iſai.*14.23.

טאב (Chald. Heb. טוב) well pleaſed, chearful, good, *Dan.*6.23,24.

טב to be good, amiable, pleaſant, &c. to do good, or well; good, goodneſs; --- יטב to be good, well, right; chearful, agreeable; do right, well, &c. מיטב the beſt. חיטיב well.*

טבה to butcher, ſlay; a cook that kills and dreſſes meat, 1 *Sam.*8.13.9.23. טבחים guards, who execute ſtate priſoners. טבחה טבח ſlaughter.

טבל to dip, immerge, plunge; tinge. טבלים died attire, ~~Exod.~~23.15.†*Ezekiel 23.15. 2 Kings 5.14 Job 9 -*

טבע to ſink, penetrate. טבעת a ring into which a finger, &c. is received.

טבר, טבור (elevated) the navel, an hill, middle, higheſt part of a country, *Judg.* 9.37. *Ezek.* 38.12.‡

טבת the month Thebeth, which falls in part of December and January, *Eſt.*2.16.

טהר to be pure, clean, clear, bright; purify, cleanſe: clearneſs, cleanſing, purification. מטהר brightneſs, glory, *Pſ.*89.44.∥

טורה to ſpin, *Exod.*35.25,26. מטוה what is ſpun. §
טוב, טוח, טור, טוש *ſee* טב &c. without the ו
טה, טוח to overlay, 1 *Chron.*29.4. cover, plaſter;

---

* Der. W. da.   † Dabble, dapple.   ‡ Tuber, tuberous.
∥ λαθαρος, καθαιρω, καθαρος clean.   § τιθω ſpin. W. edau.

                daub.

daub. טיח the daubing, *Ezek*.13.12. מטוח the reins, kidneys, inward parts (covered with fat) *Job* 38.36. *Pf.*51.6.---מטהוי *fee* מטח.*

טחן to grind, טחנה grinding, *Eccl.*12.4. †

טחר (to contract, ftrain) טחור the anus, emrods, piles, 1 *Sam.*6.11,17.

טיט (to fpot) טיט mire or clay.‡

טפף (to faften) טטפת frontlets, *Exod.*13.16.*Deut.* 6.8:11.8.

טל, טיל, יטל to caft down, fend forth: the dew. טלא, טלה a young kid (fpotted) 1 *Sam.*7.9.*Ifai.* 40.ר1:.66.25. טלא fpotted, *Gen.*30. 32,33,35. patched, clouted, *Jofh.*9.5. fpotted with divers colours, *Ezek.*16.16. (טלל Chal. for צלל to co-ver, *Neh.*3.15. to be fhaded, take fhelter, *Dan.*4. 9,13) טלטל caft out violently, carry away, cap-tivity, *Ifai.*22.17. נטל to have a burden impofed or laid on, *Lam.*3.28. to bear, fupport, *Ifai.*63. 9. take up, *Ifai.*40.15. to (offer) lay upon,2*Sam.* 24.12, heavy, *Prov.*27.3. נטילם carriers, bear-ers, *Zeph.*1.11. נטל Chal. to lift up, raife, ele-vate, *Dan.*4.31:7.4.‖

טמ־ה to be unclean, polluted, vile. טמא to pol-lute, defile; unclean, טמאה uncleannefs, pollu-tion.§

טמן to hide, cover up. מטמון hid treafures.

טנא Chal. to be wet, moift: a bafket made of moift twigs, *Dan.*26.2,4: 28.5,17. טינא mire, mud, *Dan.*2.41,43.

טנף to defile, dirty, *Cant.*5.3.

טע־ה to feduce, miflead,*Ezek.*13.10.--נטע to plant,

---

* Der. Tego, cover. Τυχος, trua, trulla, trowel; alfo thick, thatch; tache, attack; tack, tackle. † Spa. Atahona. thin. ‡ ιταχος, τηθυς Tethys the earth. ‖ Θαλλω pullulo. Soλος tholus, tutulus, peak. tilt. W. taflu. Ταλαω tollo. § Tamino, contamino, con-taminate. Temno, contemn.

fettle;

fettle; fix as a tent, *Dan.*11.24. *Ifai.*51.16. to infix as nails, *Eccl.*12.11.   נטע, נטיע, מטע a plant,
planting, plantation.

טעם to tafte; a tafte, favour; intellectual tafte,
judgment, difcretion, underftanding, reafon, advice, behaviour. Chald. a decree, ordinance.
טעמם dainty meat.*

טען to goad, *Gen.*45.17. ftab, *Ifai.*14.19.†

טף (to fport, wanton) children, little wantons.
טפוף fporting, moving wantonly, tripping child-
ifhly, *Ifai.* 3.16. --- נטף to diftil, drop; a drop :
ftacte, liquid myrrh which drops from the trees
fpontaneoufly, *Exod.* 30.34.   טף a drop.   הטף,
הטיף to drop inftruction, prophecy, *Mic.*2.6,11.
מטיף a prophet.   נטיפות drops, pendents for the
ears, *Judg.*8.26. *Ifai.*3.19.‡

טפח to fpread out, extend with the hand: to ftroke
gently with open hand as mothers their childrens
limbs, *Lam.*2.22. tenderly ftroked, and treated,
*Lam.*2.20. to expand a roof, *Ifai.*48.13.   טפהות
the coping, 1 *Kings* 7.9.   מטפחה a loofe expanded veil, *Ruth* 3.15. *Ifai.* 3.22.

טפל to annex, add, *Job* 14.17. connect, contrive
lies, *Job* 13.4. *Pf.*119.6,9.||

טפסר (from טפס to quiet, and סר a ruler) a captain, *Jer.*2.27. *Nah.* 3.17.

טפר Chal. for צפר the nails, *Dan.*4.30,33: 7.10.

טפש made grofs or fat, *Pf.*119.70.

טר־ה (order, regularity) טור a row, regular feries,
a mountain, *Dan.* 2.35,45.   טריה frefh, moift,
*Judg.*15.15. *Ifai.*1.6.   טירה a palace, caftle, of
a regular ftructure.   טירות rows, ranges.---נטר
to watch, obferve; watchful againft, *Nah.*1.2. *Jer.*

---

* Der. W. tam.   † Θαινω. Onus, thorn.   ‡ W. dafn. Tip,
tap. || Tabula, table, tablet.

78   יוד   '   טרד

3.5. keep a watchful eye over, *Lev.*19.18. מטרה
מטרא *Lam.*3.12. a mark, butt; prison.*

טרד (continual violent impulse) violent, impetuous, *Prov.*19.13: 27.15. Chald. to drive away,
thruſt out, *Dan.*4.22,29,30: 5.21.†

טרח to tire, weary, wear away, *Job* 37.11. fatigue,
*Deut.*1.12. *Iſai.*1.14.‡

טרם a particle of time: before that; not yet, e'er.

טרף to tear off, tear to pieces; or take food, provender. *Prov.* 31. 15. *Mal.*3.10. prey, ravin; a
leaf or branch torn off, *Gen.* 8. 11. *Ezek.* 17. 9.
הטרף made to give or take food, *Prov.* 30. 8.
טרפה that which is torn.‖

טוש to fly ſwiftly, *Job* 9.26 from.---נטש to let go,
let looſe, to let alone, leave, forſake, permit : to
loofen the tackle of a ſhip, *Iſai.*33.23. to draw a
ſword, free it from the ſcabbard. *Iſai.*21.15. leave
uncultivated, *Exod.* 23. 11. ſpread abroad in a
looſe unguarded manner, *Judg.* 15. 9. 1*Sam.* 30.
16. 2*Sam.*5. 18, 22. battle joined, *i. e.* let looſe,
1*Sam.*4.2. ſtretched out, diffuſed, free from reſtraint, *Iſai.*16.8.   נטישות wild ſpreading branches,*Iſai.*18.5. *Jer.*48.32. extenſive battlements,
*Jer.*5.10.

טת, טות faſting, *Dan.*6.18,19.

'

יוד ſignifies an hand or paw of a beaſt, and in the
Samaritan the form is not ill preſerved; but in

---

* Der. Tower, tier, tree. W. tŵr; tref and tre, an houſe or town,
with the name of the Britiſh proprietor ſubjoined, as Tre-degar, Tref-
Ithel. τηρεω guard.   † Trudo, truſion, intrude, trufs ; thruſt :
tread, dread.   ‡ τειρω tire; tear.   ‖ Δρεπω rapio. Fr. attraper.
trap. τριβω tero, tear. τρεφω nouriſh. δορπον meal. Turf, and with
ſ prefixed, ſtrip. Lit. tr. W. praidd.

the

the modern Hebrew we have only the leaſt of its
members, perhaps the digitus index.   It alſo ſignifies any thing thrown from the hand, as a javelin, which form it bears in the Greek and modern languages.   This letter is the 4th vowel,
ſounded as *ee* in *meet*; but before another vowel
becomes a conſonant, and ſhould be ſounded as
y in *year*.

י is a ſervile, in numbers it ſtands for 10; when
prefixed (from the 3d pronoun) it (1.) forms the
3d perſon maſculine of all verbs, (2.) appellative
nouns and proper names.   Inſerted (3.) it forms
many nouns, if inſerted after the firſt radical it
denotes the conſequence of the participle active,
as ריח odour, *the conſequence of air in motion*; if
inſerted after the ſecond radical, it implies the
conſequence of the participle paſſive, as קציר harveſt reaped, from קצור cut down; and (4.) the
conjugation Epoil הפעיל; (5.) poſtfixed the
name of a people, as עברי an Hebrew; (6.) the
ordinal numbers, as שלשי the third, &c.   (7.)
the ſecond perſon fem. future and imperative;
(8.) plural maſc. in regimine; (9.) to a noun
my, to a verb *me*.   It is alſo,

Paragogic where it heightens the ſenſe. --- (1.) It
is annexed to feminine adjectives, as in *Pſ.* 110.
4. על דברתי after the *moſt excellent* order. *Lam.*
1.1. רבתי עם ſhe that was *ſwarming* full with
people.   (2.) It is annexed to the affixes, as *Pſ.*
103.3. עונכי thy *vaſt* iniquities.   (3.) It is annexed to verbs, as *Ruth* 3.3. ושמתי and put *carefully* on.   (4.) In the ſame manner it is added
to both participles and to the infinitive.

As this letter is regularly dropped and changed,
the greateſt part of the roots are to be found under the remaining letters.   יא־ה

יא־ה to be fuitable, become fit,   *er.* 10.7.

יבש earth.   *fee* בש *Dan.*2,10.

יגר an heap.   Jegar, *Gen.*31.47.

יה Jah, the LORD, emphatically the Effence, from
היה to be.

יהד, יהודיא Chal. Judea; Jews. *fee* דח

ים (the fame הם tumult) the fea, from its tumultuous motion; the weft: the Mediterranean
fea lieth to the weftward of Judea. ימה weftward.

ים, יום a day, wherein men buftle; plu. יומים,
ימום, ימים days. שנתים ימים ים two years of days,
or two full years, *Gen.*41.1. 2 *Sam.*13.23:14.28.
*Jer.*28.3,11.   ימים year, years, or years of days,
Amos 4.4. *Lev.* 25.29. *Num.*9.22. 1 *Sam.* 27.7.
where *year* feems to be underftood. ימים Emims,
a gigantic people, *Gen.*36.24.

יון mire, clay, *Pf.*40.2: 69.2.   a pidgeon, dove.

יין wine.

For the other roots reject the י and fee the remaining letters.

כ

כף* the eleventh letter in the Hebrew alphabet is
thought to have derived its form from the hollow of the hand or cup; but it is more probable,
from its form in the Samaritan and Phœnician alphabets, to have been the abridged fymbol of the
bow or fling. The found of this letter is that of
the afpirated *k*, a found familiar to the Welfh;
as a numeral the initial כ ftands for 20, but the
final ך for 500. This letter is alfo a fervile when
prefixed (from כה thus, fo) *like as, as it were*;
if prefixed to an infinitive, *as foon as*, ככלתו *as*

* Der. καὶ and, even.

foon

foon as he had made an end. When poftfixed to a noun *thine*, to a verb *thee*, e. g. דברך thy word. פקדך he vifited thee.

כא־ה to be fmitten in fpirit, to make fad. --- נכא *fee* נכה. נכאת fpices pounded, *Gen.*43.11. fpicery, *Gen.*37.25. *fee* כת. כוין window, *Dan.*6. 10,11.

כאב to hurt, mar, fpoil, wafte: mar land, 2 *Kings* 3.19. to rot, be wafted, *Job* 14.22. be fore, painful, *Gen.* 34. 25. to hurt, to ache: מכאוב, כאב pain, grief, forrow.* ·

כאר to pierce, penetrate, *Pf.*22.16. כארי particip. benoni. agreeing with עדת or the plu. noun מרעים and may be rendered *The congregation of the wicked have furrounded me,* piercing *my hands,* &c.

כב־ה to quench, extinguifh, put out, as a fire, lamp, &c.

כבר to be heavy, weighty, honourable, rich, &c. be dull, heavy, obftinate, ftubborn: the liver, heavieft of the bowels; glory, to make weighty, *i. e.* honour, glorify. כבוד glory, honour. כבדה heavinefs, heavily, *Exod.* 14. 25. כבודה heavy luggage, *Judg.*18.21. כבוד יהוח the glory of Jehovah, a vifible appearance of fire, light and fplendor, which fhewed Jehovah to be peculiarly prefent.†

כבל (Syr. and Chald. to bind) a chain, fetters, *Pf.* 105.18: 149.8. כבול 1 *Kings* 9.13. a name given in difguft, worthlefs, from כ *like* and בול nothing.‡

כבס to wafh, cleanfe as fullers do; כובם a fuller.‖

---

* Der. αχος ache. W. gofid.   † Gravidus, heavy: copia, abundance.   ‡ Cable; cavil. W. gafael.   ‖ Vas, veffel, bafin.

כבע ,כּוֹבַע. an head piece, or helmet.

כבר to be numerous, multiply, *Job* 35.16. frequently, often, *Ecclef.* 1.10: 2.12, *&c.* כביר copious, numerous, abundant, *Job* 36.5. much,
many, mighty: a kind of coarfe hair cloth for a
pillow, 1 *Sam.* 19.13,16. כברה a fieve. מכבר a
grate; alfo a coarfe ftuff full of holes, 2 *Kings* 8.
15. כברת a little way, fmall fpace, *Gen.* 35.16:
48.7. 2 *Kings* 5:19. *fee* בר־ה †

כבש to fubdue, fubject: a footftool: a lamb, from
its tamenefs. כבשן a furnace, which fubdues by
fire; *Gen.* 19.28. *Exod.* 9.8,10: 19.18.

כד (to emit, dart out) a veffel, pitcher, barrel.
כיד fudden deftruction, *Job* 21.20. כידון a lance,
fhort fpear, javelin. כידוד fparks, flames darting forth, *Job* 41.19. כדכד fome fparkling ftone,
diamond, cryftal. ----- נכד pofterity, progeny, remote offspring; grandfon, *Gen.* 21.23. nephew,
Job 18.19. *Ifai.* 14.22. ‡

כדב (for כזב) a lie, lying, *Dan.* 2.9.

כדר (agitated, precipitate) כידור battle, affault,
Job 15.24. כדור a ball, *Ifai.* 22.18. round a-
bout, *Ifai.* 29.3.

כהיה to reftrain, reprefs, 1 *Sam.* 13.3. to fhrink,
contract as the eyes of old perfons do, be dulled,
Gen. 27.1. *Deut.* 34.7. *Job* 17.7. 1 *Sam.* 3.2. *Zech.*
11.17. to faint or fail, *Ifai.* 42.4. *Ezek.* 21.7.
heavinefs, fainting, *Ifai.* 41.3. a particle of re-
ftriction, thus, in this manner, in this place, in
this time, on this fide; hence the prefix כ like,
as, about; and כי becaufe, for, therefore, when,
tho', although, but. כהה, כהות dark, deadifh,
perhaps ftopt from fpreading, *Lev.* 13.6, 21,26,

---

† Der. Creber, frequent; cribrum, a fieve. Crib.   ‡ καδος ca-
dus, cafk; cado, cadence, cafe, cafual. W. cawdd.

28,39,56. healing, stopping, *Nahum* 3.19. burning dimly, smoking, *Isai.*42.3. ---- כוה to burn, corrode; be burnt, *Prov.* 6. 28. *Isai.* 43. 2. כי, מכוה, כויה burning, scorching. כוין windows, *Dan.*6.10. --- נכה to smite, strike, slay: stricken in the feet, lame, 2 *Sam.*4.4: 9.3. contrite, *Isai.*46. 2. נכים lame, abjects, *Ps.*35.15. מכי slain, *Jer.* 18.21. נכת spicery pounded. --- נכא to strike, smite very much, stricken, *Isai.* 16. 7. to make sad or break the heart, *Ezek.*13.22. be grieved, *Dan.*11.30. broken in heart, *Ps.*109.16. *Prov.*15. 13: 17.22. broken, vile, *Job* 30.8.*

כהל to be able. כהלין they could, *Dan.*5.8,15.

כהן to adjust, fit, fit on; deck, adorn, array with splendid ornaments, as the high priest was, *Isai.* 61. 10. a priest, to perform the priest's office. כהנה the priesthood, priest's office: a principal officer in civil affairs, 2 *Sam.*8.18: 20.26. 1 *Kings* 4.5. *Job* 12.19.†

כויה and כוא *see* under כהי ‡

כה (to spit, spit out) כוח radical moisture; vegetable moisture, or the prolific virtue of the earth, *Gen.*4.12. vigour, power, force, strength, ability, *Ezra* 2.69. substance, wealth, *Job* 6.22. *Prov.*5. 10. fruits produced by vegetation, *Job* 31. 39. A lizard, by the Arabs called Guaril, remarkable for its vigour in destroying serpents, *Lev.*11.30. --- יכח to argue, dispute with, prove, convince, confute, reprove, rebuke, chastise, correct, mark out, demonstrate, *Gen.* 24.14,44. תוכחה, תוכח reproof, rebuke, argument, reasoning, chastisement, correction. --- נכח right straight, direct;

* Der. χαος; chaos; cæcus, blind. -icio, percutio, ictus, νεικος, νει-χαω, quia. † κονεω serve; διακονος, deacon. ‡ καιω.

84   כל־ה   כחד

right on, oppofite: נכחה, נכח right, equity, uprightnefs; fet right, 2 *Sam.* 15.3.*

כחד to cut off, remove, hide, conceal.†

כחל to colour, paint the eyes with lead ore, *Ezek.*
23.40. ‡

כחש to fail, be deficient, *Pf.* 109.24: *Hof.* 9.2. *Hab.*
3.9. weaknefs, leannefs. *Job* 16. 8. deficient in
truth, to lie, diffemble; a lie; lying.‖

כי a particle; becaufe, &c. (alfo burning, *Ifai.* 3.
14.) *fee under* כה

כיד, כיל, &c. *fee* כד, כל without the י

ככה a particle; thus. The fame as כה *which fee.*

כוכב, ככב (to fhine) a ftar; ftream of light.

ככר (to extend around) a round loaf, cake: an extent of country environed with hills: round piece
of lead, *Zech.* 5.7. talent, or round mafs of filver
or gold; its weight 3000 fhekels, equal to about
113 lb. 10 oz. troy. Talent of gold reduced to
modern value is 5075*l.* 15*s.* 7*d.* of filver, 353*l.*
11*s.* 10*d.*

כל־ה to finifh, complete, accomplifh, confume,
fail, fully determine, make clean riddance, make
full end of, take all away: pluck out, *Pf.* 74.11.
altogether, full end, confumption, clean riddance.
כל all, every. הכול, כול comprehend, contain,
hold, receive, able to abide. כלה a bride, mar-
ried woman, who has compleated her virginity,
daughter-in-law. מכלה a prifon, fold, pen, *Hab.*
3.7. כלי, כיל, כילי a clofe man, churl, a gripe-
all, *Ifai.* 32.5,7. כלי a veffel, inftrument, furniture, ftuff, jewel, or utenfil prepared for man's
ufe. כלל to complete entirely, make quite per-

---

* Der. W. Hoch; gwych: κικις, κικυς, ισχυω, queo. hawk
to fpit. † κηυθω, occulto; hide; hood. Cædo, fcindo. W. cuddio.
‡ Coloro, colour. Coal. ‖ γασος deceive; κακος evil. Quafh.

fect.

fect. כלול efpoufals, *Jer.* 2. 2. כליל perfect,
wholly; holocoft, burnt-offerings, *Deut.* 33.10.
Pf. 51.19. מכלול, מכלל, כלילה perfection. כליון
confumption, *Ifai.* 10.22. failing, *Deut.* 28.65.
תכלית, תכלה מכלה an end, perfection. כליות
the kidneys or reins, wonderfully prepared for
the laft fecretion of urine; fecret thoughts, *Pf.*
16.7. כלכל to nourifh, fupport with food; fuftain, guide, manage, provide fuftenance. כלא
to reftrain, confine, fhut up, refrain. כלוא, כלא,
מכלא a prifon, fold. כלאים a mixture of things
of different nature, confined as it were together.
---יכל, יוכל to be able, can prevail. מיכל a brook,
or fhallow water, a ford, 2 *Sam.* 17.20. יכלכל to
be adequate, equal, able to fupport, *Prov.* 18.14.
Mal. 3.2. --- נכל to contrive deceitfully, deceive,
a deceiver, *Mal.* 1.14. beguile, *Num.* 25. 18.
התנכל to deal fubtily, *Pf.* 105.25. confpire, *Gen.*
37.18. נכלים wiles, *Num.* 25.18. --- מכלת food,
1 *Kings* 5.11. from אכל. להכיל to confume,
Ezek. 21.28. for להאניל.*
כלב (to keep clofe) a dog. כלוב a bafket, *Amos* 8.
1, 2. a cage, *Jer.* 5.27.†
כלח (beyond perfection) old age, *Job* 30. 2. full
age, *Job* 5.6.‡
כלם to be afhamed, blufh, turn afide, reproach,
fhame: כלמה fhame, confufion.‖
כלף (to impel) כילפים hammers or axes, *Pf.* 74.6.§
כמה (related to חמה) to burn with defire: long
for, *Pf.* 63.1. כימה pleiades, or feven ftars, per-

---

* Der. Qualus, bafket. All; ολος whole: κωλευω hinder; κλειω fhut
up; celo, conceal, κοικον cœlum. kill. cell. W. Cŵlen, caill,
καλλος beauty.   † κελ or κερϐερος, Cerberus. καλυϐιον cabin. κλωϐος.
κλουϐος cage for birds. Clip, cleave, and perhaps whelp. ‡ W. Cellach,
‖ Calumnia, calumny.   calamity.   W. cywilydd.   § κολαπτω,
κολαπτερ hammer.   Cleft. collop. club.

haps the light, making the *fire*, the *fpirit*, and the *light*. Job 9. 9. Canft thou bind the active particles of *light*, or loofen the active particles of *fpirit*? Compare ver. 38. That maketh the *light* and the *fpirit*, and turneth, &c. Amos 5.8. This verfion feems more appofite than the rabbinical. כמן Cummin, a feed *warm* in quality, *Ifai.* 27. 25,27. מכמנים treafures.*

כמו like as; *fee* כה and ניה

כומז, כומז fome female circular ornament, bracelet, girdle, necklace, *Ex.*25.32. *Numb.*31.20.

כמן (to hide, hoard) מכמנים hidden treafures, hoards, *Dan.*11.43. כמן *fee* כמה

כמס (to lay up) laid up, *Deut.*32.34.

כמר (to convolve) to yearn, have the bowels rolled together, *Gen.*43.30. 1 *Kings* 3.26. *Hof.*11.8. parched, or contracted in rolls as the fkin by famine, *Lam.* 5. 10.   כמרים idolatrous priefts, 2*Kings* 23.5. *Hof.* 10.5. *Zeph.* 1.4.   מכמרת a net, toil, which taketh prey by being contracted together.   כמרי, כמרר thick convolved darknefs, *Job* 3.5.†

כמש (to be fwift, active) כמיש כטוש the obfcene idol of the Moabites and Amorites.‡

כן, כון to fit, adopt, prepare, adjuft, machinate, eftablifh, confirm, ordain, frame, form, fafhion, &c. כן a particle, fo, thus, well, right, now. לכן therefore.   מכונה, מכון, כן an eftablifhment, ftation, bafe, place, foot. תכונה fafhion, *Ezek.* 43.11. feat *Job* 23.3. ftore, furniture, preparation, apparatus, *Neh.*2.10. כנה fettlement, colony, *Pf.* 80.15. כנות companies of men com-

---

* Der. μαω long for. κυμινος cúminus.   † Cremo, burn. κιμμις; mauros. moor.   ‡ Κωμος κωμη revellings. κωματζω comeffatio, reval.

missioned,

miffioned, *Ezra* 4. 7. כנה to eftablifh, reft, depend on, not to *furname*, &c. *Job* 32.21,22. *Ifai.*
44,5: 45.4. כונים cakes offered to the queen of
heaven or air, *Jer.*7.18: 44.19. כיון, *Amos* 5.26.
an idol reprefentative of the machine of the heavens. כנים lice, gnats, or fome fmall infects
which fettle on the bodies of men and beafts.
אכן an affirmative particle, denoting *certainty.*
יכין Ichin direction, 1 *Kings* 7.21. 2 *Chron.* 3.17.
and בעז the name of two pillars placed by Solomon in the porch of the temple, and containing
perhaps fome reprefentation of the univerfe. כנן
to prepare, adapt, eftablifh, confirm entirely or
completely.*
כנמא particle thus, in this fort, *Ezra* 4.8: 5.4,11.
from כן thus, and מא what.
כנס to gather, heap together, wrap up, collect.
מכניסים fwathes, bandages that wrap the body
clofe.†
כנע to bring down, bow down, humble onefelf.
כנען Canaan, humbled; named from the curfe
of Noah! the Canaanites were traders, hence it
fignifies, a trader or merchant. כנעה wares, mer-
chandize, *Jer.*10.17.‡
כנף (to furround, inclofe) wing, fkirt, to remove,
be removed, fly away, *Ifai.* 30.20.‖
כנר (concave) כנור a lute, guitar, harp.§
כנש to gather together, *Dan.*3.2,27. *fee* כנס
כס־ה to inclofe, include, cover, conceal, hide,
number, affefs, *Exod.*12.4. מכסה number, *Ex.*

* Der. Καρνος, κικνια lice. κανων canon, canonical. μηχανη machina,
machine. κονεω, διακονος, deacon. Conn, Count, Canton, cunning,
kind, king, queen. Cano, canto, cant, chaunt. W. hagen. † κοι-
νος communis, common. Fr. caneçor, breeches. κανης, κανατρον ca-
niftrum, canifter; κωνος cone. ‡ Genu, knee. kneel. ‖ Canopy,
camp. § Κιθυρα Cithara: guitar, canorus.

12.4. the worth, value, *Lev.*27.23. מכס tribute, affeſſment, ſhare. כס, כסה, כסא a throne covered with a canopy. כסא, כסה new moon, *i. e.* concealed, *Pſal.*81.3. *Prov.*7.20. כוס a cup or goblet with a cover; an Owl which hides itſelf, *Lev.*11.17. *Deut.*14.16. *Pſal.*102.6. כיס bag, purſe. נכסים riches, wealth. כסוי, כסות, מכסה covering, raiment, veſture, clothing. כסתות *ſee the root* כסת *

כסח to grub up, cut down, *Pſ.*80.16. *Iſai.*33.12. כסוחה as dung, not torn, *Iſai.*5.25. from כ like as, and סחה

כסל (crooked, tortuous, oblique) the joints of the back, the flanks, loins, *Lev.*3.4. *Pſ.*38.7. *hence* ſupport, ſtrength, confidence, *Job*4.6. *Prov.*3.26. hope, *Job* 8.14: 31.24. *Pſ.* 78.7. כסל folly, crookedneſs, perverſeneſs; to be fooliſh, wicked, perverſe, *Jer.* 10.8. כסיל a fool, fooliſh, perverſe: the air or atmoſphere, but tranſlated Orion, *Job* 9.9: 38.31. *Amos* 5.9. כסלי planets, *Iſai.*13.10. כסלו Chiſleu, *Neh.*1.1. *Zech.*7.1. the ninth month which begins with the new moon in November.†

כסם to cut or clip the hair, ſhave, *Ezek.*44.20. bearded corn, rye, &c. *Exod.* 9. 32. *Iſai.* 28. 25. *Ezek.*4.9.‡

כסף paleneſs; to be pale or wan, pine as with deſire, *Gen.*31.30. *Job* 14.15. *Pſ.*17.12: 84.2. pale with fear, *Zeph.*2.1. pale mettal, ſilver, money.‖

כסת a cuſhion, pillow or covering, *Ezek.*13.18,20. *ſee under* כס־ה

כען now, now then, *Dan.*3.15.

---

* Der. κασιω. Fr. chaiſe. Caſa, caſe. Cenſus — κασυς the numeral termination in Greek. Caſh. † κοζουλια folly. ‡ κοσμος, κοσμεω adorn. Coſmetic. ‖ Concupiſco, to deſire or long for.

כעס and כעש to anger, vex: be vexed; provocation, wrath, anger, grief.*

כפ־ד to bend, bow down; bend back, pacify, *Prov.* 21.14. a bending branch : the palm of the hand, fole of the foot, hollow of a fling, 1 *Sam.* 25. 29. hollow of the thigh, *i.e.* acetabulum : a fpoon. כפות hollow handles, *Cant.* 5.5. כפים clouds, hemifpheres, *Job* 36.32. כיף, כפים hollow caves, rocks, *Job* 30.6. *Jer.* 4.29. אכף for כף the hand, *Job* 33. 7. כפף to bow or bend greatly.†

כפל to double; fold back. כפלים twofold, double, *Job* 11.6. *Ifai.* 40.2.‡

כפן (to hunger, be hungry) hunger, famine. *Job* 5.22: 30.3. כפנה *Ezek.* 17.7. bend, turn as it were, from כ and פן ‖

כפס (to connect) כפים a beam, rafter, *Hab.* 2. 11.

כפר to cover, overfpread, pitch, *Gen.* 6. 11. the pitch or turpentine tree, *Cant.* 1. 14: 4. 13. a village, covert, to (cover fin) expiate, atone, appeafe; purge, pacify, pardon; ranfom, bribe, fatisfaction, atonement: to difannul, render ineffectual *Ifai.* 28.18. כפור, כפר a bafon, veffel with a cover: hoar froft that covereth the earth, *Exod.* 16. 14. *Job* 38. 29. *Pf.* 147. 16. כפיר a young lion which hides himfelf in coverts. כפרת the cover of the ark, the propitiatory, mercy feat. §

כפש to deprefs, cover, plunge in, *Lam.* 3.16. ¶

כפת to bind, *Dan.* 3.20,21,23,24.

---

* Der. Κυζω, κυζομαι enrage. W. Câs. † Κυφος cup. Καμπτω bend. Cave, Cope, Cap, Coop, Cove. Capio. ‡ Copulo, Couple. W. dyblyg. ‖ Pine. § Cover. Κυπρος Cyprefs. Coffer. W. Cwfert. ¶ Κυπας, Κιβος, Cibus.

כפתר (from כף to bend, and תר to turn round,) a round knob, refembling pomegranates: lintels with fpherical ornaments on the top of two of the pillars in Solomon's temple, *Am*.9.1. *Zeph*.2.14.

כר־ה to cut, penetrate, cut up, dig, bore, pierce; cut off: a grazed pafture: pafture, fheep or lambs; to provide, prepare, procure: provifion, 2 *Kings* 6.23. a captain, furniture, *Gen*.31.34. to grieve, אתכרית was grieved, *Dan*.7.15. כרים battering rams, perhaps chiefs or captains, *Ezek*.6.23. כרת cottages; holes in the rock, *Zeph*.2.6. מכרת habitations, *Gen*.49.5. מכרה a falt pit, *Zeph*.2.6. כור a furnace, (dug in the ground) a crucible. מכורה the birth, nativity, original of a perfon, *Ezek*.16.3: 21,30: 29.14. כר a meafure for folids or liquids, the fame as the Homer; a large round pannier, *Gen*.31.34. כיור, כיר the laver in the tabernacle and temple: Solomon's fcaffold, 2 *Chron*. 6. 12. the hearth, *Zech*.12.6. pans, pots, 1 *Sam*. 2. 14. *Lev*. 11.35. אכר hufbandman who digs. כרכר to leap, fkip, move nimbly, dance, 2 *Sam*. 6. 14, 16. כרכרות dromedaries, fwift beafts, *Ifai*.66.20. --- נכר to be diftinguifhed, difcern, know, acknowledge, regard; to mark or diftinguifh himfelf as different from what he is, to diffemble; to feign to be another: a ftranger, foreigner, eafily known; to eftrange, act or treat as a ftranger; deliver, give up, alienate, 1 *Sam*.23.7. נכרי ftrange, ftranger. מכר acquaintance. הכרה fhew, or diftinguifhed appearance, *Ifai*.3.9. The Epoil or Hiphil of נכר generally fignifies to acknowledge.*

* Der. Καρ, Καςνος, Αςνος lamb. Καςανος, Καςαιω. Fr. Garenne, Warren. Κςιος; ram. Κυριος; Κοιρανος;. Car, Cart, Carry, Chariot. Curro. Current. χορτος;. W. Gwair. Fr. Créufer. Κοςιω.

כרב,

כרב, כרוב a cherub, כרובים cherubim, the forms
are defcribed *Ezek.*ɪ. and feem to be emblematic
figures reprefentive of every part of nature, annexed to the ark of God, which from its form
and having wheels was perhaps not unlike a triumphant car, intimating that every part of nature was fubject to the Divinity that was fuppofed to be feated on the ark.

כרבל to clothe, inveft, ɪ *Chron.*ɪ5.·27.   כרבלת
fome upper garments, *Dan.*3.2ɪ.* -

כרז to cry aloud, *Dan.*5.20. an herald, *Dan.*3.4.†

כרך (to involve) תכריך an outward garment, *Eſt.*
8.ɪ5.‡

כרכב area, compafs, circuit.

כרכם (from כר to cut and כמה to be warm) faf-
fron.‖

כרם (to prune) a vine, vine dreffer, vineyard.§

כרמל (from כר pafture, and מל־ה to fill) Carmel,
a fruitful field, full ears of corn.   כרמיל crimfon
or purple fiſh taken near mount Carmel, 2*Chron.*
2.7,ɪ4: 3.ɪ4.

כרם a throne, *Dan.*7.9.

כרסמן to extirpate, root up, *Pſ.*80.ɪ4.

כרע to bend, bow down, couch.   הכריע to fubdue,
bring down.   כרעים the legs (which bend) ¶

כרפס fine linen, *Eſth.*ɪ.6.**

כרש (to contract) the belly or maw, *Jer.*5ɪ.34.†‖

כרת to cut off, as a branch, or by death, to chew
meat, *Num.*ɪɪ.33. to cut in pieces as a facrifice.

כריתות, כריתת a divorce.·· מכרתי ſwords, *Gen.*

---

* Der. Crupellarii, foldiers covered with iron armour.   † Κραζω,
Κηρυσσω, Κηρυξ. ‡ Κροκωτος carracalla. ‖ Κροκος Crocus. § Καρμα,
muſtum. Κουρμι beer. Charm. Carmen. Crumb. ¶ Crus, leg, Cringe,
Crank, Crook, Crouch.   ** Καρβασος carbaſus.   †‖ Γαςηρ belly.
W. Croth.

49.5. כרת ברית to make a covenant, ratify, as defcribed *Gen.*15.10,18. *Jer.*34.18,19. *fee* ברת ‖‖‖

כש־ה to cover, be covered, fame as כס־ה *Deut.*32. 15. כוש Æthiopia, the country of Chufeftan. כושי an Æthiopian. כושית an Æthiopian woman.

כשב a fheep or lamb.*

כשר, כשרי a Chaldean.

כשל to ftumble againft an obftacle, fo as to produce fome diftafter; to fall, ftumble. כשלון a fall, *Prov.*16.18. מכשל a ftumbling block. כשיל an ax, mall, pick-ax, crow, fome inftrument for pulling down buildings, *Pf.*74.6.†

כשף (to difcover) to ufe inchantments, forcery; a forcerer. מכשף an inchanter. מכשפה an inchantrefs, witch.‡

כשר to be or proceed *right:* right, agreeable. כשרון equity, rectitude. כושרות right convenient feafons, or as the Syriac, with profperity, *Pf.*68. 6. כישות a fpindle which directs the thread, *Prov.*31.19.

כת to pound, beat, deftroy. כתת to beat over and over, to deftroy by repeated beatings. כתות beaten, fpoken of oil obtained by pounding. מכתה burfting, breaking, *Ifai.*30.14. ---- נכת, נכאת (pounded) fpicery, aromatics; precious things, *Gen.*37.25: 43.11. 2*Kings*20.13. *Ifai.* 39.2.‖

כתב to write, defcribe, record, prefcribe, a writing. מכתב regifter. כתבת infcription, *Lev.*19. 28. §

כתל (to confine) a wall, *Cant.*2.9.

כתם to engrave, embofs. ככתם marked, *Jer.*2.

‖‖‖ Der. Κειρω, Κουριζω Curtus, whence Curt, Curtail, Curtlefs; and with ſ prefixed the Danifh Skorter and Englifh Short. W. Cwtta.
* Ger. Schaf. Sheep.   † Joftle.   ‡ Βασκαινω.   ‖ Cut, κοττιω.
§ Lit. tr. πυκτις book.

22. כתם joined with words expreſſive of gold, it means gold emboſſed. מכתם golden; in the title of the Pſalms : a golden wedge, *Iſai.*13.12. כתנת, כתן a coat. *

כתף the ſhoulder, ſhoulder-blade; ſhoulder-piece, ſide of a building, 1 *Kings* 7.30,34. ſide of a country, a portion.

כתר to encloſe, ſurround; beſet, crowned; a crown, diadem. כתר לי, ſtay near me, *Job* 36.2. כתרת, כיתות a chapiter of a pillar. †

כתש to bray or pound in a mortar, *Prov.*27.22. מכתש a mortar, *Prov.*27.22. an hollow place in the ground, or perhaps a large tooth, a grinder, *Judg.*15.19.

ל

למד the twelfth letter is a ſervile; its form has been conjectured to have been taken from a plough-ſhare. ל prefixed (from אל) 1. to, unto. 2. With a V. infinitive, to, for to, as לפקד to viſit, until, *Lev.* 24. 12. after that, *Exod.* 19. 1. 3. into. 4. for, becauſe. 5. after, *Gen.* 7. 10. 6. according to. 7. of, concerning, touching, *Gen.* 20.13. 8. for, inſtead of; as it were, *Lam.*1.7. 9. a particle of time; at, about. 10. a particle of nearneſs; at, about, before, with. 11. with, together with, *Gen.*46.26. 12. of, out of, *Iſai.*54.12. *Pſ.*12.7. *Exod.*35.34. *Lev.*7.26.

לא״ה to be tired, fatigued, to loathe, be grieved, faint. תלאה travel, fatigue. לוא, לא not, nay, no; none, without; ſometimes put for לו to him; and for לו if, 2*Sam.*18.12. 1*Sam.*14.30. oh! that, *Iſai.*48.11.*

* **Der.** Χιτων. Coat.   † Κιταξις, Κιδαξις, Cidaris.   ‡ Laſſo, Laſſus.

לאב

לאב to be dry, thirſty. תלאובת great draughts, *Hoſea* 13.5.*

לאט to hide, involve, 2*Sam.*19.4. concealment, ſe-crecy, *Judges* 4. 21. בלאט ſecretly, in ſecret. לאט ſlowly, gently. *ſee* אט†

לאך (to ſend, ſerve) מלאך an agent, meſſenger, angel, ambaſſador. מלאכות a meſſage, *Hag.* 1. 13.‡

לאל (from ל and אל) in the power of, interpoſi-tion of.

לאם (to meet together) לאום a people, nation.‖

לב, לבה, לבב (to vibrate, move to and fro, or up and down) the heart, mind; middle: to raviſh, delight the heart, *Cant.*4.9. to be wiſe in heart, *Job* 11.12, to turn up and down on the hearth, 2*Sam.*13.6,8,10.----לבת for להבת a flame,*Exod.* 13.2. ---- לביא, לבא a lioneſs, ſo called from her *heart, i. e.* courage. §

לבט to fall, tumble down, *Prov.*8.10. *Hoſ.*4.14.¶

לבן to whiten, be white; whiteneſs, white. לבנה a white brick or tile; the clay in Ægypt and Ca-naan when burnt is white: to make brick: the white ſilver paleneſs of the moon, *Cant.* 6. 10. *Iſai.*24.23: 36.26. Frankincenſe, of a white co-lour, the white poplar. לבנת paved curiouſly with brick, *Exod.* 24. 10. מלבן brick wall or building; brick-kiln. לבנון Lebanon, or white mountain, on the north of the land of Iſrael, du-ring one ſeaſon of the year much covered with ſnow.**

---

* Der. Lybia. W. Llafur.   † Lateo, Latent, Lot.   ‡ Le-gare, Legate, Legacy. Fr. Laquais.   ‖ Λαος, Loam, tenacious earth. Loom.   § Life, Lubet, Libet, Libido, Libidinous, Leap, Librate, Liber, Love. W. Llew.   ¶ Labor, Lapſus, Lapſe.   ** Al-bus. Alpes. W. Lleuad. Peithyn.

לבש to clothe, put on, inveſt, array. לבוש, לבוש, מלבוש
תלבושת veſture, garment, apparel.**

לוג, לג (to ceaſe) a log, (a meaſure one-72d of an
Epha) containing about three-qrs. of a pint.*

אלגביש great hail. *ſee in* א

אלגם, לגם *(ſee in* א*)* Algum, timber trees which
grew on mount Lebanon, written in 1 *Kings* 10.
11, 12.   אלמג Almug.

ילד, לד to produce young, beget or bear, gender,
bring forth, travail with child, be delivered of a
child; to do the office of a midwife, *Exod.* 1. 16.
ילד, ולד a child.   ילדה a girl.   ילדות childhood,
youth.   לדה birth.   מילדת a midwife.   התילד
to make out ones pedigree, *Num.* 1. 18.   הולדת a
birth-day.   מולדת kindred, nativity.   תולדות
generations.   יליד he that is born.†

לה to fail, faint: be outragious, *Gen.* 47. 13.
מתלהלה an outragious madman.----לו/--לוה *ſee*
נלה to complete, make an end of, *Iſai.* 33. 1.   מנל
perfection, completion, *Job* 15. 29.   נול Chaldee
to defile.

להב (to burn, flame) שלהבת, להבה flame; the
glittering blade of a ſword, *Judges* 3. 22. or head
of a ſpear, 1 *Sam.* 17. 7.   שלהבתיה a violent raging flame, the flame of Jah, *Cant.* 8. 6.   *ſee in* ש ‡

להג ſtudy, meditation, *Eccl.* 12. 12. from ל and הג
meditate.‖

להט to burn, ſet fire, ſcorch up, *Gen.* 3. 24.   להטים
inchantments, *Exod.* 7. 11. *ſee* לט §

להם, מתלהם a wound : others, to be mild, ſoft,
gentle, *Prov.* 18. 8: 26. 22.¶ .

** Λωπος thin garment. Limbus, border.   * Lag, Lack. Λα-
γυνον galon.   † Yield. Ειλειθυια Ilythia or Lucina : Lad, (with Sin
prefixed) Child. W. Herlodes.   ‡ Λαμπτω, Δαμπρος, Λαμπας,
Lamp. W. Llafu.   ‖ Λεγω, Lego.   § Light. Lantern.   ¶ Lamb.

להן

לחן the fame as לכן therefore, *Dan.*2.6,9. befides, except, *Dan.*2.11: 3.28. but *Ezra* 5.12.

להק, להקת (to increafe) company, 1*Sam.*19.20.

לו־ה to join, add; lend, borrow, and fo mutually united and obliged. לוית ornament, addition, wreath, diadem, *Prov.*1.9: 4.9. ליות addition, united figures, Cherubim. לוי joined. Levi, Levite. לויתן Leviathan (from לוי coupled, and תן dragon) a crocodile, whale, or monfter. לות with, *Ezra* 4.12. לו, לוא O that! would to God! affuredly. לולי, לולא except, unlefs, from לו and לא *

לוג, לוז, לוח fee *without the* ו   •

לז, לוז to turn apart, decline, afide, *Prov.*3.21: 4. 21. the almond, hazel or nut tree, perhaps from its flexibility, *Gen.*30.37. הלז, לוז, לז this, that, pronoun demonftrative.---נלוז perverfe, froward, *Prov.* 2.15: 3.32: 14.2. נלוז לזות perverfenefs, *Prov.*4.24. *Ifai.*30.12.†

לח־ה (fmooth) לוח a fmooth table, block of wood or ftone. לחה, לח natural viridity or juice, fmoothnefs of complexion, *Deut.* 34.7. green, moift, with its natural moifture in it. לחי the lower jaw bone.‡

לחך to lick, lick up.‖

לחם to cut, hack with teeth or with fword : to eat, fight, make war; food, bread, meat; a feaft, *Dan.*5.21. נלהם to fight, make war. מלחמה battle.§

לחן, לחנות concubines; perhaps from לח fmooth, delicate.

---

* Der. Fr. Allier. Γλια Gluten. αλλειω. Lend, Loan. † Λιαζω Loofe, Leaze, i. e. lie, decline from the truth. ‡ Λαχαιω, Leck, Χλοα grafs, Levis. W. Gwlychu. ‖ Λειχω, Lingo, Lingua, Lick. W. Llyfu. § W. Lluniaeth, Milwyr.

להץ to prefs, fqueeze, crufh, thruft; opprefs, oppreffion.

לחש to fpeak foftly, whifper, mutter, 2*Sam*.12.19.
Pf.12.7. a muttering inchantment, *Eccl*.10.11.
Jer.8.17. foft perfuafion, *Ifai*.3.3. foft humble
prayer, *Ifai*.26.16.   לחשים ear-rings, fome tin-
kling ornament worn as an amulet or charm,
Ifai.3.20.   מלחשים charmers, *Pf*.58.3. *

לט, לוט, לאט to enwrap, involve, 1 *Kings* 19.13.
2 *Sam*.19.4. *Ifai*.25.7. to be covered over, 1*Sam*.
21.9. fecret, *Job* 15.11.   לאט gently, 2*Sam*.18.
5. בלט, בלאט fecretly, privily, foftly.   לטים,
להטים enchantments, tricks, which cover real
appearances and impofe falfe ones, *Exod*.7.11,12:
8.7,18.   לט myrrh, laudanum, *Gen*.37.35: 43.
11.   לטא, לטאה a lizard, like a newt.†

לטש to polifh, fharpen, whet, 1*Sam*.13.20. to glif-
ten with anger, *Job* 16.9. a whetter, inftructor,
Gen.4.22.   מלטש fharp or fharpened, *Pf*.52.2.

ליות addition. *fee* לוה

ליל, ליש &*c. fee without the* י

ילך (לך) the fame as הלך to go, walk, &*c*. הוליך
lead, bring, carry.

לכד to take in war, by lot, by fnare, catch. מלכדה
a trap, *Job* 18.10.

לל to wind, turn, move round.   לול winding
ftairs, 1 *Kings* 6.8.   לילה, ליל the night. לילית
bird of night, fcriech-owl.   לולי, לולא except,
unlefs, from לו if, and לא not. --- ילל to fhriek,
howl.   אללי woe, *Mic*.7.1. *Job* 10.15.   תוללינו
they that wafted us, made us howl, *Pf*.137.3.‡

למד to learn, teach, be taught.   תלמיד a fcholar,

---

* Der. Λακαζω Illicio.   † Λनθω Lateo, Latent. W. Lleidr.
‡ Lull, Loll. W. Ellyll. Ολυλω Ululo. Eλεω; Ulula, Owl. Yell.
Howl.

1*Chron.*25.8. למדים difciples, *Ifai.*8.16. מלמד a goad for oxen, *Judg.*3.31.||

לן, לון to abide all night, lodge; abide, remain; to murmur or growl as beafts in the night. מלונה, מלון an inn, lodge. תלונות murmurings, growlings *

לץ, לוץ to abforb, fwallow up, *Job* 6. 3. fwallow down, *Obad.*16. devour, *Prov.*20.25. the throat, gullet. יעלעו for ילקו fuck up, *Job* 39.30.†

לעב to deride, fneer, mock, 2*Chron.*36.16.‡

לעג to deride, laugh to fcorn, ftammer; fcorning, ftammering.||

לעז barbarous language or pronunciation, *Pfal.* 114.1.§

לעט to gulp, tafte, fwallow, eat. הלעיט feed, give me a fup of, *Gen.*25.30.¶

לען (to reject, deteft) לענה wormwood.**

לף (ילף, ילפיד (to ftick, adhere) a fcab, fcabbed, *Lev.*21.20: 22.22.----מלפנו who teaches us, *Job* 35.12. for מאלפנו from אלף

לפד (to fhine) לפיד a burning lamp, light, torch, brand; lightening, *Exod.*20.11.††

לפת to incline or be turned afide, *Job* 6.18. turn himfelf, *Ruth* 3.8. take hold of, *Judg.*16.29. to embrace.‡‡

לץ, לוץ to fcorn, fcoff at, mock, deride; a fcorner, מליץ, לצץ a fcorner. התלוצץ to be mockers, *Ifai.* 28.22. לצון fcorning. מליצה a taunting pro-verb.----מליץ an ambaffador, interpreter, teacher, advocate, interceffor, mediator. מליצה interpre-tation. *fee* מליץ||||

מלצר, לצר houfe fteward or butler, *Dan.*1.11,16.

|| Der. Μανθανω.   * Luna; Lunar.   † Gula.   ‡ Λιβιναι.
|| Γελαω Laugh.   § Βλαισος Blæfus.   ¶ Γλυζω Glutio; Lautco.
Lit. tr. Glut, Gloat.   ** Loon (fcoundrel).   †† Λαμπας Lim-pidus, Limpid.   ‡‡ Λαφος Lævus. |||| Λασθω Λασκω deride.

לק to

לק to lick or lap as a dog, *Judges* 7.5. 1 *Kings* 21.
19: 22.38.   לקק to lap up again and again.   ילק
a fpecies of locufts, &c.

לקח to take, receive, catch, fetch, &c. &c. (this
root drops its firft letter) learning, doctrine; fair
fpeech, *Prov.* 7. 21.   מקה taking, 2*Chron.* 19.7,
קוח a prifon.   מקחות things received for ufe,
wares, *Neh.* 10. 31.   מלקוח prey, booty taken;
jaws which catch prey, *Pfal.* 22.15,   מלקחים a
pair of tongs, fnuffers, *Exod.* 37.23.*

לקט to collect, gather up, glean;   a gleaning.
ילקוט a fcrip into which things were gathered,
1 *Sam.* 17.4c.†

לקש to gather the latter fruits, *Job* 26.6. the latter math, *Amos* 7.1.   מלקוש the latter rain which
in Judea falls about May.

לש, לוש to knead.   ליש a lion of the fierceft kind,
Job 4.11. *Prov.* 30.30. *Ifai.* 30.6.   לשון, ילשון a
tongue, language; to betongue, flander, accufe,
Pf. 101.5. *Prov.* 30.10. a bay, *Jofh.* 15.2,5: 18.
19. a lingot or wedge of gold, *Jofh.* 7. 24. a
tongue or flame of fire, *Ifai.* 5.24. compare *Act.*
2.3.‡

לשד (to be moift) moifture, *Pf.* 32.4. *Numb.* 11.8.
לשך, לשכה a chamber, parlour, room. ‖
לשם a Ligure, precious ftone which fparkles, *Ex.*
28.19: 39.12.

לשן (to turn about, twift) לשון tongue. *fee above*
under לש

לתח, מלתחה a veftry, wardrobe, 2*Kings* 10.22,
לתך an half Homer, about 38 gallons, *Hof.* 3.2.
לתע to break in pieces.   נתעו for נלתעו are broken, *Job* 4. 10.   מלתעות the great teeth or grin-

---

* Der. Ἀηχω, Λειγω Colligio. Laqueus.   † Δηκύθος veffel.
‡ Γλωσσα. Λαζω flander.   ‖ Λεισχη.

100

מ מ מם

ders, *Pf.* 58.6. מתלעות the fame, the letters being tranfpofed, *Job* 29.17. *Prov.* 30.14. *Joel.* 1.6.

מ

מם the thirteenth letter is a fervile and a confonant; the found of this letter, as well as form
of it in the Samaritan alphabet, feems to have
been taken from the rolling of the fea, and refembles the undulation thereof. מים fignifies water, in Ægyptian Mω whence the Greek Mυ in Tyrian מיא as well as Greek Maια is mother, as
faith *Euftatius*, water being the mother of all
productions. This letter is a liquid labial; as a
numeral מ ftands for 40, but the final ם 500.
As a fervile מ (1.) prefixed, from מן or מנה
to diftribute, is the particle *from, with, by*; (2.)
forms the participle of Epoil, Epol, and with ת
Etpol; whence (3.) it forms nouns fignifying
the *inftrument, means,* or *place of action,* as מגן a
fhield; (4.) to an infinitive, מפקד *from vifiting;*
(5.) it alfo expreffes a fimple degree of comparifon
as טובה חכמה מפנינים, *Prov.* 8. 11. *wifdom is
good before pearls,* i.e. better, here it fupplies the
place of מן as טובים שנים מן אחד *two are better than one;* (6.) poftfixed (from הם them) to a
noun *their,* to a verb *them,* as דברם *their word,*
פקדם *he vifited them;* (7.) with ו forms fome
nouns פדיום *redemption;* (8.) alfo fome adverbs,
as יומם *by day.*
מ a particle, an abbreviation of מן from מנה to
diftribute, 1. from, by; 2. without; 3. at, near,
toward; 4. before, in the prefence of; 5. againft;
6. of, concerning, for; 7. from, out of; 8. rather than, more than; 9. becaufe of, by reafon
of; 10. according to; 11. with an infinitive, left
that,

that, not, *1st, Gen.*2.2. *Hof.* 7. 4. *2d, Job* 21.9.
Micah 3.6. *3d, Gen.*3.24. *Ex.*33.6. *4th, Numb.*
32.22. *Jer.*51.5. *5th, Jer.*3.20. *Dan.*11.8. *6th,*
*Lev.*6.18. *Josh.*22.24. *7th, Gen.*2.23, &c. *8th,*
*Deut.*14.2. *Judg.* 2. 19. *9th, Exod.* 6. 9. *10th,*
*Ezek.*7.27. *11th, Gen.*31.29.

מאד‎ ftrength, might, ability, *Deut.*6. 5. *2 Kings*
23. 25. very, very much, greatly, exceedingly.
It expreffes the higher degrees of comparifon, as
טוב מאד‎ very good, *Gen.*1.31.*

מאיה‎ an hundred.   מאתים‎ two hundreds.

מואל‎ for מול‎ over againft, *Neh.*12.38.

מאוי‎ defire, from אוה‎

מאם‎, מאום‎,מאומה‎ any thing, any, the leaft thing,
a fmall matter, *Gen.*22.12. *Job* 31.7.   מאום‎ for
מום‎ a blot or blemifh, *Dan.*1.4.   *fee* מום‎

מאן‎ to reject, refufe; refufe, refufing.   מאני‎,מאנוא‎
from מן‎ veffels, inftruments, utenfils, *Ezra* 5.14.
*Dan.*5.2.

מאס‎ to reject with contempt, to naufeate, caft off,
abhor, become loathfome, *Job* 7. 5. (put for מס‎
melt away, *Pfalm* 58. 7.†

מאר‎ to fefter, rankle, fret ; applied to the fcratch
of a briar, and to the leprofy.   ממאיר‎ pricking,
*Ezek.*28.24.   ממארת‎ fretting, *Lev.*13.51,52: 14.
44.‡

מאר‎ light,   *fee* אר‎
מבא‎ entry, income,   *fee* בא‎
מבזה‎ vile,   *fee* בז־ה‎
מבט‎ expectation,   *fee* נבט‎ in בט‎
מבוכה‎ perplexity,   *fee* בוך‎
מבול‎ deluge,   *fee* בל‎
מבנה‎ a frame,   *fee* בנח‎

---

* Dcr. Αδην.Αδεω. Mad.   † Μισεω.   ‡ Mæreo. Mar. Mur-
rain.

מבוסרה a treading down, *fee* בס

מבוע a fpring, *fee* נבע in בע

מבוקרה void, *fee* בק

מבשים the fecrets, *fee* בש

מג to diffolve, melt. מגג to diffolve, melt very much, *Pf.*65.11. *Ifai.*64.7.‖

מגד (to excel, exceed) delicacies, valuable produce, precious fruits. In Chaldee to deftroy, *Ezra* 6. 12. מגדנות the fame.*

מגיד a meffenger, *fee* נגד in נד

מגל a fickle, *Joel* 3.13. *Jer.*5.16. from גל, named from its circular form and motion. מגלת a volume.

מגן to deliver up, give, prefent, *Gen.*14.20. *Prov.* 4.9. *Hofea* 11.8. alfo a fhield, *fee in* גן

מגפה flaughter, plague, from נגף *fee in* נף

מגר to thruft or throw down, *Pfalm* 89.44. thruft down, *Ezek.*21.12. *fee in* גר †

מד to meafure; a meafure fem. מדה: tax or tribute, *Neh.*5.4. a long robe, fuit of armour commenfurate with the body; plu. מרות, מדים, and מדוים. מרד to meafure entirely or completely; be gone or meafured, *Job* 7. 4. מדין ftature, *2Sam.*21.20.‡

מריבת caufing forrow, from דאב

מדוה languor, difeafe, *fee* דוה

מדח ruin, *fee* דח

מדי from, ever fince, *fee* די

מדכה a mortar, *fee* דך

מדן a province, jurifdiction.

מדינה the fame, *fee* דן

מדין, מדון ftrife, &c. *fee* דן

מדן wages of whoredom, *fee* נד

‖ Der. Muck. Mug. Muggy, i.e. moift, damp. W. Mwg. * Μαϰ-τυαι Maftya. W. Myged. † Migro, Emigrate. ‡ Μετϱω Metior. Μοδιος, Μετϱον Modus. Mcct. Metc. Metre. Mode. W. Medr. Μανδυη Manteau, Mantle.

מדין ſtature, ſee מד

מדע why, how, ſee ידע *in* דע

מדור a pile, ſee דר

מדיש threſhing, ſee דש

מה to be amazed, aſtoniſhed: the pronoun, who, which, what: the particle how? what? מזה what is that, *Exod.* 4. 2. תמהון aſtoniſhment, *Deut.* 28. 28. *Zech.* 12. 4. התמהמה, מהמה to delay, linger, tarry; loiter on, *Iſai.* 29. 9.*

מהל to mix, mingle, *Iſai.* 1. 22. --- מחלל praiſe, from הל †

מהומה trouble, ſee המה

מהר to haſten, make haſte, be expeditious: to endow, a dowry, given to haſten marriage, *Gen.* 34. 12. *Exod.* 22. 16, 17. 1 *Sam.* 18. 25. מחרה, מהר quickly, ſhortly, ſuddenly. מהיר ready, diligent. נמהר haſty, precipitate, *Hab.* 1. 6. carried headlong, *Job* 5. 13. raſh, *Iſai.* 32. 4. fearful, hurried in mind, *Iſai.* 35. 4. ‡

מו pronoun *them*; the ו here is paragogic: it is alſo a ſyllabic adjection uſed after and annexed to the particles ב, כ, ל

מוג, מוה, מוט ſee מג, &c. without the ו

מום a ſpot or blemiſh, natural or ſpiritual, *Lev.* 21. 17, 18. 2 *Sam.* 14. 25. *Deut.* 32. 5. ‖

מזי, מזה to conſume, burnt, dried up, *Deut.* 32. 24. מזה what is that? from מה זה מא to heat with fire, *Dan.* 3. 19.

מזוי pantries, ſee וו

מזוזה a door poſt, *from* זוז

מזג to mix or mingle, mixed liquor, *Cant.* 7. 2. §

מזה, מזיח a girdle, *Pſ.* 109. 19. ſtrength, *Job* 12. 21. *Iſai.* 23. 12.

* Der. Μαω quæro.　† Fr. Meler. Mingle. pele-Mele, pell-Mell.　‡ Μειρω, Μερος part. Μωρος raſh. Marry.　‖ Μωμος. Maim.
§ Μισγω Miſceo, Mix, Mixture. W. Myſgu.

מולורה

מזלות planets, *fee* ינזל in זל

מזמה device, *fee* זם

מזן meat, fed, *fee* זן

מזור, כמזור fpurious, a baftard, *Deut.* 23. 2. *Zech.* 9. 6.

מזר, מזרות, מזרים *fee* זר

מחה wipe away, to blot out: to fmite; deftroy; to reach, *i. e.* take a fweep by the fide of the fea, *Numb.*34.11. מחי a Catapulta, a Balifta, a war-like engine for deftroying fortifications, *Ezek.*26. 9. מח, מוח fat, marrow, *Job* 21.24. מחים, מיחים fat ones, fatlings, *Ifai.* 5.17. *Pf.*66.15. ממחים full of marrow, *Ifai.*25.6 מחא to rub the hands together for joy, to clap hands, *Ezek.*26.6. *Pfal.* 98.8. *Ifai.*55.12.*

מחבת a pan, *fee* חב

מחיה fuftenance, *fee* חיה

מחוגה compafs, *fee* חוג

מחזה a vifion, *&c.* from חזה

מחל ficknefs; dance, *fee* חל

מחנה a camp, *fee* חנה

מחסה a refuge, *fee* חסה

מחץ to fink deep, deprefs, to give a deep wound; to embrue the hand, foot, fword in blood; to pierce through, to wound; a ftroke or gafh, *Ifai.* 30.26. *fee alfo under* חץ

מחק to break, fmite off, *Judg.*5.26.

מחר, מחרת (to exchange) to-morrow, the next day. מחיר fomewhat given in exchange; price, worth, value; hire, *Mic.*3.11. gain, *Dan.*11.39. †

מחתה ruin, terror; fire-pan, cenfer, *fee* חרה

מט מוט to decay, rot, be moved fo as to be difor-dered or difappointed; to fhake, nod, totter. המיט to caft, *Pf.* 55. 3. ‡

---

* Der. Μυελος Medulla. Mucus, Mucid.   † Αυριον, Morrow, Morn, Morning. W. Forn.   ‡ Mud.

מוט ה

מוטה, מוט a pole, bar, lever, yoke, &c. by which heavy burdens are moved and carried. מטה, מטא to reach unto, come upon, *Dan.* 4. 8: 17. 21.

מטה a bed, couch, below: *fee* נטה to incline.

מטט, התמוטט to be diffolved intirely, totter exceedingly, *Ifai.* 24. 19.*

מטוה what is fpun, *fee* טוה

מיטב the beft, from טב

מטח, מטחוי a bow-fhot, *Gen.* 21. 16.†

מטל, מטול (to hammer) a forged bar.‡

מטר to rain ; a fhower. ‖

מטרה a prifon, *fee* טר

מי pron. perfonal and relative, who. It has fometimes a negative or prohibitory fenfe; leaft, 2 *Sam.* 18. 12. take care who מי *i. e.* leaft any one.

מי for מים waters.

מים, מין, מיין *fee* מם &c. without the י

מך, מוך to decay, fall to ruin; grow poor, be brought low.§

מכה ftroke, &c. מכוה burning. *fee* כה

מכל perfection ; prifon, *fee* כל

מכל for מאכל food, 1 *Kings* 5. 11. *fee* אכל

מיכל a brook, *fee* יכל in כל

מכן a bafe; place, *fee* כן

מכס number; covering, *fee* כס

מכר to deliver up, fell; ware, price, fale, felling; that which is fold. ממכרה, ממכר the fame. *fee* כר ¶

מל־ה to cut off, divide, break; circumcife, cut off the forefkin ; to divide the voice into breaks, articulate, talk, fpeak, utter. מלין, מלים pl. מלה מליֹם

---

* Der. Motus, moved. Νευω nuto, Μεθω temetum, Μεθη, Μεθυω temo, a team. Mute; Moth. Mud. W. Mwyd, Symmud, Ymmod. Matta, Mat. Meta. † Mitto. ‡ Mettal. ‖ Mother, Mothery. § Μικκος, Μικρος little ; Macies, emaciate : Muck, Meek. ¶ Lit. tr. Merx, Mercari. Market, Merchant.

talk, fpeech, a word: tumult, confufed talking
together, *Jer.* 11.16.   מלל to cut off intirely:
fpeak.   מלילת ears of corn, *Deut.*23.25.---מול
and נמל to circumcife; cut off, deftroy, cut down.
מול the fore front; overagainft, before; it is written מואל *Neh.*12.38.   מולת circumcifion.   נמלה
an ant, *Prov.*6.6. plu. נמלים *Prov.*30.25. (the
ants crop off the buds from their corn). --- מלא
fulnefs, completion; to fill, fulfil.   מלוא, מלאה
מלו fulnefs.   מלא יד to fill the hand, confecrate.
איל מלאים a ram of confecration.   מלואים filling, confecration.*

מולד kindred,   *fee* ילד in לד

מילד midwife,   *fee as before.*

מלח to diffolve, melt away, be diffolved as falt in
water, *Ifai.*51.6. falt; to feafon with falt, purify.
מלחה faltnefs or barrennefs, becaufe where the
foil abounds with too much falt it is barren.
מלחים falt-water-men, mariners; alfo rotten rags
wafted with wearing, almoft diffolved, *Jer.*38.11.
בריתמלח a covenant of falt, *i. e.* a purification
facrifice.†

מלוח this by fome is placed by fome under the
former root, and rendered mallows, *Job* 30.4.
better perhaps thus; cropping off מלוח the green
of the fhrubs for food, from לח frefh.

מלט to deliver, refcue, efcape, fet free, leap out,
Job 41.19. to deliver, bring forth, lay eggs, *Ifai.*
34.15. an hiding place; not clay, *Jer.*43.9.‡

מלך to reign, be a king; monarch, king: the idol
Moloch. מלכה a queen.   ממלכה, מלוכה, מלכות,
ממלכות a kingdom.   וימלך לבי עלי then my heart
reigned over me, *i. e.* I took courage, *Neh.* 5.7.
courage or counfel, *Dan.*4.27,24.

---

* Der. Multus, Μυλλω, Λαλιω, Λαμυρος.   Maul, Mall, Mill, Meal:
to Mell, old Engl. to fpeak.   W. Amledd. Mallu.   † Mullock or
Molluck, W. Halen.   ‡ Melt.

מלמעל above, upwards, *see* על

מלון an inn, from לן

מלץ to affwage, fweeten, be agreeable, delightful, *Pf.*119.103. מליץ an advocate, ambaffador, interceffor, mediator. מליצי interceffors, priefts, *Ifai.*43.27. embaffadors, 2 *Chron.*32.31. מליצה fweetnefs of difcourfe, *Prov.*1.6.*

מלף for מאלף who teaches, *see* אלף

מלק to pinch, wring off, *Lev.*1.15: 5.8.

מם, מים a fpot or blemifh.†

מים, מי waters, *see* ימ

מנ־ה to adjuft, diftribute, affign; tell, number, ordain, appoint, prepare. מני, מן a particle: from, among, out of, &c. *fee* מ. מן *Exod.* 16. 15. for מה *what*, manna. מנא, מנה an affigned portion. מנים times, *Gen.*31.7,41. מנה the Maneh, equal to 60 fhekels, or 7 *l.* 1 *s.* 5 *d. Ezek.*42.12. מנים pounds, each 100 fhekels in weight (compare 1 *Kings* 10.17. with 2 *Chron.*9.16.) מני the name of an idol, tranflated, that number, *Ifai.*65.11. תמונה, מון a fimilitude, image, or likenefs. מין a fpecies or kind. מנים *Pf.*150. 4. kinds, various kinds of mufic in concert; others, ftringed inftruments adjufted and tuned.---ימן, ימנית, ימני right, in oppofition to left. ימין the right hand; to ufe the right hand, 1 *Chron.*12.2. המין, ימן, ימין to go or turn to the right hand, 2 *Sam.* 14. 19. *Ezek.* 21. 16. *Gen.* 13. 9. *Ifai.* 30. 21. תימן the fouth, on the right hand when looking eaftward.‡

מנוד a fhaking, *fee* נד

מנה, מנחה a prefent, offering, meat offering, *fee* נח

---

* Der. Μαλισσω Mulceo, Μελισσα a bee. Μελι Mel. W. Melus.
† Μωμος, ‡ Μηνυω Mien. Numero, Number, Many. Μηνη Moon, Μονα, Mina, Μονας, Μονος, Monad. Mon-achus Monk. Manna. Main. Amain; Mean. Mens, W. Môn, the Welfh name for Anglefey, the Mona of the Romans.

108 מוסר מנך

מֵנֵך a chain, collar, *Dan*. 5.7,16,29.

מֵנֵל perfection, *see* נלה in לה

מֵנוֹן a fon, *see* נון

מֵנוֹם flight, refuge, *see* נס

מֵנֵע to withhold, keep back, reftrain, hinder, refrain.§

מֵנַעֲנֵע Cornets, *see* נע

מֵנַקִית cups, *see* נקה in קה

מֵינַקֵת a nurfe, *see* ינק in נק

מֵנוֹר, מֵנֹר a weaver's beam, 1 *Sam*. 17.7. 2 *Sam*. 21. 19. 1 *Chron*. 11.23: 20.5.*

מֵנוֹרָה candlefticks, *see* נור

מֵס־ה to melt, diffolve, faint, be difcouraged. מסס to be greatly terrified, &c. מס a levy of men draughted out and difunited from the reft. נמס refufe, what is good for nothing, 1 *Sam*. 15.9. (*Pf*. 58.7. it is written מאס) מסת trial, wafting, *Job* 9.23.†

מֵסֵה trial, *see* נסה in סה

מֵסֵב round about, *see* סב

מוסָד a foundation, *see* יסד in סד

מַסְוֵה a veil, *see* סוה

מֵסָך to mix, mingle, mixture: to drink ftrong mix'd liquors, *Ifai*. 5.22. מֵמְסָך mixt wine, *Prov*. 23.30. mixt drink offering, *Ifai*. 65.11. מֵסֵכָת the web formed by intermixture of threads, *Judg*. 16.13,14.‡

מֵסָך covert, *see* סך

מֵסָל caufey, path, *see* סל

מֵסֵע journey, *see* נסע in סע

מֵסְפוֹא provender, from ספא

מֵסָר to deliver, give up, fupply, *Numb*. 31.5. to deliver, teach, inftruct, *Num*. 31.16. perhaps from יסר

מוסָר inftruction, *see* יסר

§ Der. Nego. Monor. Minus. Minifh. * Minerva. † Miꜱꝛꝺ Mefs, Mafh, Moift. ‡ Miꜱʏw Mifceo, Mix. Mafque.

מוסר

מוסר, מסות מסוה a bond, from אסר

מעים, מע־ה the bowels. מעתוי *Ifai.*48.19. fhould
be rendered bowels, *i. e.* like the bowels of the
fea, or the numerous fry of fifhes, *fee* עו־ה

מעי a heap, *Ifai.*17.1. *fee* עיה

מעבה thicknefs, from עב

מעוג a cake; feaft, *fee* עג

מעד to totter, fhake, flip, flide, 2 *Sam.*22.37. *Job*
12.5. *Pfal.*18.36: 26.1: 37.31. חמעד make to
totter or fhake, *Pf.*69.23. מועדת out of joint,
lame, tottering, *Prov.*25.11. מעדנות tremblings,
fhaking; 1 *Sam.*15.32.

מועד fet time, from יעד in עד

מוז fortrefs, &c. *fee* עז

מעט to diminifh, leffen, make few, little; give or
take a few : a few, little. כמעט as it were a little, almoft; in a little time, fhortly.*

מעך to comprefs, fqueeze, crufh, prefs upon, *Lev.*
22.24. ftick, 1 *Sam.*26.7. preffed, *Ezek.*23.3.

מעל to trefpafs, tranfgrefs, deviate from rule or
law: a trefpafs, tranfgreffion.†

מעיל robe or mantle, a furtout, *fee* על

מען (to remain, dwell) מעונה, מעין, מעון manfion,
dwelling·‡

מען whence למען *fee* ענה עה

מעונן an obferver of times, *fee* ענה

מעין fpring, well, *fee* עין

מעף dimnefs, *fee* עף §

מעצה counfel, *fee* יעץ in עץ

מעקה a battlement, *fee* עקה

מועקה affliction, *fee* עק

מער a cave, den, cavern; and alfo

מער a meadow, *Judges* 20. 33. *fee* ערה

---

* Der. Mote, Mite, Moth.   † Malum, Male, Malice.   ‡ Μενω,
Μονη Maneo, Manfion.   § Mope.

מער nakednefs, &c. *fee as above.*

מעשה work, *fee* עשה

מפו, מפה on this fide or that, *fee* פה

מופז pure fine gold, from פז

מפח breathings out; bellows, *fee* נפח in פח

מפל refufe, ruin, *fee* נפל in פל

מפץ flaughter, a maul, *fee* נפץ in פץ

מופת a prodigy, *fee* יפת in פת

מצות,מץ to fqueeze, prefs, wring, milk out. מצ־ה unleavened bread, cake. מוץ chaff. מיץ to prefs forcibly, rendered churning, wringing, forcing, *Prov.*30.33. מץ an extortioner, *Ifai.*16.4. מצא to catch, feize, find. המציא to prefent, caufe to find, caufe to come.

מוצא a going out, *fee* יצא in צא

מצב ftation, pillar, *fee* יצב in צב

מצד, מצרה, מצודה a fortrefs, ftrong hold, muni-tion, *Pf.*66.11. *Prov.*12.12. *Ezek.*12.13: 17.20. a net or fnare, *fee* צד

מצוה a command, from צו־ה

מצח the front, forehead. מצחת 1 *Sam.* 17. 6. greaves, plates of brafs adapted to the fhins, *fee* צח

מצל fhadowing, deep, *fee* צל

מצע a bed, *fee* יצע in צע

מצפה watching, watch-tower, *fee* צפה

מצק ftraitnefs, pillar, pipe, *fee* צק

מצר *fee* צר

מק, מוק to putrify, rot, corrupt, wafte, pine. מוק ftink, rottennefs, *Ifai.*3.24: 5.24.*

מקבת a hammer, *fee* נקב in קב

מקוה, מקוא hope: linen yarn, *fee* קו־ה

מקל a ftaff, rod, from קל

מקום place, ftation, *fee* קם

מקנה what is bought, &c. *fee* קנ־ה

מקצה end, from קצה

    * Der. Muck.   מקר

מקר cooling, chance, fountain, *fee* קר

מקש beaten, *fee* קש

מר־ה to be bitter; bitter: to be bitter in mind, provoke, imbitter, grieve, rebel. מרר to be very bitter, offenfive, revolt, rebel,&c. התמרמר,מרמר. to be moft bitterly provoked, *Dan.* 8. 7: 11. 11. מור, מרור, מר myrrh, a bitter gum. מר, מרור, מריר bitter. מרר, תמרור, מרירות, מרה, ממר bitternefs. מרא מררה gall. מרי rebellion, bitter, rebellious. מוראה provoking, irritating, *Zeph.*3. 1. מריא the Buffalo, a furious implacable animal remarkable for fat, 2 *Sam.* 6. 13. המריא Chald. to rife up, ftand erect, *Job* 39. 18. מרא Chald. a fovereign, lord, *Dan.*2.47: 16.21: 5.23. ימרוך *Pfal.* 139. 20. they fpeak againft thee, for יאמרוך *fee* אמר. מורה teacheth, *Job* 36. 22. from ירה. מורה a rafor, *Judg.* 13. 5: 16.17. 1*Sam.*1.11. *fee* in רה --- ימר to exchange, alter, change. מיר to change; remove, *Pfal.* 46. 2. תמורה changing, exchange, recompence, *Job* 15. 31. reftitution, *Job* 20.18. ימר boaft, *Ifai.*61. 6. from אמר --- נמר (to variegate) a pard, leopard. מר a drop or fpot of water, *Ifai.*60.15.*

מרב much ftrife, *fee* רב

מרג to impel, drive forward; a threfhing inftrument, 2*Sam.*24.22. 1*Chron.*21.23. *Ifai.*41.15.†

מרד to rebel, revolt. מרדת, מרד rebellion.

מרוד reduced, rather than caft out, *Ifai.*58.7. mifery, dejection, *Lam.*1.7: 3.19. מורד defcent, *fee* ירד in רד.

מרדך Merodach a Babilonifh idol.

מרה to crufh, comprefs. מרוח bruifed, broken, *Lev.*21.20· מרח to lay on a plaifter or poultice, *Ifai.*38.21.‡

* Der. Μυρм. Amarus, Morofe. Marrow. W. Marw. Αμαρτανω. Fr. Maraud. † Merga, Mergo. ‡ Mark.

מרט to pluck, rub off; excoriate, *Ezek.* 29. 18. peel; furbish, polish; pluck off the hair, *Neh.* 13.25. ימרט hair fallen or rubbed off.

מרך faintnefs, from רך

מרום high, upwards, *fee* רם

מרמה deceit, *fee* רם

מרע pafture; neighbour, *fee* רע

מרף flothful. מרפיון feeblenefs, from רפ־ה

מרץ troublefome, *Job* 6.25. grievous, fore, heavy, 1 *Kings* 2.8. *Mic.* 2.10. המריץ embolden, *Job* 16. 3. the tranflations make the meaning, ftrong, forcible.

מרוץ a race, running, &c. from רץ

מרק to fcour, cleanfe, purify, *Lev.* 6.28. furbifh, *Jer.* 46.4. מרוק bright, fcoured, 2 *Chron.* 6.16. תמרוק, מרוק cleanfing, purification. מרק broth, liquor made from the pure juices of the meat, *Judg.* 6.19,20. *Ifai.* 65.4.*

מורש poffeffion, *fee* ירש in רש

מש־ה to remove, withdraw, retire, go back, depart: draw out. משה Mofes: to draw with gentle hand, *Exod.* 2.10. 2 *Sam.* 22.17. *Pfal.* 18.16. משי filk curioufly drawn out, *Ezek.* 16. 10, 13. משה a creditor, &c. from נשה under שה. משש to remove repeatedly.---ימש־ to feel, fearch, grope, handle. ימשש to grope.†

משא defolate, burden, *fee* in שא and שה

משובה backfliding. מושב a feat, *fee* שב

משגה error, ignorance. *fee* שגה

משח to anoint; משחה ointment, anointing, oil, *Ezra* 7.22, &c. משיה the anointed, Mefliah.‡

משוט an oar, from שוט

משך to draw, draw out, protract, prolong: to draw in a yoke: allure, entice: delineate; con-

---

* Der. W. Marc. Ομογγνημι, Αμεγνω. † Μαϛομ. Μυϛ. Mus, Moufe. ‡ Mefliah.

tract,

tract, draw together: defer, *Prov.* 13.12. forbear, *Neh.*9.30. the price, or rather attraction,
Job 28.18. precious; rather basket whence the
seed is drawn, *Pfal.*126.6. to draw forth, as the
sower his seed, *Amos* 9.13. scatter, be drawn different ways, *Ifai.* 18.2, 7.   משכות bands, con-
tractions, *Job* 38.31.

משוך, משכית hedge, picture, *see* שך
משל to rule, govern; speak in proverbs or weighty fentences, and with authority: to compare,
liken, be like: a proverb, parable or simile, remarkable for their force. ממשל, ממשלה dominion.*

משמה aftonifhment, defolation, from שם
משנה double, &c. *fee* שנה
משסה fpoil or booty, from שסה
משע afpect. מושע faviour; falvation, *fee* שע
משק to move about, run to and fro, *Ifai.* 33.4.
ממשק breeding or fpreading; according to others,
drynefs; defert, *Zeph.*2.9.   בן משק fon of moving, a fteward, *Gen.*15.2.
משק a butler, from שקה
משר a faw, from נשר to cut, *Ifai.*10.15.
משר government; a finger; equity, *fee* שר
מושש joy, &c. *fee* שש
משתה a feaft, banquet, from שתה
מרת to die, kill, flay; ממתה, ממות, מות death;
מת dead. מתה, מתית mortals, men.
מתי when, from. מה what time, and יחי fhall it
be?

מתת a gift, from, נתן in תן
מתג a bit of bridle.†
מתה to extend, ftretch out, diftend, *Ifai.* 60.22.
אמתחה a fack or bag diftended by filling.‡

* Der. Mufculus, Mufcle.   † Mataxa.   ‡ Tractus.

O   מתלהלה

מתלהלה a madman, from להוֹה

מתם foundnefs, from תם

מתן (to ftand ftill, be firm) מתנים the loins.

מתן a gift, from נתן in תן

מתק to be fweet; agreeable: fweeten, *Pfal.* 55.14.
feed fweetly on, *Job* 24. 20. מתק, מתיק fweet,
fweetnefs.   ממתקים fweet things, fweetneffes.

מותר refidue, *fee* תר

מיתר cord, *fee* תר

נ

נון the fourteenth letter, is a confonant; it is uncertain from whence the original form of this
letter was taken. It is a liquid labial, and a fervile; as a numeral it ftands for 50, the final ן
ftands for 700. Nun is only ftrictly radical,
when followed by א, ה; ו, ח, ע, or when the fecond radical is doubled.

נ as a fervile, 1. when prefixed (perhaps from נוה
to reft) forms the preter of *Nepol:* 2. from the
firft pronoun forms the firft perfon plural of
verbs: 3. forms proper names, as נמרד Nimrod;
alfo appellatives, נרגן a whifperer: 4. ן poftfixed,
(from אתן) *them, their* feminine: 5. alfo forms
many nouns, efpecially with ו preceding, as שכרון
drunkennefs: 6. it is paragogic where it fometimes encreafes the fignification, and fometimes
diminifhes it; thus *Pfal.* 11.2. ידרכון קשת fimply
tranflated is *they fhall bend the bow*, but it means
more, *they fhall bend the bow* with an hoftile in-
tention. In *Gen.* 2.17. God threatened the dif-
obedience of our firft parents in thefe ftrong
terms, מות תמות *thou fhalt furely die*; this *Gen.*
3.3. is foftened by the woman, God bade us not
eat

eat of that tree, fays fhe, פן ומתון leaft *perchance*
ye *fhould* die : in verfe 4, the Devil purfuing the
idea, ftill weakens it with לא מות תמתון No,
ye *furely will not* die.

נא to fail, fall fhort: to difannul, fruftrate, to dif-
allow, *Numb.*30.5,8,11. render ineffectual, *Pfal.*
33.10. break, make fore, or raw ; (in *Pf.* 141. it
is written יני) difcourage, *Numb.* 32.7,9. תנוא
breach of promife, *Numb.* 14. 34. occafion for
quarrel, *Job* 33.10. to be raw, not boiled, *Exod.*
12.9. נא, אנא a particle of defire, I pray thee,
fee אן *

נאה, נאות comely, defireable, *fee* אוה

נאד (to pour forth) a bottle, bag of fkin to hold
wine, milk, *&c.* †

נאל *fee* אל

נאם to affert, affirm folemnly. ‡

נאף. to commit adultery; worfhip falfe gods, *i. e.*
fpiritual adultery. נאפים adulteries. נאפופים
repeated fcandalous adulteries.

נאץ to defpife, abhor, reject, treat with contempt
and fcorn ; provoke: blafpheme. נאצה provocation: blafphemy. ינאץ fhall flourifh, *Eccl.*12.
5. rather, fhall be loathed; even the beauty of
the almond tree fhall yield no pleafure to old age.||

נאק to groan as in anguifh. נאקה groaning.

נאר to caft off, caft away, abolifh in mind ; rendered abhor, *Lam.*2.7. make void, *Pfal.*89.39.

נארים curfed, *Mal.* 3.9. from אר

נואש defpair, from יאש in אש

נב־ה to bud out, fhoot, grow as plants, increafe,
bring forth fruit. תנובה ניב fruit, increafe.
נבב to caufe to grow, increafe. ינובב fhall grow
in vigour, *Zech.*9.17.----נבב to be hollow, *Exod.*

* Der. Νυν Nunc, Now.   † Νυδυς.   ‡ Ονομα, Nomen, Name.
‖ Nauci, Naufea, Naufeate.

27.8: 38.7. *Jer.* 52.21. empty, vain, *Job.* 11.12
fee בב   נבו a Babiloniſh idol.

נבא to prophefy, *fee in* בא *

נבזבה a gift, reward, *Dan.*2.6: 5.17.

נבח to bark as a dog.†

נבחז Nibbaz, 2*Kings* 17.31. the idol of the Avites,
from נבה and חזה to fee.

נבט to look, attend to,   *fee in* בט

נבל to run off.   מבול deluge.   *fee* בל‡

נבע to guſh forth, ſpeak fluently, &c.   *fee* בע
אבעבעת puſtles.

נברש (to ſhine, be inflamed) נברשתא a candle-
ſtick, *Dan.*5.5.

נג־ה ſorrowful, afflicted, *Lam.* 1.4. *Zeph.* 3. 18.
fee נגה in יגה

נגה light, ſplendor, morning, *Dan.*6.19,20. *fee* גה

נגב (to be dry, parched) the ſouth,   *fee* גב

נגד (to be dry, parched) the ſouth, *fee* גב

נגד declare; to ruſh forth, flow rapidly, *Dan.*7.10.
before, towards, *fee* גד ‖

נגה to be bright, ſhine; ſplendor, *fee* גה §

נגח to butt, gore, *fee* נח

נגן to ſtrike; play on muſic, *fee* גן

נגע to touch, reach, occur, ſmite, a ſtroke, plague,
fee גע

נגף to ſmite, daſh violently, a violent ſtroke, *fee* גף

נגר to diffuſe, pour out, ſpread, *fee* גר

נגש to approach, ſqueeze, extort, oppreſs : a taſk-
maſter, *fee* גש ¶

נד־ה to move, agitate; wag as the head, *Jer.* 18.
16. move, tranſmigrate, remove : to be agitated
in mind; to compaſſionate, condole.   ניך, נידה

---

* Der. Knop. Knob. Nubo. W. Eb.   † Anubis, the Egyptian idol.   ‡ Fall. Nebulo. Νιφιλη Nebula.   ‖ W. Myncgi.
§ Γαυxω.   ¶ Εγγυς, Εγγιαζω. W. Agos.

a moving,

a moving, motion, wandering, *Job* 16.5. *Lam.* 1.
8. מָנוֹד a fhaking, *Pf.* 44.15. נד a vagabond,
vagrant, fugitive, *Gen.* 4.12, 14, 16. נדה removal, feparation, on account of legal uncleannefs :
unclean, uncleannefs, efpecially that of a men-
ftruous woman. נדן, נדה the wages of whoredom, confidered as filthy, *Ezek.* 16.33. נוד to
fhake, remove; condole, bemoan. נד an heap.
מנדה a tax, *fee* מד. נדד to move repeatedly as
a bird its wings, *Ifai.* 10.14. or as the body agitated in joy, *Jer.* 48.27. or in the toffings of a
reftlefs night, *Job* 7.4. or as exerted in running,
to flee, depart, vanifh; wander hither and thither. מדד begone, *Job* 7.4. perhaps meafured,
from מד *

נדב to incite, be willing, *fee* רב †

נדה to impel naturally or morally, *fee* דה ‡

נדן a fheath; the body, *Dan.* 17.15. *fee* דן ‖

נדף to force, expel. דפי a ftumbling block, *Pfal.*
30.20. *fee* דפ §

נדר a vow, folemn promife to God.

נהה to lament, bewail. נה, ני, נהי, נהיה lamentation or wailing. נהיה *Mic.* 2.4. and elfewhere, .
to become, *fee* היה --- ינה to opprefs by fraud or
violence. יונה, יון a pigeon or dove, naturally
defencelefs and expofed to rapine. יין wine. יון
mud. ¶

נהג to lead, guide, bring, drive. מנהג a driving,
marching. **

נהל to lead gently and with care: tend, take care
of. נהללים *Ifai.* 7.19. *fee* in הל

נהם to roar, moan, cry out. נהם, נהמת roar-
ing, difquietude.

---

* Der. Λovεω.   Nod.   † Donavit. W. Pendefig.   ‡ Need.
‖ W. Noddyn.   § Dab.   ¶ Ovoω. Nænia.   ** Aγω.   Nag.
Fr. Manege.

נהק to bray, like the wild afs when in want of food, *Job* 6.5. to make a doleful noife, *Job* 30.7.
נהר to flow together: to be lightened, the light flowing upon them, *Pf.* 34.5. a river, conflux of water. נהרה conflux or ftream of light: fplendor, *Job* 3.4. מנהרות caverns, letting light flow into the earth, *Judges* 6.2. נהרא Chald. a river, *Ezra* 4.16. נהורא light, *Dan.* 2.22. נהירו light, illumination, *Dan.* 5.11,14.*

נו־ה to dwell, inhabit, fettle, ftay at home: to make (the Lord) a refting place, *Exod.* 15.2. an home, fettled habitation. הנוה *Jer.* 6.2. a woman, that from delicacy, keepeth at home, others fuppofe it for נאוה comely, from אוא †
נוא, נוב, נוד &c. *fee* נא &c. without the ו
נוד to fod or boil. נזיד pottage, *fee* זד
נזה to be fprinkled. *fee* זח ‡
נזל to flow, diftill, *fee* זל
נזם a pendant, jewel for ear or nofe, *fee* זם
נזק Chald. to hurt, injure, damage; lofs, *fee* זק ‖
נזר to be feparated, a Nazarite, *fee* זר
נח־ה to reft, ceafe from motion; lead gently, guide, bring, order. נוח abide quietly, to caufe to reft, to quiet. מנהה, מנוח, ניהוה, נחת, נוח reft, quiet: מנחה an offering or prefent made with a view of appeafing God or man: ניחוח fweet odours, things agreeable, *Ezra* 6.10. *Dan.* 2.46. --- ינח to leave, permit, let alone, *Ifai.* 28.2. to put, place, lay up, let alone, let remain: pacify, leave (offences) unpunifhed, *Eccl.* 10.4. מנה what is left. §

נחל to inherit, caufe to inherit; a valley, torrent, *fee* חל ¶

---

* Der. Run. Νηρευς Nereus. † Ναιω. W. Annedd. ‡ Νιζ.
‖ Nocco, Noxious. § Νυχ, Νυξ, Nox, night. ¶ Λ-χη, Λ-γ-χαιω. Νειλος Nile.

נחם to relieve the mind; comfort, repent. נחם,
נחום repentance. תנחום, נחמה comfort, con-
folation.

נחנו, אנחנו We, pron. plu. of אני

נחץ to haften, precipitate, require hafte, 1 *Sam.* 21.
8.*

נחר to fnort as in anger. נחרת fnorting, *Jer.* 8.
16. *Job* 39. 20. נחר, נחיר the noftrils, *Job* 41.
20.†

נחש to view attentively, to make a difcovery, 1
Kings 20.33. to learn by experience, *Gen.* 30.27.
to divine, ufe Auguries, ufe inchantments ; inchantment : a ferpent, remarkable for eying its
object. נחשה, נחשת, נחושה copper, native brafs,
named from its colour which refembles fome
kinds of ferpents. נחוש brazen. נחשת a brazen
chain or fetter : poifonous filth like verdigreafe,
the folution of copper, not brafs money, *Ezek.*
16.36. ‡

נחשתן Nehufhtan, from נחש to divine, and תן ferpent, 2 *Kings* 18. 4. Now *(Hezekiah)* brake the
ferpent of brafs which Mofes made, becaufe even
to thofe days the children of Ifrael were burning
incenfe to it, and (they) had named it Nehufhtan.

נחת to fink into, penetrate: rendered, come down,
Jer. 21.13. 2 *Kings* 6.9. *Joel* 3.11. go down, *Job*
21.13. ftick faft, prefs upon, *Pf.* 38.2. fettle, or
penetrate, *Pf.* 65.10. enter, *Prov.* 17.10. break,
2 *Sam.* 22.35. lighting down, תחת under : inftead of, for; becaufe of. מתחת underneath,
from under. תחתים lower. תחתון lower, nether. תחתירת, תחתיה lower, loweft.‖

נטה to ftretch out, fpread; to incline, bend onefelf; lean in any particular direction, turn afide,

* Der. lit. tr. Haften.   † Nares, Noftril.   ‡ Νους. Nofco. Νεισι.
‖ Beneath. Nether.

bow

bow down, decline, pervert, &c.   נוט to be moved, *Pf.*99.1.   מטה perverſeneſs: a bed or couch: a rod or ſtaff: a tribe branching from the original ſtock: below, beneath.   למטה downward. מלמטה underneath.   מטות ſtretchings out, *Iſai.* 8.8.*

נטל to lay on, impoſe, load : lift up,   *ſee* טל †

נטע to plant, ſettle, infix,   *ſee* טע

נטף to diſtil, drop, flow ; myrrh,   *ſee* טף ‡

נטר to watch, obſerve, guard,   *ſee* טר ‖

נטש depart, leave, forſake,   *ſee* טש

נִי wailing, *ſee* נהה. יני ſhall break,*Pf.*141.5. *ſee* נא

נין ,ניק, ניר   *ſee* נן without the י

ניסן Niſan, *Neh.*2.1. *Eſth.*3.7. ſame as the month Abid, which falls about March or April.

נכ־ה to ſmite, lame, ſlay, wound,   *ſee* כה §

נכד poſterity, grandchild,   *ſee* כד ¶

נכה equity, right; for, before,   *ſee* כה

נכל to conſpire craftily,   *ſee* כל **

נכס poſſeſſions, riches, goods,   *ſee* כס ††

נכר to know; eſtrange, alienate; ſtrange, *ſee* כר‡‡

נכת   *ſee under* נכ־ה and כה

נל־ה complete; conſummate; to defile.   נולו a dunghill,   *ſee* לה

נם to ſlumber, doze.   תנומה, נומה drowſineſs, ſlumber.‖‖‖

נמל to cut off, circumciſe,   *ſee* מל

נמר a pard, leopard,   *ſee* מר

נן ,נון, נין to propagate, be continued by offspring, *Pf.*72.17. a ſon, *Gen.*21.23. *Job* 18.19. *Iſai.*14. 22. מנון ſon, *Prov.*29.21.--- נינם let us deſtroy them, *Pfal.*174.8. from ינה

---

* Der. Τεινω. Nuto. Nct.   † Ταλαω Tollo.   ‡ W. Dafn.
‖ Τηρεω.   § -icio, Percutio. Νηκος, Νηκαω.   ¶ Nepos, Nephew.
** Κηλεω Callide.   †† Cenſus.   ‡‡ Κεινω Cerno.   ‖‖‖ Numb, Benumb.

נְסִ׳ה to fignalize in any manner ; to tempt, prove, try, attempt; to flee away, depart: נָס abated; fled away, *Deut.* 34.7. חֲנִים make to flee, put to flight: to hide from, *Judg.* 6.11. מַסָּה temptation, trial. מָנוּס, מְנוּסָה flight, refuge. נָסַס to erect a ftandard. נֵס a fign, fignal, enfign, ftandard, *fee* סָח *

נָסַג to take hold, to turn or go back, *fee* in סָג

נָסַה to pull or pluck away, *Ezra* 6.11. *fee* סָח

נָסַך to pour out, to anoint, to fufe, *fee* סָך †

נְסָן, נִיסָן Nifan, the fame as the month Abib, fo called from נָס to fly ; in this month the Exodus fell out.

נָסַע to remove, journey, depart, *fee* סָע ‡

נָסַק to afcend, go up, *Pf.* 139.8. *Dan.* 3.22: 6.23. ‖

נִסְרָך Nifroc, an Affyrian idol, 2 *Kings* 19.37. *Ifai.* 37.38.

נָע to move, reel, be agitated, moved, fifted; wander, fhake, fcatter, ftagger; be promoted; or ramble about, among, *Judg.* 9.9,11. a fugitive, *Gen.* 4.12,14. מְנַעְנְעִים Siftrums, mufical inftrument played on by fhaking.

נָעַל to faften, make faft, nail; fhoe, bolt, lock ; a fhoe or fandal. מַנְעֻל a bolt or lock. §

נָעֵם to be pleafant, fweet, agreeable. נְעִמוֹת pleafures. נֹעַם beauty, pleafantnefs. נַעֲמָן pleafant. מַנְעַמֵּי dainties, *Pf.* 141.4.¶

נָעַץ to infix. נַעֲצוּץ a thorn, *Ifai.* 7.19: 55.13.

נָעַר to move brifkly; to fhake vehemently; tofs up and down; fhake off, &c. raifed up, excited to vigorous activity, *Zech.* 2.13. to roar, yell as a lion, *Jer.* 51.38. the Vulgate renders it, fhall *fhake their manes:* a young active man, lad or boy. נַעֲרָה a

---

* Der. Nice.   † Ἀναξ, Ἀνασσω to reign. ' Soak.   ‡ Νισσομαι. ‖ Scando, Afcend.   § Nail.   ¶ A-mænus.

P   maiden,

maiden, damfel. נעור youth. נערת tow, dreſt
by various agitations, *Judg*.16.9. *Iſai*.1.31.*
נף to brandifh, wave, agitate, fhake, &c. lift, *Iſai*.
30.28. יפה נוף *Pſ*.48.2. having a beautiful waving branch, rendered fituation. תנופה a wave-
offering, fhaking. נף to perfume or fprinkle,
Prov.7.17. נפת a fieve, *Iſai*.30.28. alfo a partition, or tract of country, *Joſh*.11.2: 17.11: 12.
23. 1*Kings* 4.11. honey; *Pſ*.19.10. *Prov*.5.3: 24.
13: 27.7. *Cant*.4.11. in the two laſt fenfes it feems
to come from פת. נפף to agitate repeatedly,
Iſai.10.32.†

נפח to breath, blow, blaſt, pant, *fee* פח ‡
נפך an emerald, precious ſtone, *fee* פך
נפל to fall, fall off, an abortion, *fee* פל ||
נפץ to difperfe, diffipate, loofen, *fee* פץ
נפק to go, come, bring into action: go forth, iffue,
Dan.2.13. bring forth, *Ezra* 5.14: 16.5. נפקתא
expences, *Ezra* 6.8.
נפש to breathe; a foul, man.§
נצה to ruſh, flee away, *Lam*.4.15. an hawk remarkable for flight: to ruſh upon, attack, contend, ſtrive: to be broken, deſtroyed: to fend
forth buds, *Cant*.6.11: 7.12. נצה, נצן a flower,
bloſſom, *Gen*.40.10. *Job* 15.33. *Cant*.2.12. *Iſai*.
18.5. נצץ to emit fparks, fparkle. ניצוץ a fpark
or blaze, *Iſai*. 1. 31. נצא to fly, flee away, *Jer*.
48.9. *fee* צה ¶
נצב a pillar, garrifon, officer: ſtrength, *Dan*.2.41.
fee יצב in צב
נצה to urge on, forward a work 'till overcome;

---

* Der. Νεαρος youth. W. Når.
now.   ‡. Πνεω Puff, Snuff.
§ Φως man.   ¶ Noify. Neſt.

† Vannus, Vane, Fan, Win-
now. || Σφαλλω, Εδνσπαλιζω Nobles.

prefide,

prefide, overfee; conquer; eternity: preferred, *Dan*.6.3,4. *fee* צח

נצל to fpoil, plunder; efcape, *fee* צל *

נצר to preferve, guard; a branch, *fec* צר †

נקה to make innocent, guiltlefs, cleanfe. ינק, ניק to fuck, fuckle. מינקה a nurfe. יונקת ,יונקת ,יונק a fucker, young twig, branch. נקק ,נקיק an hole, cavity in a rock, *Ifai*.7.19. *Jer*.13.4: 16.16. נקא innocent, pure, *Dan*.7.9. *fee* קה and קיק ‡

נקב to pierce, perforate; exprefs, define; curfe: hollow; a female, *fee* קב ‖

נקד a point, fpotted, nicked, marked: a fhepherd, *fee* קד §

נקם to avenge, revenge, punifh, defend, *fee* קם

נקע alienated, *fee* יקע in קע

נקף to furround, enclofe, cut off, *fee* קף ¶

נקר to dig out, perforate, pluck out an eye; a clift, cavern, *fee* קר

נקש to infnare; to dafh, fmite, *Dan*.5.6. *fee* קש

נר (to fplit, feparate) a lamp, or candle. נור; ניר the fame. ניר to till, plough, break up, *Jer*.4.3. *Hof*.10.12. tillage or fallow ground,*Prov*.13.13. *Jer*.4.3. *Hof*.10.12. מנורה a candleftick. נור, נורא fire, *Dan*.3.6,24: 7.9,10, &c.

נרגל Nargal, the Aleim of the men of Cuth, 2 *Kings* 17.30. from נר fire, and גל to revolve.

נרד Nard, fpikenard, *Cant*.1.12: 4.13,14.**

נש־ה to bear, lift, remove. נשים women, wives which bear children. נשה to fhrink, *Gen*.32.32. to forget, caufe to forget; to convey: lend, *Jer*. 15.10. נשיה forgetfulnefs, perhaps removal, *Pf*.88.13. to lend. נשא to bear, fupport, lift,

* Der. Συλαω. Ληςης, Ληςευω fteal. Afylum. † Servare. ‡ Innocuus, Innocency. a Keck, Kex or Keckfy. ‖ Cavo. Nuncupo. W. Cauo. § Nick. ¶ Κοπτω. Fr. Couper. ** Nard. Ροδον Rofa.

take up. מַשָּׂא a carrying, bearing; a burden : doom or prophecy. נשא to lay a burden upon another; an ufurer or oppreffive creditor, alfo the perfon oppreffed: to bear fin ; be regarded as a finner : to bear it in a vicarious manner : to receive, obtain, *Efth*.2.15. *Pf*.24.5. to raife, lift up, elate; deceive, feduce; be elated; feduced: receive; carry, take up: bear, bring forth; fetch, carry off: number, give, prefent. שִׂיא, שְׂאֵת elevation, exaltation; tumour, fwelling. נשִׂיא a prince, a noble. נשיאים נשאים vapours. מַשְׂאֵת rifing column of fmoke, *Judg*.20.38,40. נשׂאת a gift, prefent, 2*Sam*.19.42. מַשְׂאֵת the fame, *fee* in שׂהה and שׂא.

נשב perhaps for נשׁף to breathe, blow, *Pf*.147.18. *Ifai*.40.7. ישׁב *Gen*.15.11. he fat down, *fee* ישׁב in שׁב

נשׂג to overtake, reach, attain to. שׂיג an overtaking, *fee* in שׂג *

נשׁך to bite, pierce with the teeth; to lend on ufury; biting-ufury. נשכה a chamber, fame as לשׁכה *fee* שׁך †

נשל to take, caft, or flip off, *fee* שׁל ‡

נשׁם to breathe. נשמה breath, the foul. נשמות fouls. תושׁכת the Chamæleon, alfo a fpecies of the owl, *fee* שׁם ‖

נשׁף to blow : the twilight: morning dawn when the breezes are felt. ינשׁוף a bird of twilight, the owl. אשׁפים conjurers, *fee* שׁף

נשׁק to kifs, touch gently ; to fnap, crackle as fire doth, to burn. נשׁקות kiffes. משׁיקות kiffing. נושׁקי clafhing with armour. נשׁק the din of arms. *fee* שׁק §

* Der. Sequor, Affequor, Seek.   † Νυσσω.   ‡ Solvo.   ‖ Αυμος; Animus. Mens.   § Κυω, Κυσσω Kifs.   W. Cufanu.

נשׁר

נשר to tear, faw; an eagle. משור a faw, *see שר*

נשת to dry up, fail, perifh. נשתונא, נשתון a letter, an epiftle (נושת in Perfic is to write) *see* שת

נתב (Arab. to raife) נתיבה a caufeway, path, *fee*
תב

נתח to cut in pieces; a piece cut off, *fee* תח †

נתך to pour out, fufe, melt, diffolve, *fee* תך

נתן to give, grant, yield, make, caufe, deliver to,
&c. אתנה, אתנן, מתן, מתנה a gift, reward,
prefent. נתינים perfons given to the priefts for
fervile offices.‡

נתם to break, deftroy, fpoil, *Job* 30.13.

נתע *fee* לתע

נתץ to break down, deftroy, demolifh, *fee* מץ

נתק to pull, draw, pluck afunder, to burft, break,
be broken: a dry fcale which pulls off the hair,
and makes a rupture in the fkin, *Lev.* 13, and
14.54. אתוק, אתיק a gallery, feparate from the
reft of the building, *Ezek.*41.15,16: 42.3,5.

נתר to loofen; move freely: fhake off, *Dan.* 4.
11, 14. to leap, be moved, to unlóofe, diffolve:
the Natrum or nitre of the ancients, *fee* תר ‖

נתש to root up, extirpate, raze, deftroy, *fee* תש

ס

סמך the fifteenth letter, it fignifies a bafis or fupport: this letter is an afperate fibilant, as a numeral it ftands for 60.

סא־ה (to meafure, mete) a meafure equal to about
two gallons and an half. סאסאה to return meafure for meafure, *Ifai.* 27.8.§

סאן

סאן to conflict, strive: a warrior: battle, *Isai.*9.5.*

סב to turn, turn aside, bring or compass about; סבב turn about, turn round, encompass entirely. סבה the cause that bringeth about, 1 *Kings* 12. 15. סביב about, round about. סביבות environs, places round about. נסבה environs, 2 *Chro.* 10.15. מסב round about, 1*Kings* 6.29. a table round which we fit, *Cant.* 1. 12. מוסב a winding about, *Ezek.*41.7. מסבות about, *Job*37.12. סבא to stagger, reel, be drunk, *Isai.*56.12. intoxicating liquor, wine, drink, *Isai.*1.22. *Hof.*4. 18. סובא a drunkard. סבא a yew tree, or the like, whose branches intwine each other, *Nahum* 1.10. וכסבאם סבואים like *yew trees intwined.*†

סבך to interweave, be entangled, wrapped, folded together, as a thicket, or the bushy boughs of of trees: a thicket. סבכא an harp thick strung, rendered sacbut, *Dan.*3.5. *see* שבך ‡

סבל to bear, carry a burden; be a porter: a burden; charge, 1*Kings* 11.28.‖

סבן a napkin or towel. §

סבר to believe; think, *Dan.*7.25.

סג to recede, turn back; a backslider. סנים, סיג, drofs, סג Chald. to inclose, hedge round. סוגה *Cant.* 7. 2. fet about; perhaps סוגה בשושים might be better rendered, *retired* among the lillies. --- נסג to remove from its place. In *Job* 24.2. ש is put for ס and *vice versâ* in *Mic.*6.14.

סגד to fall proftrate, reverence, *Isai.*44.15,17,19. 46.6. *Dan.*2.46.

סגל to appropriate. סגלה peculiar treasure; property. ¶

* Der. Σαννον Sono, Sound. † Σαβασιος Bacchus. Σαβος prieft. Σαβοι acclamation. Σαβαζω. Sabinus. Sapa vel multum. ‡ Spoke. ‖ Bajulo. Sabulum, Sand from its weight. § Σαξανον Sabanum. ¶ Singularis, Single.

סגן a Chaldee or Affyrian ruler or noble.*

סגר to fhut up, clofe; deliver; caufe to be fhut up.
סוגר ward, clofe confinement, *Ezek.* 19.9. סגור
the pericardium, the caul inclofing the heart,
*Hof.*1.3. alfo fine gold, which has been fhut up
and purified in the fire.   מסגר a prifon; alfo a
fmith; lockfmith, 2*Kings* 24. 14, 16. *Jer.* 24. 1:
29.2.   מסגרת border, inclofure.   סגריר *Prov.*
27.15. very rainy, ftormy; when men fhut themfelves up.†

סד ftocks, fetters, *Job* 13.27: 33.11. from---יסד to
fix, eftablifh, found, lay a foundation; to take
counfel, *i.e.* lay a foundation for action, *Pf.*2.2:
31.13. appoint, ordain, *Efth.*1.8.   סוד a counfel; an affembly met for confultation. מוסד, יסוד
a foundation or bottom.

סדין (to loofen) loofe garments; fine linen, *Prov.*
31. 24. *Ifai.* 3. 23. fheets, fhirts or wrappers,
*Judg.*14.12,13.‡

סדר order, regularity; row, *Job* 10. 22.   מסדרון
porch or portico, rows of pillars, *Judg.*3.23. *fee*
שדר ‖

סה *fee* נסה to attempt, prove, try; tempt. מסה
temptation, trial.

סהר round, *Cant.* 7. 2. a prifon, round houfe.
סהרא moon.

סויה (to cover) סות a garment, *Gen.*49.11.   מסוה
a vail, *Exod.*34.33,34,35.

סוג, סוד, סוך, *&c. &c. fee* סג *&c.* without the ו

סח־ה to fweep, fcour off, *Ezek.*26.4.   סוחה dung,
filth, *Ifai.*5.25. סחי refufe, off-fcouring, *Lam.*
3.45.--- נסח to extirpate, demolifh, deftroy, raze,

---

* Der. Σωγανη Infignis.   † W. Efgid.   ‡ Σινδων, Satin.
W. Sidan.   ‖ Συνεδριον Sanedrim. Sedere. Con-fidero, Confider.

break

128   סך   סחב

break down, 2 *Kings* 11.6. *Prov.*15.25. pluck up, *Deut.*28.63. *Pf.*52.5. root out, *Prov.*2.22.*

סחב to drag, draw along, to tear by dragging, pull in pieces, 2 *Sam.*17.13. *Jer.*22.19: 49.20: 15.3. סחבות rags, caſt clouts, tails of robes worn out by trailing on the ground, *Jer.*38.11,12.†

סחף to ſweep along or away, *Prov.*28.3. *Jer.*46. 15.‡

סחר to go about as tradeſmen, pedlers; to trade or traffick : a market: merchant.   מסחר סחרה merchandiſe.   סחרה a buckler; target moved round to guard off blows, *Pf.*91.4.   סחרת ſome precious ſtone with irregular veins, rendered black marble, *Eſth.*1.6.   סחרחר to pant, flutter, *Pf.*38.10. ‖

סחש to ſprout, grow of its own accord.   סהיש corn ſo growing, 2 *Kings* 19.29.

סטיה for שטיה שטים they that turn aſide, *Pſal.* 101.3.

סך to cover.   מיסך, מסך, סכות, סכה, סוך, סך a co-vert, tabernacle, booth, pavilion; hanging co-vering, vail.   הסך את רגלים to cover the feet, *i. e.* to eaſe nature; rather to be laid down to ſleep, *Judg.*3.14. 1 *Sam.*24.3,4. compared with *Ruth* 3.7. סכות־בנות Succoth Benoth, 2 *Kings* 17.30. the tabernacle of young women or of Ve-nus, either a lewd idol or pavilions for proſtitu-tions. מסכת a web, *Judg.*16.13,14.   בסך *Pf.* 42.4. with the multitude; the meaning here is uncertain. שכו his tabernacle, *Lam.*2.6. the ש for ס.   סוך to anoint, *Dan.*10. 3.   אסוך a pot of oil, 2 *Kings* 4.2.   מסוכה a thorn hedge, *Mic.* 7.4. the ס for ש.   סוך to cover completely. סכסך

* Der. Scopo. ᴢⱳ, Sack.   † Shove. W. Yfgubo.   ‡ Sweep, Swoop, Scoop.   ‖ Ware.

to

to arrange, set one before another, to mingle, *Isai.*9.11: 19.2. --- יסך to pour upon, *Exod.* 30. 32. ---- נסך to pour out, as water or wine in an offering. נסך, ניסך a drink offering; to pour out as oil in anointing kings, &c. *Ps.*2.6. *Prov.* 8.22. נסיך a prince or duke: to pour out liquid mettal, as a founder in casting. מסכה molten, a molten image.*

סבל to pervert, turn away from the true end and purpose; act foolishly, make foolish; a fool. סכלות folly, an ש for ס *Eccl.*1.17.†

סכן to foresee, attend to, provide for, cherish, be serviceable or profitable to; be accustomed and acquainted with : to be endangered, or to attend upon, *Eccl.* 10. 9. a purveyor, steward, *Isai.* 22. 15. מסכן one poor or impoverished, *i.e.* needing attendance or supply, *Eccl.*4.13: 9.15.16. *Isai.*40. 20. מסכנה scarcenefs, *Deut.*8.9. מסכנות store-houses.‡

סכר to close, shut up, *Gen.*8.2. *Ps.*53.11. *Isai.*19. 4. שכר for סכר sluices; to stop water, *Isai.*19. 10. ‖

סכת to listen, attend, *Deut.*27.9. סכות a taber-nacle, *see* in סך §

סל־ה to strew; beat down, lay prostrate, tread down, weigh down, sink, deprefs, *Psal.*119.118. *Jer.*50.26. *Lam.*1.15. to value, *i.e.* lay or weigh one thing with another, *Job* 28. 16, 19. סלה mind this, Selah. סלן the dew briar. סלל to make a plain road, which is done by raising it; hence to raise and exalt in mind. סללה a mili-

---

* Der. Σκεπω Tego. Σκια Shade, Σκιαδιον Shadow. Σηκος Stabu-lum. Σαγος Sagum, Succus. W. Cyfgod. Gwifg. † Σκολιος per-verfe. ‡ Scan, Scant, Skink. W. Afgen, Yfcler. ‖ Scrinium, Sacer. Secret Σχιρρος Schirrus. Secure. § Old Fr. Efcouter Scout, Aufculto.

tary bank caſt up for beſieging a town. מסלה,
מסלול a cauſey, path, highway. סלסל to conſider again and again; others, exalt, *Prov.*4.8.
סלא compare, comparable, *Lam.*4.2.*

סלד to be hardened, *Job* 6. 10. harden; burn,
pray. †

סלח to ſpare, pardon, forgive. סליחה forgive-
neſs. ‡

סלם a ladder, *Gen.*28.12.

סלון, סלן a kind of briar or thorn, *Ezek.*2.6: 28.
24. *ſee* סלה ‖

סלע (to cut, break) a rock.§

סלעם (to ſwallow) a ſpecies of locuſts, *Lev.*11.22.
from סלע and עם

סלף to pervert, overthrow; perverſeneſs.¶

סלק to aſcend, go up, *Ezra* 4.12. *Dan.*2.29,&*c.***

סלת (to cleanſe) fine flour, meal.

סם (to put, place) סמים a compoſition of *ſweet
ſpices.* אסמי barns, ſtorehouſes. †‖

סמדר (from סם and דר) the vine bloſſom, *Cant.*2.
13,15:7.12.

סמך to lean, lay, reſt, ſtay upon, ſuſtain, uphold;
followed by על or אל to oppreſs, diſtreſs.†§

סמל an image, *Ezek.*8.3,5. a figure, *Deut.*4.16.
idol, 2*Chron.*33.7,15.‡‖

סמן to mark; appoint, *Iſai.* 28. 25. נסמן millet.
This root ſeems to belong to שם.‖‖

סמף, סומפניא *Dan.*3.5: 10. 15. a muſical inſtrument, the bag-pipes. §‖

---

* Der. Ital. Azzolare.   † Solidus, Solid.   ‡ Slack, Slacken.
‖ The fruit Slan or Slone; Slow tree.   § Λαας Silex; Sling, Slain.
¶ Slip, Slope.   ** Scàla, Scalo. Fr. Eſcalade.   †‖ Sum.
†§ Σκυμπτω, Σκιμπτω, prop. Σκιμβος lame.   ‡‖ Similis, Similo, Si-
milar. Fr. Sembler, Semble, Semblance. af-Semble, &c.   ‖‖ Ση-
μαινω, Σημιῶ, Signum.   §‖ Συμφωνια Symphony.

סמר to ſtand upright, as the hair in terror, *Job* 4.
15. to tremble, be in terror, *Pſ.* 119.120. rough
with hair, *Jer.* 51.27. מסמר nail, ſpike, ſtrait or
upright, 1 *Chron.* 22.3. 2 *Chron.* 3.9. *Iſai.* 41.7.
Jer. 10.4. משמר *Eccleſ.* 12.11. the ſame, ש for ס*

סניה (to hurt, wound) a thorn, buſh, tree with
buſhy top, *Exod.* 3.2,3;4. *Deut.* 33.16. סיני mount
Sinai adjoining to where Moſes had the viſion.
אסון hurt, miſchief. ניסן *Niſan* ſee in נ. סנסני
a bough, the palm tree, *Cant.* 7.8,†

סיפניא *Dan.* 310. ſame as סומפניא in סמך

סיון *Sivan*, a month which falls in May or June,
from סוה to rejoice, *Eſth.* 8.9.

סנפיר (from סנה and פר) fin of a fiſh, *Lev.* 11.9,
10,12. *Deut.* 14.9,10.

סנר (to blind) סנור blindneſs, *Gen.* 19.11. 2 *Kings*
6.18. confuſion of ſight.

סס a moth, *Iſai.* 51.8. סוס an horſe. ססתי a company of horſes, *Cant.* 1.9. סוס, סיס the ſwallow,
Iſai. 38.14. *Jer.* 8.7. ſo called from its note.---נסס
ſee in נס ‡.

סעה a ſtorm, *Pſal.* 55.8.--- נסע to pull up in order to remove to another place: to decamp, remove, ſet forward; take a journey. מסע journey: a dart, miſſil weapon diſcharged with violence, *Job* 41.26. hence סעה a violent ſtorm.

סער to prop, ſupport, keep from falling or fainting; comfort, refreſh, ſtrengthen. מסעד a prop,
1 *Kings* 10.12.

סעף (to project) סעיף the top of a rock; the projecting branches of a tree: to lop off, *Iſai.* 10.33.
סעפים lofty thoughts or opinions, *Pſal.* 119.113.

---

* Der. Σμιϱδνος terrible.   † Sentis bramble.   ‡ Συς. Souſe.
Pega-fus.

1 *Kings* 18. 21. perhaps here the ס is changed with שׁ *

סער to be turbulent, tumultuous; a ſtorm, tem-peſt, whirlwind; ſtormy, *Ezek.*13.11,13. to be tempeſtuous, *Jonah* 1.11,13. tempeſt toſſed, *Iſai.* 54.11. driven with a whirlwind, *Hoſ.*13.3. come out as a whirlwind, *Hab.* 3. 14. ſcatter with a whirlwind,*Zech.*7.14. be fore troubled,2*Ki.*6.11.

ספ־ה to take away, ſweep clean away, conſume, periſh, deſtroy. סַף a cup, baſon, bowl, hollow veſſel: the threſhold, door, poſt, gate. סוּפָה a ſweeping whirlwind. סוּף to conſume; an end, 2*Chron.*20.16. *Eccl.*3.11: 7.2. concluſion, *Eccl.* 12.13. end, extremity, *Dan.* 4.8,19, סוֹפָא the ſame, *Dan.*6.26: 7.26,28. סוּף a bulruſh,weeds, flags: the papyrus; the place where they grow, *Ex.*2.3,5. יַם סוּף the ſea of weeds, *i.e.* the red ſea. סַף the hinder part, *Joel* 2.20. סַף gathered together. תֹסֵף takeſt away,*Pſ.*104.29. סַפַּף to lodge at the threſhold, *Pſ.*84.10. מִסְפּוֹא, סְפָא provender. --- יָסַף to add, increaſe, repeat, or do a thing.†

סָפַד to moan, lament, bewail. מִסְפֵּד lamentation, mourning, wailing.‡

סָפָה to join, adhere, unite. מִסְפַּחַת a ſcab adhering to the fleſh. סָפִיחַ corn; which in harveſt falls to the ground and ſprings the following year. מִסְפָּחוֹת veils, kerchiefs, turbans, *&c. Ezek.*13. 18,21.‖

סֵפֶל a bowl or diſh, *Judg.*5.25: 6.38.§

סָפַן to cover, ceil, *Deut.*33.21. *Jer.*22.14. *Hag.* 1.4. cover, 1*Kings* 6.2: 7,3,7. סְפֻן the ceiling,

---

* Der. Sepes.   † Σιφων Siphus. Vas. Veſſel. Sap. Ship, Skiff. Σποδος aſhes. Σφιδνο; intenſe.   ‖ Speck, Spike.   § Simpulum, Πυελος Pelvis. Φιαλα Phial, Vial.

1 *Kings* 6. 15. ספינה a decked veffel; perhaps the cabin, *Jonah* 1.5. שפן to hide, *Deut.*33.19. the ש for ס

ספק to fmite, ftrike, clap hands: to wallow, *Jer.* 48.26. ספקו his fufficiency, *Job* 20.22. ס for ש and *vice verfâ.* ספק ftroke, *Job* 36. 18.§

ספר to count, enumerate, number, declare, tell, relate; an enumeration, account in writing, book, regifter, letter, writing. ספר, ספור a writer, fcribe, notary. מספר a faphire, a precious ftone with a number of gold fpots.*

סק --- נסק to afcend or climb, *Pf.*139.8.

סקל to ftone to death, caft ftones : to gather out ftones, *Ifai.*5.2: 62.10.†

סר־רה to turn afide, remove; turn or take away: revolt, rebellion: wrong, *Deut.* 19. 16. סרר to be refractory and ftubborn. סרה, סרין a brigandine, coat of mail which turns afide the darts, *Jer.*46.4: 51.3. סור to depart, turn afide, &c. סר heavy or difgufted, turning himfelf away, 1 *Kings* 20.43: 21.4,5. four, *Hof.*4.18. *i.e.* turned off. סורי degenerate, *Jer.*2.21. סרת without, devoid, remove from, *Prov.*11.22. שור depart, for סור. סיר a pot or caldron, to remove meat to or from the fire. סרים thorns which prick and make animals turn afide, *Eccl.*7.6. *Ifai.*34. 13. *Hof.*2.6. *Nah.*1.10. סירות fifh-hooks, *Amos* 4.2.---יסר to correct, chaftife, reprove, inftruct. מוסר, יסור inftruction, correction, difcipline. מוסר, מסרת a bond or toil, from אסר to bind. ‡ סרב a nettle or briar, *Ezek.*2.6. סרבל to cover; robes, mantles, *Dan.*3.21.

---

* Der. Sufficio, fufficient.   † Ζαφειρος Saphire. Cypher. Suffragium, Suffrage. Σφεαγις a Seal.   ‡ Scopulus, a rock.   § Sour, Surly. W. Sarrug. Suro.   ‖ Scrub.

סרה to fpread out, be redundant or fuperfluous; fpreading, luxuriant, ʾEzek. 17. 6. hang over, ftretch beyond, Exod.26.12,13. exceeding,Ezek. 23.15. abounding with fuperfluities, Amos 6.4,7. luxuriant, ufelefs, proud; rendered vanifhed, Jer. 49.7, furplus, remnant, Exod.26.12.||

סרך prefidents over other governors, Dan.6.§

סרן (perhaps from שׂר) a prince or noble of the Philiftines: a plate, 1Kings 7. 30.   סרין a coat of mail ; the two laft fenfes from סר־ה*

סרס (to ferve) סריס an officer,chamberlain,eunuch. .

סרעף long waving branches, Ezek.31.5. from סר to turn, and עף to vibrate.

סרף to burn, Amos 6.10. (for שׂרף) an uncle; cryer, undertaker of funerals. The Jews fometimes burned the bodies of their dead when too putrid to embalm.

סרפד a fpreading thorn or briar, Ifai.55.13. from סיר and רפד

סת,ᶾ סות, סית to remove, withdraw; entice, incite, perfuade. סית remove, take away, Job 36. 16, 18. סות clothes, Gen. 49. 11.   סתו winter, which removes the beauty of plants, Cant.2.11.†

סתל (to cohere, ftick) סתלל to ftick clofe to, retain, detain. מסתולל detaining, Exod.9.17.‡

סתם to clofe, ftop, fhut up: hidden, Pfalm 51.6. סתום a fecret, Ezek.28.3.||

סתר to hide, conceal: fecret, hiding place, a covert, a den: backbiting, Prov.25.23. to deftroy, Ezra 5.12,   מסתר a fecret place. סתרה hiding or protection. מסתרתא fecret things,Dan.2.22.§

ע

עִיִן the sixteenth letter, from its name and form in the old Samaritan and Phœnician alphabet, seems to signify an eye, of which perhaps it was a symbol. It is a liquid palatine, and as a numeral stands for 70.

עבד־ה to be thick, grow thick; עב thickness, thicket, a thick plank or beam, a thick cloud, or the density at the extremity of the system. עבי, מעבה thickness; עוב or עיב to cover with a thick cloud, *Lam.* 2.1.*

עבד to serve, labour, work, till: Chald. to make, form, do: be made. עבדות, עבדה bondage, service. מעבד work.†

עבט to pawn, lend or borrow upon pledge, *Deut.* 15.6: 24.10,13. a pawn or pledge; to turn awry, distort, break rank, make crooked, *Joel* 2: 7. Chaldee for עבת

עבטיט (from עב thick, and טיט mud) thick clay, *Hab.* 2. 6.

עבר to pass or move from place to place; to pass on, thro', over, away, by, or beyond; to transgress: a passage, or side: to make a partition by bars passing across, 1 *Kings* 6.21. to die: beyond, on the other side: to conceive, *Job* 21.10. שורו עבר ולא יגעל *Vacca ejus (semen maris in uterum) transire facit, & non evomit.* עברה a ferry-boat, 2 *Sam.* 19.18. מעברה a ford or passage. עבור corn of the last year, *Josh.* 5.11,12. בעבעור because; for the sake of. עברות, עברה wrath, rage which overbears all bounds. התעבר to be exceeding angry; be transported with rage.‡

* Der. Web, Weave. Hub of a wheel. Heap.   † Οπαδευω Obedio, Obey. Fr. Obeïr.   ‡ Πειρω, Πορος, Υπερ supper. Over. Βαρις. Υβρις. Aber. Hebrew. Γεφυζα, Οπωρα and with the Hebrew name for

nation

עבש to be rotten or mouldy, *Joel* 1.17.*

עבת to twine, twift together, wreathe; bufhy, wreathen; thick branch: a cord or rope: to wrap up, involve, *Micah* 7.3.

עג־ה to bake cakes, *Ezek.*4.12. עגה, מעוג a cake; a feaft, *Pfal.*35.16.†

עגב to be charmed, delighted with: to love; luft after; dote upon, *Ezek.*23.5,6,9,12,16,20. עגבה inordinate love, *Ezek.*23.11. עגבים lovers, *Jer.* 4.30. much love, *Ezek.*33.31. very lovely, *Ezek.* 33.32. עוגב an organ which charms the ear.‡

עגל (to roll) to be round, circular; a young bull or heifer, becaufe either fit for the waggon, or to tread out the corn in a circular motion. עגיל a round ear-ring. עגלה a car, chariot, waggon which rolls uqon wheels. מעגל way, path track-ed out by wheels: a trench or place where car-riages were laid, 1 *Sam.*17.20: 26. 5,7. מעגליך thy paths; rather thy circulators, *Pf.*65.11.||

עגם grieved, tortured, anxious, *Job* 30.25.§

עגן to be detained, ftay, *Ruth* 1.13.

עגר, עגור a Crane, a bird of paffage, *Ifai.* 38. 14. *Jer.*8.7.¶

עד־ה to pafs on without limitation, or to fome point of time or place. עדיה, עדן, עדי, עד yet, befides, again, until, to, whilft, 'till when, how long, &c. unto a place, or until a time; while, as yet, for ever, eternity: to teftify, fupport by evidence, proteft, bear witnefs; to pafs by, *Job* 28.8. take away, *Prov.*25.20. rob, *Pfal.*119.61.

nation added, we have the Roman Aborigines Αβοριγῖνις gens transfuga. W. Aber, the fall of a leffer water into a greater, whence the names of towns fituate near their fall, as Abergwily, Aberyftwith, Aberdeen.

* Der. Σαπρος, Σηπω.   † Coquo. Cook. Cake.   ‡ Αγαπαω.
|| Magalia. Αγαπα. Waggon. Ogle. Goggle.   § Αγων, Αγωνια A-gony.   ¶ Γιρανος Grus. Crane.

עד a witnefs; a prey, *Gen.* 49. 27. *Ifai.* 33. 23.
*Zeph.*3.8. עדי ornaments; rendered the mouth,
*Num.*23.18. *Job* 32.19. *Pf.*22.9: 103.5. the two
firft paffages are better tranflated *teftimonies*, or
to, unto: the third paffage, thus : עדיו their *ornaments confift* in bit and bridle. *Pf.*103.5. *thus* fa-
tisfying with good עדיך *even thee*. עדים f.lthy,
torn, *Ifai.*64.6. עדה, עדות, תעודה a witnefs,
teftimony. עדא to pafs away, עדד to fupport,
preferve, continue, *Pf.*20.8: 146.9: 147.6.---יעד
to appoint, conftitute; betroth: affemble: meet.
עדה an appointed affembly, company, congregation. מועד a folemn feaft, or affembly, a fet
time, folemnity: דברים, עדת *Jud*16.8. a fwarm
of bees. ¶

עדן to pleafure, delight: pleafure. עדינה pleafure.
מעדנים delicacies. מעדנות delicately, 1*Sam.*15.
32. fweet influencies, *Job* 38. 31. עדן, עדנא
Chald. time, occafion, opportunity. †

עדף to remain, over and above; fuperabundant.

עדר to difpofe, order, to hoe, *i.e.* difpofe the earth
round the roots of the vines, *Ifai.*5.6: 7.25. an
orderly collection of cattle, a flock, or drove: to
keep an army in array; 1*Chron.*12.33,38. as a
difpofition in one place caufes a deficiency in
another. נעדר in the paffive fignifies to be deficient, to lack, fail, *&c.* ‡.

עדש lentils a kind of pulfe which boiled make a
pottage of a chocolate colour, *Gen.*25.34. 2*Sam.*
17.28: 23.11. *Ezek.*4.9.

יעה fee the next root.

¶ Der. Ad. At. Decus. Oδενω. Vado. Add. Aid. Yet. Oath. W.
Etto. Hyd. † Ἡδονη Idoneus, Δην Diu, Eden. ‡ Oρθοω Order.
Other. Lit. tr. Herd. Heart.

עו־ה to turn out of its fituation, turn away, make crooked, pervert, act perverfely; be iniquitous; be troubled, bowed down, diftorted, *Pfal.* 38. 6. *Ifai.* 21.3. perverfenefs. עון iniquity, and its punifhments. עוענים repeated perverfeneffes, *Ifai.* 19.14. מעי, עי, עיה an heap, bullock; a grave, *Job* 30.24. מעותי gravel, or pebbles, *Ifai.* 48.19. מעי the bowels.--- יעה to clear away, *Ifai.* 28.17. יעים fhovels. §

עוב, עוג &c. &c. *fee* עב, עג &c. without the ו.

עז to be ftrong, vigorous, ftrengthen, prevail, harden, be mighty: a goat. עוז, עז power, ftrength. מעוז, משזן fortrefs, forces, ftrength. עזניה the ftrong black eagle, *Lev.* 11.13. *Deut.* 14.12. עיז to haften, or gather together for fafety, *Exod.* 9. 19. *Ifai.* 10.31. *Jer.* 4.6: 6.1. עזז to make exceeding ftrong; ftrengthen very much: great power, or ftrength. --- יעז, נועז ftrong, fierce, robuft, *Ifai.* 33.19. *

עזאזל (from עז and אזל to go away) a fcape goat, *Lev.* 16.8,10,26. ‡

עזב to leave, forfake, leave off: difpatch, finifh an affair, as it may be rendered, *Neh.* 3.8: 4.2. *Ezod.* 23.5. עזבון wares left at a mart to be exchanged, *Ezek.* 27.12,14. &c.

עזק to fence round, *Ifai.* 5.2. Chald. a ring which furrounds the finger, *Dan.* 6.17. ¶

עזר to help, aid, affift; help. עזרה affiftance, alfo the great court of the temple, 2*Chron.* 4.9: 6.13. the fettle, or the inbenching of the alter, *Ezek.* 43.14,17,20: 45.19.

§ Der. High. Ho. Hoe. Haw, old Englifh for hill and mountain, and with m prefixed, to Mow. Fr. Mouë, wry mouth.   * Αιξ. Ιζαιη a goat's fkin coat, hence Zany. Ις Vis. Αζω Ox.   ‡ Gazella. ¶ Hufk.

עט־ה

עט־ה to move fwiftly, fly, rufh: to cover haftily, put on: turn afide as one afhamed, or veiled, *Cant.*1.7. עט a pen, or ftyle. עיט to attack, or fly upon fiercely, 1 *Sam.*14.32: 15.19: 25.14. a rapacious bird, or beaft.---עיט to cover, *Ifai.*61. 10. מעטה a garment, *Ifai.* 61. 3. Chald. from יעץ, to counfel, advife, *Dan.*6.7. עטא counfel, *Dan.*2.14. יעטין counfellors, *Ezra*7.14,15. *

עטלף (from עט to fly and עלף in obfcurity) a bat, *Lev.*11.19. *Deut.*14.18. *Ifai.*2.20.

עטן, עטיני breafts, or rather bowels, *Job* 21.24. his bowels are full of חלב fat: others, milk-pails.

עטף to obfcure, cover, be covered, overwhelmed, faint, fwoon: be feeble, weak, *Gen.*30.42. עטפים weak, faint, מעטפות mantles, *Ifai.*3.22. †

עטר to encompafs, crown. עטרה, עטרת a crown. ‡

עטש, עטישות fneezings, *Job* 41.18. ||

עוה &c. fee above in עו־ה

עיב, עין &c. &c. *fee* עב, עו without the י.

עכבר a moufe, *Lev.*11.29. 1 *Sam.*6.4, &c. *Ifai.*56. 17. perhaps from Arab. עך to turn, and Arab. כבר nimbly.

עכביש a fpider, *Job* 8.14. *Ifai.*59.5. perhaps from Arab. עכב nimbly, and כבש to fubdue.

עכס to amble, mince ones gait, trip along, *Ifai.* 3.16. compedes, or fhackles worn by women to give them a fafhionable gate, *Ifai.*3.18. the ftocks, *Prov.*7.22. rather thus as the foolifh (animal) *trippeth* into the toils.

עכר to trouble, difturb, ftir: trouble. נעכרת the fame. §

עכשוב the afp, adder, *Pf.*140.3. perhaps from עך to bend, and שוב involution.

* Der. Tego. Εσθης Veftis, Veft. Αττω Αιτος.   † Fr. Etoffe, ftuff.   ‡ Τιαρα Tiara. || Tuffio & Tuffis. W. Tiffio.   § Οκριαω.

R 2   על־ה

על־ה to afcend, go, or come, up; mount up, or climb; take, or offer up; fpring, leap, rife, get, bring, caft, carry, fetch, fet, light; light, or lift *up*: to grow, excel, increafe; and the like. עלה על לב to afcend upon the heart, *i.e.* to come into the mind. על on high. עלה a burnt offering, which afcends in flame, or fmoke: an afcent. עלי a peftle; working above the body bruifed by it. עליה an upper chamber. עלית upper. עליון uppermoft, fupreme, moft high. עלה, עלי fing. a leaf, branch, or fhoot, upon a tree. תעלה an aqueduct, trench, watercourfe, conduit, canal: alfo a cure or healing, *i.e.* the advancing of health; perhaps it fhould be, profit, advantage, *fee* יעל below. על, עול a yoke, laid on the neck: in a metaphorical fenfe, flavery, fervitude, fubmiffion. עול (fem. עילה) oppreffion, injuftice, iniquity: to opprefs, act unjuftly, be wicked, oppreffive. עויל unjuft. עלה, עלוה, עלתה, עולה unrighteoufnefs, iniquity. עול to bring up, be with young, to nurfe, or fuckle: an infant. עילים fucklings, little ones. עולה, עויל, עולל, תעלול, מעולל an infant, young child, babe. מעל, מעלה a ftep, ftair, degree; above, upon, upwards. למעלה, מלמעלה, מלמעלה the fame. מעיל furtout, upper garment. עלי, על a prepofition; upon; of, *concerning*; for the fake of; againft; over, beyond, more than; befides; at, near; to, towards; by, according to; together with; for, inftead of: and with מ prefixed מעל from; near, by; againft, from above; more than; on account of; above. על־ה Chald. to enter, or come in. העלה and הנעלה to introduce, bring in. עלא Chald. above, עלל to glean grapes by afcending the vines repeatedly: to do, accomplifh, perform, effect; according to the

עלם עלג 141

the Lexicons, but in this reduplicate form it may
more accurately be rendered, *to reach, come up to,
come upon*, and denotes not *only* the actual *event*
of a thing, but its being *unlikely, unforeseen and
unexpected* before it happened. Chald. to enter,
go, or come in, *Dan.*44. 5: 8. 10. to cause to
enter, put or thrust in, *Job* 16.15. התאלל eminently to exalt one self (by good or bad deeds)
so it should be rendered, *Exod.*10.2. 1 *Sam.*6.6.
*Pf.*141.4. *Num.*22.29. *Jer.*38.19. *Judg.*19.25.
1 *Sam.*31.4. 1 *Chron.*10.1. עלולה, תעלל a work,
action, occasion, doing. תעלל delusion, device,*If.*
66.4. עללות gleanings. עליל a crucible, where
in the drofs of metal is made by fire to ascend.
יעל to profit, ascend advantageously. תעלה profit, advantage. יעל the Ibex, or a kind of wild
goat that ascends and browses on the higheft
mountains. *

עלג to stammer. עלגים stutterers, *Isai.*32.4.
עלז to exult, rejoice with exultation. עליזה joy-
ous, rejoicing. †

עלט darkness, the twilight, *Gen.*15.17. *Ezek.*12.
6,7,12. ‡

עלם to hide, conceal: a young unmarried man,
who lives in a concealed state. עלמה a virgin.
עלם, תעלמה somewhat hidden or secret. עלומים
youth. עילם, עולם time indefinite, hidden or
concealed from man as to duration or length:
ever, perpetual, of old, everlasting, ages. עלמות
in *Pf.*9. tit. perhaps from על over and מות death.‖

* Der. Altus. Αλλομαι Folium. Ala. Hail. Heal. Fr. Haut. W.
Uchel. Golo. Ελιουν the Gods of the Phœnicians; and the Alonim
Alonuth of the Carthaginians. See Plautus's Pænulus, Act 5. Sc. 1.
† Elysium, fields of joy; from this root and the Hebrew word that sig-
nifies Light, may be derived Glister, Glitter. ‡ Αλιτεω to fin. How-
let. ‖ Olim. Whilom. Oleo, Olefco. Whelm. Gloom. Iflandic
Hiima to cover. Saxon Helm, Helmet.

עלם

עלם to exult, leap for joy, *Job* 20.18. התעלם to solace or delight oneself, *Prov.*7.18. נעלסה to flutter, *Job* 39.13. spoken of the wings of the oftrich which uses this motion to catch the wind, and increase her speed.

עלע to swallow down, *Job* 39.30. Chald. plu. עלעין a rib, *Dan.*7.5. from the Hebrew צלע *

עלף to cover all over, invelop, *Cant.*5.14. *Gen.*38.14. to be overcome, be faint, swoon, *Isai.*51.20. *Ezek.*31.15. *Amos* 7.13. *Jonah* 4.8.†

עלץ to exult, rejoice (the same as עלז and עלם) עילצת triumph, rejoicing, *Hab.*3.14.

עלק (Arab. to stick) עלוקה a leech, horse-leech, *Prov.*30.15.‡

עם (to associate) a people, a collection of men, a society; also a preposition, with; in; against; like as; before; near to; as long as: with a verb infinite, when. מעם a particle, from, with, unto, before. עים collected strength, force, *Isai.* 11,15. עמית a neighbour or fellow. עמם Chal. to hide, conceal, *Ezek.*28.3: 31.8. to obscure, become dim. ויעם dim, obscured, *Lam.*4.1.‖

עמד to continue, stand, stand still, cause to stand, appoint, support, sustain, &c. עמוד a pillar. עמדה a standing. מעמד station, office, attendance. עמדי with me, or standing near me.

עמל to toil, labour, travail, afflictive labour, travail, weariness, misery, trouble, perverseness, mischief, a wicked person who causes trouble; painful, laborious, *Pf.*73.16.§

עמס to load, poke, borne, sustained, *Isaiah* 46. 3. עמסה a load, burden, *Zech.*12.3.

---

* Der. Swallow.   † Velop. Gulf. Wolf.   ‡ Leech.   ‖ Aμα, Oμου. Saxon Ham, whence Hamlet, Home.   § Molior. Emolument; and the old Oscian word Farnel, a slave.   Famulus, Family.

עמק

עמק to be deep, profound, sink deep; a valley : depth, abyss. מעמק depth.*

עמר to gather or prefs together; to bind the sheaves, *i.e.* pick up handfuls after the reaper, *Pfal.*129.7. a sheaf or handful. עמיד the same. עמר an O-mer, the tenth part of an Epha, equal to three quarts; the quantity of corn a sheaf yielded. התעמר to make merchandife, pick up gain. עמר Chal. wool, *Dan.*7.9. for Hebrew צמר

עמש to load, for עמס *Neh.*4.17.

עמת next to, anfwerable to, over againft. כל עמית in all points, anfwerable in all refpects, *Eccl.*5.16. עמית a neighbour : all thefe words feem to be on-ly derivative from עם †

ענ־ה to act upon; to plough; to afflict, humble; be oppreffed; to have to do with a woman; to re-ply, anfwer, fing alternately. מענה an anfwer. מענה, עינה a furrow, ploughed field, 1*Sam.*14.14. *Hof.*10.10. *Pfal.*129.3. עונה cohabitation, duty of marriage, *Exod.*21.10. עין the eye; fight; face; colour; object of fight. מעין, עין a well, fountain or fpring, *i.e.* an eye of the earth. עינה, יען an owl or oftrich, or fome bird that anfwers its mate with its cries. מעון, עון a dwelling, den, habitation. עון iniquity, *fee* עו־ה. יען becaufe, for as much as, *i.e.* in anfwer to. למען, מען be-caufe, for anfwer, for the fake of, therefore, to the end that. עני poor, humbled; affliction. ענו meek, afflicted; ענוה meeknefs, humility; ענות affliction, *Pf.*22.24. תענית heavinefs, *Ezra*9.5. עון to eye attentively, 1*Sam.*18.9. ענן, a cloud; to bring a cloud, *Gen.*9.14. to augur, or divine by clouds; rendered to obferve times; a cloud-monger, an obferver of times, a foothfayer, in-

* Der. Μυχος.   † Mate.

chanter.

chanter. מעונן the fame. ענין afflictive labour, fore travail, *Eccl.*‡

ענב (to clufter) a grape.

ענג delight, pleafure; luxurious delicate. התענג to delight onefelf, be voluptuous. תענוג delight. מענג delicate.*

ענד to bind round, *Job* 31.36. *Prov.*6.21.†

ענף (to fhoot out) a branch or bough. ענפה full of branches, *Ezek.*19.10.‡

ענק to encircle; a chain worn as a badge of honour, *Judg.*8.26. *Prov.*1.9. *Cant.*4.9. to compafs as with a chain, *Pf.*73.9. to furnifh, cloathe, in token of honour, *Deut.*15.14.‖

ענש to mulct, fine; a fine, punifhment.

ענת Chal. time, opportunity, occafion. Heb. עת

עם to trample; עסם to tread down, *Mal.*4.3. עסים juice forced out by treading, *Cant.*8.2. fweetnefs, new wine juft trodden in the prefs.§

עוע perverfenefs, *Ifai.*19.14. *fee* עוה

עער to raife up, *Ifai.*15.5. *fee* ער־ה

עפ־ה to flutter, fly; turn or whirl about; to fly eagerly upon, *Prov.* 23. 5. be brifk and active, *Job* 11.17. עוף a fowl. מעוף מועף dimnefs, *Ifai.* 8.22: 9.1. עיפה, עפתה darknefs, *Job* 10.22. *Amos* 4.13. alluding to dimnefs of fight occafioned by a vertigo. עפי Chal. foliage, leaves or branches, waving with the wind, *Dan.*4.9: 11.18. עפף to flutter, move, fly away *fwiftly:* to brandifh, *Ezek.* 32.10. עפעפים the eyelids, from their motion: the eyelids of the morn; the dawn or beams of day, *Job* 1.9: 41.9. עפא a leaf, branch, foliage.

‡ Der. Ωοy a chamber; with Mem prefixed, Μινω Maneo, Remain. Cano, fing. Αινος praife. Οπμι, help. Ονοω, Ονοταζω blame Ανα forrow. Onus, a burden. Yean.   * Γανο;, Γανοω. Sax. Hunig, whence Honey.   † Wind. Wend. Lit. tr. Nodus, Knot.   ‡ Imp, Hump. ‖ Αναξ king. Wing. Hank.   § W. Gwafgu.

--- יעף

--- יעף to diſſolve, melt, diſtribute; to be tired, weary, faint; ſuch ſwiftneſs as occaſions weari-neſs, *Dan.* 9. 21. tired, ſpent. עיף the ſame. תועפות meltings, weight of ſilver that has been melted, *Job* 22.25. weariſome high hills, *Pſal.*95. 4. indefatigable ſtrength, which will weary out others, *Num.*23.22: 24.8.*

עפל to be lifted up, *Hab.* 2. 4. preſume, *Num.* 14. 44. be arrogant, haughty, proud, daring: a fort, tower; eminence. עפלים the anus; the piles.†

עפר duſt, mortar, earth, rubbiſh, powder; to caſt duſt, 2*Sam.* 16. 13. a young hart, roe, or goat, *ſprinkled* with ſpots, *Cant.*2.9,17: 4.5: 7.3: 8.14. עפרת lead; it has a great mixture of earth and calcines to powder. ‡

עץ to fix, make firm, *Prov.*16.30. a tree, wood, timber, ſtick, ſtalk: the back bone or *os ſacrum*, being firmly fixed. --- יעץ to adviſe, conſult, give or take counſel; עצה, מעצה counſel, deſign. ||

עצב to grieve, vex; wreſt, torture, *Pſal.*56.5. an idol that brings diſtreſs inſtead of help. עציב la-mentable, *Dan.*6.20. עצב, עצבון, מעצבה ſorrow, grief.

עצר to ſharpen, edge. מעצר an ax, file, *Iſai.* 44. 12. *Jer.*10.3. §

עצל to be idle, ſlothful; a ſluggard: עצלה, עצלות ſloth, idleneſs. ¶

עצם ſubſtance, ſolidity, firmneſs; a bone; to be or become mighty, ſtrong, powerful: might: break the bones, bone him, *Jer.* 10. 17. to ſhut ſtrongly, *Iſai.*29. 10: 33. 15. עצם יום the body

---

* Der. Avis. Ιπταμι. Γνοφος. Οφρυς. Huff. Hop. Whip, Whipe.
† Απιλω Polleo, Piles. Απελος Iſlandic. Hybile. Hovel. Λοφος. Λοφη.
‡ Capra. Caper. || Ιοτης. Οζος. Haſta. W. Gwydd.   § Αξινα
Aſcia. Adze. Edge.   ¶ Aſſellus. Slow. Slug. W. Lleſg.

of the day, the felf fame day. עצמה ftrength,
Ifai. 40. 29. *Nahum* 3. 9. abundance, *Ifai.* 47. 9.
העצמות power, *Pf.*68.35.*

עצר to reftrain, retain, ftop, fhut up clofe, refrain;
retain ftrength; reftrain by power, reign, 1 *Sam.*
9.19. 2 *Chron.*14.11. magiftrate, *Judg.*18.7. reftrained, barren, *Prov.* 30. 16. violent reftraint,
oppreffion, *Pfal.*107.39. magiftracy, prifon, *Ifai.*
53.8.   מעצור rule, reftraint, 1 *Sam.*14.6. *Prov.*
25.28.   עצרה, עצרת folemn feaft day, when labour is reftrained.†

עק־ה, עיק to comprefs, fqueeze, to be loaded or
hard preffed, *Amos* 2.14. עקת oppreffion, *Pfal.*
4.3. מועקה affliction, *Pf.*46.11; מעקה a battlement incompaffing the roof of a houfe, *Deut.*22.
8 ‡

עקב the end or extremity of a thing, *Pf.*19.33,112.
at laft, in the end, *Gen.*49.19. becaufe, in confe-
quence of: the heel, footftep, print of the heel:
to take by the heel, *Hof.*12.3. ftay, detain, *Job*
37.4. to trip up the heels, fupplant, *Gen.*27.36.
*Jer.*9.4. deceitful, fupplanting, *Jer.*17.9. crooked, trodden into holes and inequalities, *Ifai.*40.4.
polluted, trampled with blood, *Hof.*6.8. עקבה
fubtilty, 2 *Kings* 10. 19. עקב a reward: an am-
bufh, the liers in wait, *i.e.* extremity or rear, *Jof.*
8.13. יעקב Jacob; the fupplanter.

עקד to bind: ring-ftreaked, fpotted or ftreaked,
*Gen.*30.35,40: 31.8,10,12.   בית עקד the houfe
of binding, where fhepherds bound their fheep
for fhearing, 2 *Kings* 10.12,14. unlefs the binder
is here an Idol.

עקל crooked, perverted, diftorted. מעקל wrong,

---

* Der. Σωμα. Offum or Os.   † Sero. Hawfer.   ‡ Oak. Αγχι,
Αγχος, Αχθος, Αγχαι.

wrefted,

wrefted, *Hab.* 1. 4.   עכלתין crooked, *Ifai.* 27. 1.
עקלקלית by or crooked ways, *Judg.*5.6.*Pf.*125.5*.
עקר the root or ftock of a family, *Lev.*25 47. to
root up, extirpate, *Eccl.*3.2. *Zeph.*2.4. to hough
or hamftring horfes: to render chariots ufelefs by
breaking their wheels or axles: barren, applied
to male or female: digged down, *Gen.*42.6. better, *extirpated a prince:* Chald. plucked up as
horns. *Dan.*7.8. a ftump.
עקרב the fcorpion.   עקרבים rods or whips armed
with points or thorns, 1 *Kings* 12.11,14. 2 *Chron.*
10.11,14. from עקב and רב greatly.†
עקש to pervert, diftort, be or made perverfe, froward, crooked. עקשות frowardnefs. מעקשים
crooked things, *Ifai.*13.16.‡
ערה to ftir up, roufe, raife up, wake; to pour out,
demolifh a city, make naked, bare: to fpread,
make confpicuous, *Pf.*37.35. to uncover by emp-
tying.   ער a mafter, who waketh his dependants;
a watcher, *Dan.*4.13, *&c.* an enemy, one ftirred
up to oppofe: a city.   מער proportion, difplay,
1 *Kings* 7.36. עיר a city: a fole or colt, young
afs; a fhoot of a vine, *Gen.*49.11. יער an honey-
comb, pure field honey, 2*Sam.*14.26. *Cant.*5.1.
עור the naked fkin, which pours forth the per-
fpirable matter: to ftrip, bare; to blind, to make
blind. עורון blindnefs. Chald. chaff, duft raifed and blown about, *Dan.*2.35. מער,עריה,ערוה,
מעור nakednefs, adultery, privities. מערה meadow, *Judg.*20.23. ערות paper reeds, rather mea-
dows upon naked tracts of land, *Ifa.*19.7. ערר
to excite, raife up repeatedly: to roufe onefelf;
alfo to ftrip entirely: עריר childlefs, deftitute of
children. ערר to raife up. ערער to be laid in

* Der. Σκαλος, Knuckle.   † Σκορπιος Scorpion,   ‡ Κακος.
    ruins;

ruins; utterly broken down, *Jer.* 51. 58. deftitute, entirely ſtript, *Pſ.*102.17. heath, wild ta-
marifk, a plant that grows in defert places, perhaps a blaſted tree, ſtript of its foliage, *Jer.*17.6:
48.6.---(מער, מערה a den, cavern, *ſee* מער)*
ערב to mix, mingle: the evening, when darkneſs
mixes with the light: to be darkened, obſcured,
*Iſai.*24.11. to intermeddle with; to become fure-
ty, engage for another; to mortgage, *Neh.* 5. 3.
the woof, intermixed with the warp: a mixed
multitude, ſwarm: to trade, intermix in dealing:
to be ſweet and pleaſant, where the mixtures are
agreeable: a raven frequenting defarts: the willow, it being of a mixed colour, pale on one ſide
and green on the other. ערבה a wilderneſs, where
vegetables are mixed and confuſed. ערבון,ערבה
a ſecurity, pledge. מערב a market, merchandiſe: the weſt, evening. ערבבים merchants.
תערבות pledges, hoſtages, 2*Kings* 14.14. 2*Chron.*
25. 24. ערבות the heavens, or mixtures, *Pſal.*
68.4.†
ערג to ſtretch out, extend, to defire eagerly, long
after: to pant for water when thirſty, *Pſal.*42.1.
Joel 1.20. ערוגה a dry bed or plot, where vines
are planted, and muſt be watered, *Cant.*5.13: 16.
2. *Ezek.* 17.7, 10. ערג the noiſe of a ſtag in
groyning.‡
ערד, ערור *Job* 39.5. ערדיא *Dan.*5·21. the wild aſs.
ערך to order, ordain, ſet in array, keep rank, direct, prepare; reckon up, rate, eſtimate, value,
compare: could handle, rather *ordered with* ſhield

* Der. Ἀερω, from the above root and *Am* a people, comes Ἐρημος,
Ἐρημιτης, Hermit. Ορω. Ορευω. Εγειρω. Γ. εγορεω. Ειρος. Hare. Horreo,
Horrour. Orior. Hair. Oar. Ware,Wary.Whore. W. Grûg. Gwr. Caer.
† Corvus, Raven. Ἐρεϐος, Ἀρραϐων. Arab. Arabia, place of ſweets. Orb.
‡ Οργαω, Ορεγω. Urgeo, Urge. W. Geran.

and

and ſpear, *i. e.* completely armed : eſtimation, taxation : a ſuit, ſet of garments, *Judg.* 17. 10. proportion, *Job* 41.12. price, 28.13. הֶעֱרִיך to tax, make an order, 2 *Kings* 23.35. מֶעֱרך preparation, ordering, *Prov.* 16. 1. מֶעֲרכה a rank, army, row.*

עֵרֵל a ſuperfluous incumbrance, impediment : uncircumciſed. עֵרְלה the foreſkin; to count uncircumciſed, *Lev.* 19.23. to have the foreſkin uncovered.

עֵרֹם, עֵרוֹם, עִירֹם ſtript, naked, contemptible : prudent, ſubtle. עֵרֹם an heap, properly of corn ſtripped of ſtraw and chaff. נֶעֱרֹם gathered into an heap, *Exod.* 15.8. עָרמה prudence, cunning. מֵעֲרֹם naked, 2 *Chron.* 28.15.†

עֶרמוֹן (from עֵר־ה to ſpread, and מֵנ־ה diſtribute) the plane tree, *Gen.* 30.37. *Ezek.* 31.8. ſome place this as a derivative from the former root, and Engliſh it the cheſnut tree.

עֵרֹם to knead, עֵרִסת, עֵרִיסוֹת maſſes of dough, paſte, *Num.* 15.20,21. *Neh.* 10.37. *Ezek.* 44.30.

עֵרף to diſtill, drop, flow, *Deut.* 32.2: 33.28. the hinder part of the neck thro' which the juices flow from the brain; to break or cut off the neck: break down, behead. עֵרִיפִֹם the heavens; defluctions, gloominefs, *Iſai.* 5.30.‡

עֵרפֶל dark, thick darknefs, from עֵרף and אֹפֶל thick darknefs.

עֵרץ to break, tear violently to pieces, *Job* 13.25. *Iſai.* 2.19,21. to opprefs, *Pſal.* 10.18. to terrify, fear, be affrighted: to prevail, be formidable, *Iſai.* 47.12. עֵרִיץ dreadful, terrible. עֵרוֹץ a cleft,

* Der. Work. Wright. Rectus, Right. Rank, Arrange. Ογχος. Hortus. † Γνωριμος. Γνωριζω. Gnarus. Ο;μος. Vermis. Worm, Old Eng. Earm, poor, wretched. Harm, hurt, ‡ Ορφανος Orphan.

fiſſure,

fiffure, *Job* 30.6. מְעַרִיץ, מֶעֶרְצָה a breaking off:
terror, dread.*

עֶרק to move fwiftly, fly, *Job* 30.3. עֹרְקִים the ar-
teries which conduct the blood from the heart,
Job 30.17.†

עֶרְשׂ a bed, bedftead, couch.

עשׂ־ה to act, do, perform, make; form, procure,
produce; prepare, drefs food; offer; trim: it
meaneth any kind of action, and muft be inter-
preted accordingly : to bruife, handle, disfigure,
*Ezek.*23.3,8,21. do juftice to, *i.e.* undo, *Zeph.*3.
19. עוֹשׂוּ affemble, form yourfelves, *Joel* 3.11.
יֶעֶשׂ to make, *Exod.* 25.31. עַשׂ a moth. עָשׁ, עָשׁ־יש
Arcturus, or the north pole, round which the
ftars in the northern hemifphere revolve; or Jupiter with his fatellites; or, according to others,
the *corroding* particles of the atmofphere. עָשַׁשׁ
to confume, wafte away, *Pf.*6.7: 31.9,1c.‡

עֶשֶׂב (weak) herb, herbage, grafs.

עָשַׁן to fmoke, fume; it denotes anger: fmoke, calamity.‖

עָשַׁק to prefs, rufh upon, opprefs, defraud; loaded
with, *Job* 40.23. badly rendered, drink up. עָשַׁק,
מַעֲשַׁק oppreffion, violence. הִתְעַשֵּׁק to contend,
ftrive, ftruggle.

עֶשֶׂר to give or take tithes; become or make rich;
riches: עָשִׁיר rich. עֶשֶׂר, עֶשֶׂרָה ten; the rich
number which contains all the units. עֶשְׂרִים
twenty. עָשׂוּר an inftrument of ten ftrings.
עֲשִׂירי tenth. עִשָּׂרוֹן a tenth part of the Epha.
מַעֲשֵׂר tithes. עָשִׁיר Ofiris, the enricher.§

עֶשֶׁת (this word is related to עשׂ־ה and fignifies)

---

* Der. Ἀρασσω. Ἀρης. Orts, fragments. Fr. Orage, a ftorm. Crufh.
† Ἰσχυς. Jerk. Yerk. to Rock.　　‡ Κις Cis.　　‖ Weafand.
§ Ofiris of the Egyptians.

work

work improved: *Jer* 5.28. to manufacture, po-
lith; be trim, fleek: Chal. and Heb. to think
properly, propofe, intend, *Dan*.6.3. to take careful thought, *Jonah* 1.6. fhine, *i.e.* are improved.
עשׁות bright, *i. e.* beft, moft improved, *Ezek*.27.
19. עשׁת the fame, *Cant*.5.14. עשׁתות raifed,
elevated thoughts, *Job* 12. 5. עשׁתנת improved
defigns, *Pf.*146.4.*

עשׁתי one, unity, (from עשׂה to make, and שׁת a
foundation) this word is always joined with עשׂר
ten, and fo fignifies eleven, *i. e.* one advance on
ten.

עשׁתרת (from עשׂה and תר a compafs) flocks of
fheep, *Deut*.7.13: 28.4,18,51. Afhteroth, an idol
of the Philiftines and Sidonians. †

עת time, feafon, opportunity. עת to time, or
fpeak in feafon, *Ifai*.50.4. ufed for עוה to be or
make crooked, perverfe; to fubvert, pervert, deal
perverfely with. עתה now, at this time. עתי
fit, opportune, *Lev*.16.21. התעות bow or bend
one felf, *Eccl*.12.3. עותה wrong, *Lam*.3.59.‡
עתד to prepare, make fit, *Prov*.24.27. *Job* 15.28.
be ready,*Dan*.3.15.ready. עתיד the fame. עתדות
things intended or prepared,*Deut*.32.35. עתודות
treafures, ftores for ufe, *Ifai*.10.13. עתדים the
goats, fit for every ufe: rulers, chiefs, *Ifai*.14.9.||
עתם to be burnt, darkened, *Ifai*.9.19.§
עתק to remove, transfer, tranfcribe, *Prov*. 25. 1.
to diftort, turn on one fide in contempt, *Pfal.*75.
5. perverfe, deviating from truth, iniquities, 1*Sa.*
2.3. *Pf.*31.18: 94.4. Chal. to grow old, *Pf.*6.7.
Job 21.7. עתק, עתיק durable, ancient, 1*Chron.*
4.22. *Prov*.8.18. *Ifai*.23.18. *Dan*.7.9: 15.22.¶

---

* Der. Αγιος.   † The German goddefs Eoftre or Eafter.   ‡ W.
Gwaith. || Hœdi.   § Ατμος fteam. Ατμιζω. Θυμα. Θυμαζω.
¶ Antiquus, Antique.

עתר to intreat, pray, deprecate; to ufe abundance of fweet words: to increafe, multiply, *Ezek.*35. 13. to be rich, abundant: thick, abundant and fragrant, *Ezek.*8.11. עתרי my fuppliants, *Zeph.* 3.10. עתרת abundance. נעתר frequent, ear-neft, rather than, *deceitful.**

פ

פא the feventeenth letter; its ancient form repre-fented an angle or corner, whence perhaps it was taken to fignify the mouth or lips, by which this letter is founded. As a numeral פ ftands for 80, but the final ף for 500.

פאה (diftenfion) an angle, corner, end, extremity, fide; captain; to difperfe into corners, *Deut.*32. 26. פא here, *Job* 38.11. *fee* פה †

פאר to adorn, beautify, glorify; an ornament, beauty; a turband, mitre, tire, bonnet. פארה a bough or branch of a tree, which is its beauty. פאר to go over the boughs, *Deut.*24.20. תפארת beauty, honour, glory; beautiful, glorious. פארור beauty, fhining, *Joel* 2.6. *Nahum* 2.10. all places fhall withdraw their fhining (beauty).‡

פג to intermit, *Pf.*77.2. *Hab.*1.4. to faint, fwoon, *Gen.*45.26. *Pfal.*38.8. פוגת, פוגות intermiffion, *Lam.*2.18: 3.49. פגים green figs, *Cant.*2.13:‖

פגל to defile: abominable, unclean, foul.§

פגע to meet with, reach to; to intreat, meet in a friendly manner: to meet with violence and force, flay; oppofe: an occurrence or chance, *Kings* 5.4. *Eccl.*9.11. מפגע mark or object of refentment,

---

* Der. Votare. Ουθαρ. Uber. Udder. Gather.   † Βωτιον Bout. Butt-end.   ‡ Βηρος Birrus. Fair. Fr. Parer. Parade. Pure. Worth. ‖ Ficus, Fig. to Fag. Fag-end. W. Ffigys. Παϋϋ, Φινγϋ.   § Foul.

Job

Job 7.20.   הפגיע to lay or make to meet upon,
*Ifai.*53.6. to intercede, *Ifai.*53.12.*

פגר to faint, be exhaufted, 1 *Sam.*30.10,21. a dead
carcafe.†

פגש to meet, meet together.

פדה to fever: deliver, redeem by power or price.
פדיום, פדין, פדות, פדת ranfom, redemption. פיד
feparation from happinefs; ruin, deftruction.‡
כפדן, פדן a plain; pavilion, palace, *Dan.*11.45.||
פדע to deliver, *Job* 33.24.

פדר (to wafte) the fat, *Lev.*1.8,12: 8.20.

פה (to obvert) here, hither: מפה, מפו or this fide
or that.   פה in regimine פי a mouth; fpeech;
edge of a fword; a portion, part, *Deut.* 21. 17.
2 *Kings* 2.9. *Zech.*13.18.   לפי, כפי, על־פי according to. פיפיות many edges, *Pf.*149.6. teeth of
an inftrument, *Ifai.*41.15. --- תפיני baken pieces,
Lev. 6. 21.   תפהו bake thereof, 1 *Sam.* 28. 24.
from אפה --- יפה to be fair, beautiful. יפי beauty. יפיפה to be exceeding fair, *Pf.*45.2.§

פו, מפו fee above in פה

פוג, פוח, פיך fee פג, פה, &c. without the ו

פז (folidity, compactnefs) to be confolidated, made
ftrong, *Gen.*49.24.   מופז פז, compact, fine gold.
אופז Uphaz the country of gold, *Dan.*10.5. *Jer.*
10.9.   פזז to exert the ftrength in leaping, 2 *Sam.*
6.16.¶

פזר to difperfe, fcatter, break, be broken in pieces.**

פהה to expand, fpread a fnare, to infnare, *Prov.*
29.8. *Ifai.*42.22. a governor, captain, deputy,
prefect.   פח a fnare.   פחים thin plates expanded by beating, *Exod.*39.3. *Nu.*16.38.--- פוח, יפה,

* Der. Fight.   † Piger. lit. tr. Corpus, Carcafe. Badger; from its
floth. ‡ Φειγω. Iflandic Feed; defect. Fade. || Πεδαν.   § Fari. Εϖω.
Φαω Φημι. Πιϝω. Οψ. Ομφη. Fee. Fairy.   ¶ Faft.   ** Σπιιζω.
Spa go,   Dif-perfe.

T   to

to breathe or blow, *Cant.*2.17: 4.6,16. *Ezek.*21. 31. to puff at, *Pf.*10.5. to breathe out lies, *Prov.* 6.19: 14.5: 19.5,9. פיח afhes of a furnace which may be blown away, *Exod.*9.8,10. to break out, in a way of fulfilment, *Hab.*2.3. to break out in threats, *Pf.*27.12, in lamenting, *Jer.*4.31. as the morning light, *Cant.*2.17: 4.6. --- נפח to breathe or blow; to puff or fnuff at, *Mal.* 1. 13. נפוח feething, boiling pot, fending out a vapour, *Job* 41.20. *Jer.*1.13. מפח giving up, breathing out, *Job* 11. 20. the bellows, *Jer.* 6. 29. תפוח the apple, or fome fruit or tree which fends forth a fweet fcent. בית־תפוח the houfe of fruit or ex-panfion, *Jofh.*15.5,3.*

פחד to tremble, fhake; pant, palpitate; be afraid: the penis of the Hippopotamus, *Job* 40.17. fear, tremor.†

פחז to overflow, as water, *Gen.* 49.4. extravagant, rafh, licentious, diffolute, *Judg.* 9. 4. *Zeph.* 3. 4. פהזות extravagance, *Jer.*23.32.‡

פחם (to ftifle) a dying coal, *Prov.*26.21. *Ifai.*44. 12: 54.16. ‖

פחר (to form or fafhion) a potter, *Dan.*2.41.

פחת (to dig up) a pit. פחתת a deep pitted fret of the leprofy, *Lev.*13.55. §

פטר, פטרה Topaz, a gem, *Exod.*28.17: 3910. *Job* 28.19. *Ezek.*28.13.

פטר to open, let out, *Prov.*17.14. flip away, 1*Sam.* 19.10. fet free or at liberty, 1 *Chron.* 9. 33. dif-mifs, free, fet open, 2*Chron.*23.8. a firftling open-ing the matrix. פטורי צצים open flowers, *i. e.* palm trees in bloom, 1*Kings* 6.18,29,32,35.¶

כטש

פטש (to ftrike) פטיש a large hammer, *Ifai*.41.7.
Jer.23.29: 5.23. פטשי a turband. Chald. rendered hofe, *Dan*.3.21.*

פי a mouth, fee in פה
פים, פיד fee פד and פם without the י
פך to diffolve, pulverife; to flow, run out, *Ezek*.
47.2. a vial, cruet with narrow mouth, 1*Sam*.10.
1. 2*Kings* 9.1,3. פוך beautiful painting, 2*Kings*
9.30. *Jer*. 4. 30. painted, glittering. אבן פוך
ftones veined with black; marble, 1*Chron*.29.2.
fair colours, *Ifai*.54.11. lead ore, with the powder of which the women tinged their eye-balls,
hair and eye-lids, to give a gracefulnefs to the
complexion. At this day the women, in fome
parts of the Eaft, tinge their eyes black to heigh-
ten their beauty.---נפך an Emerald, *Exod*.28.18:
39.11. *Ezek*.27.16: 28.13.†

פל־ה to feparate, fet apart in a diftinguifhed manner; to fhew, diftinguifh, *Pf*.17.7. פול a bean,
or fome kind of pulfe, 2*Sam*. 17. 28. *Ezek*. 4. 9.
תפרה a prayer. פלל to diftinguifh between good
or bad; to judge, arbitrate; to think, decide in
ones own mind, *Gen*.48.11. to intercede, medi-
ate; execute judgment, compofe an affair, *Pfal*.
106.30. פליל an arbitrator, judge. פלילה,פליליה
arbitration, judgment, *Ifai*.16.3: 28.7. התפלל
to arbitrate for one's felf; to intreat, pray.
עון פלילים a crime which an arbitrator would
condemn, *Job* 31.12,28. פלא to feparate, *Num*.
6.2. to perform, accomplifh or diftinguifh, make
a diftinguifhed vow, *Lev*.22.21. *Num*.15.3,8. to
make a fingular vow, *Lev*.27.2. to be wonderful.
פלא, נפלא, פלאי wonder, wonderful, wonderful
work, to act wonderful. נפליתי I am wonder-

* Der. Πατασσω.   † Φυκος Fucus.

T 2   fully

fully made, *Pfal.* 139. 14. מפלאות wonderful
works, *Job* 38. 16. ---- נפל to fall: an abortion,
Job 3 16. *Pf.*58.8. *Eccl.*6.3. הפיל let fall, caufe
to fall, caft down. נפלים giants, rather apof-
tates, fallen from God, *Gen.*6.4. *Num.*13.3. מפל
refufe, offal, *Amos* 8.6. מפלי flakes or fallings,
Job 41. 23. מפלה ruin, fall: fallen carcafe,
*Judg.*14.8. נפלל to fall repeatedly.*

פלג to divide: a divifion, ftream, torrent, river.
מלנה פלגה the fame.†

פילגש, פלגיש (from פל to feparate and נגש to approach) an harlot, concubine. ‡

פלד (to feparate) a torch, *Nahum* 2.3. ||

פלה to cleave, *Job* 16.13. cut, *Pfal.*141.7. fhred,
2*Kings* 4.39. ftrike through, *Prov.*7.23. to bring
forth, by parting, *Job* 39. 3. a piece, fragment.
Chald. to ferve, obey. פלחן fervice, *Ezra* 7.19.§

פלט to efcape, deliver; bring forth or be delivered
of, *Job* 21. 10. פליט one who has efcaped.
מפלט, פליטה, פלט efcape, deliverance.¶

פלך (to fupport) a ftaff, 2*Sam.* 3. 29. a diftaff,
*Prov.*31.19. Chal. a diftrict, part, region, tract.**

פלני, פלמוני (from פל to keep fecret, and נ I) *i.e.*
fecret from me; fuch an one; a certain one, *Dan.*
8.13.

פלם to adjuft, weigh, contrive, ponder; level; a
fcale or weight, *Prov.*16.11. *Ifai.*40.12.‡‡

---

* Def. Φιλεω. Bellus. Fr. Belle. Lupinus, Lupin. Aππελλαι Cha-
pels. Inter-pello. Velum, a Veil. Πελοϛος. Pull. Peel. Pill. Pillage.
Flay. Flaw. Puls. Pulfe. W. Pabl. Σφαλλω Εδιοπαλιζω Fall, Fell.
Fail. † Πελαγος Pelagus. Plug. W. Plyg. ‡ Πελλαξ,
Παλλακη. Pellex. || Field, divided ground. § Πελακυς Falx.
Φλαω, Flake. Plough (fo the above word fignifies in Chaldee, Syriac
and Arabic) Pluck. Fallow. Flock of wool, Fleece. Filch. Flitch.
¶ Φυλαττω. Flight. Flit. Fleet, fwift. Fleet, fhips. Pelt. Pellet.
** Baculus. Fulcio. Plaga. Block. Fulcrum. Place. ‡‡ Πλασσω,
Φαλαγξ. Bilanx, Balance.

פלץ to tremble, have a tremulous motion, *Job* 9. 6. פלצות tremor, terror, *Job* 21.6. *Pf.*55.5. *Ifai.* 21.4. *Ezek.*7.18. מפלצת the trembler; an idol; Simulachrum Turpiffimum, an image of Priapus, 1*Kings* 15.13. 2*Chron.*15.16. תפלצה terrible-nefs, *Jer.*49.16.*

פלש to roll in, wallow, cover. מפלשי involutions, *Job* 37.16.†

פם Chald. a mouth, aperture, *Dan.* 4. 28: 6. 17, 22: 7.5.‡

פנה to turn, turn towards, look at, refpect, re-gard; turn or look back; to turn out, *Zeph.*3.15. prepare, *i.e.* clear from incumbrance, empty: the corner or turning point of any body. פנה, פון to turn this way and that, as in great diftrefs, to be diftracted, *Pf.*88.15. hence פן leaft, a particle of doubt or caution. פנים face, faces; corner, *Zech.* 14.10. לפני before or to the face of. לפנים be-fore, afore time. מלפנים within, 1*Kings* 6. 29. פנימי, פנימה within, inner, meaning the infide of a book or a houfe which faceth the fpectators. אבן פנתה the key ftone of an arch. פנות cor-ners; chief perfons, who are the fupport of a community, as the corner ftone is of an houfe, *Judg.* 20. 2. 1 *Sam.* 14. 38. אופן, אפן a wheel. מפני refpects, views, *Prov.*25.11.

פנינים pearls or rubies cut into faces and corners.‖

פנג Pannag. balfam, delicate fpice, gum, or oint-ment, *Ezek.*27.17.

פנק to educate delicately, *Prov.*29.21.§

פס to diminifh, fail, be diminifhed, *Pf.*12.1. פסח

* Der. Pallas. Πλισσω. † Plafh. Flefh. Plafter. ‡ Φημι to fpeak. Φιμος bridle-bit. Pomum, fruit. Πωμα drink. ‖ Ποινω. Pain. Πανικον Panic. Φαινω. Πνεω. Pœnitet. Re-pent. W. Pen as in Pen-rith, i. e. the red head-land. Pennine-Alps. § Banket or Ban-quet.

a fmall

a ſmall quantity, handful, *Pſ.*72.16. פסים ſmall pieces, ſhreds, ſtripes of divers colours, *Gen.* 37. 3, 23, 32. 2 *Sam.* 13.18, 19. פס, פסא a piece or part.*

פסג rear up, to divide as hills do; ſurvey diſtinctly as from an eminence, *Pſ.*48.13. פסגה Piſgah, the mountain whence Moſes ſurveyed the land of Canaan.

פסח to paſs over; leap over: the Paſſover: Paſcal-offerings: limping, lame; to be lame, 2 *Sam.* 4. 4. to halt or leap from ſide to ſide, 1 *Kings* 18. 21. to leap up and down, 1 *Kings* 18.26.†

פסל to hew, cut: an idol, a carved or graven i-mage, פסיל the ſame: a quarry whence ſtones are hewed, *Judg.*3.19,26.

פסנטר, פסנטרין (from פש to touch) ſtringed muſical inſtruments, pſalteries, *Dan.* 3.6,7,10,15.

פעה to cry or ſhriek out, *Iſai.*41.14. אפעה a viper or adder, from the ſhrillneſs of its hiſs, *Job* 20.16. *Iſai.*14.29: 59.5. אפע the male viper, *Iſai.* 41.24.--- יפע to ſhine with bright and full ſplendour. יפעה brightneſs, *Ezek.*28.7,17.‖

פעל to work, make, do, ordain, prepare, *Pſ.*7.13. work, act, deed. פעלה, מפעל, מפעלה the ſame.§

פעם to ſtamp, beat, move, agitate, ſtrike repeat-edly, ſmite alternately: to trouble, be troubled: an anvil, *Iſai.*41.7. the foot: alſo a turn or time, now, once, twice, thrice; counting as it were the ſucceſſion: hence an orderly rank, 1 *Kings* 7.4,5. in order, *Ezek.*41.6. פעמת corners, which re-gularly correſpond, *Ex.*25.12: 37.3. 1 *Kings*7.30. פעמים feet, ſteps, footſteps, *i.e.* the treading of

---

* Der. Piece.   † Paſcha. Paſchal. Paſs. W. Paſg.   ‖ Beav. Pungo, Pungent, &c. Pang. Heaven.   § Beav. Polio; Poliſh. Po-lite. File. Fangle. Bungle.

the

the feet: wheels, *i.e.* steps of a chariot, *Judg.* 5.
28. פעמן a bell, struck with the clapper; or perhaps from the sound.*

פענח Paaneah, *Gen.* 41.45. צפנת פענח *i. e.* the
comfortable enlightener, or revealer of secrets,
from צפן hidden, יפע to enlighten and נח rest,
comfort.

פער to gape, open wide, *Job* 16.10: 29.23. *Ps.*119.
131. *Isai.*5.14. בעל פעור Baal-Peor, an obscene
idol of the Moabites.†

פצה to open; set free, deliver, *Psal.*144.7,10,11.
פצץ to be burst, riven, opened. התפצץ shatter-
ed to pieces, *Hab.* 3. 6. --- נפץ, פוץ to scatter,
break, dissipate, dash in pieces: overspread or scat-
tered abroad, *Gen.*9.19. to be discharged, *i.e.* broken up, or taken to pieces, 1*Kings*5.9. dispersion,
dissipation. מפץ slaughter, breaking to pieces,
*Ezek.*9.2. מפיץ a maul, *Prov.*25.18. mace, battle ax, &c. *Jer.* 41. 20. תפוצה dispersion, *Jer.*
25. 34. נפצץ or יפצפץ to shatter exceedingly,
Job 16.12.

פצם to break, *Micah* 3.3. to break forth with the
voice, *i.e.* make a noise, *Ps.*98.4.

פצל to take off the bark, pill, peel, *Gen.*30.37,38.
פצלות strakes or pillings.‡

פצם to burst or break open; riven, *Ps.*40.2.

פצע to wound, beat, bruise, crush; a wound.

פצר to rub hard upon, press, urge, force, compel;
persuade: stubbornness, *i.e.* obstinate pressing or
persisting, 1 *Sam.* 15. 23. פצירה a rubber, file,
1*Sa.*13.21. rather פים פצירה a bluntness of edges,
i.e. the edges of their plough shares were blunted.||

* Der. Foam.
‡ Φοιζώ. Φλοιω. Peel.
Freeze, Frost.
† Aperio. Pore. Pario. Parent. Furrow.
|| Force. Press, Pressure. Com-de-op-press.

T 4   פק

פֻּק, פוק to totter, ſtagger, *Iſai.*28.7. move, *Jer.*
10.4. פִּיק ſtriking of the knees in fear, ſtaggering, *Nah.*2.10. פוּקָה offence, grief, ſtaggering,
1 *Sam.* 25. 31. --- נפק to go, come, bring forth,
ſupply, *Pſ.*144.13. get, obtain, *Prov.*3.13: 8.35:
12.2: 18.22. to further, ſucceed, encourage, *Pſ.*
140.8. draw out for ſupply, *Iſai.*58.10. Chald.
to go forth, iſſue; bring forth. נפקתא expences,
Ezra 6.8.*

פקד to viſit, review, overſee; puniſh: take care of,
notice, take account of: to number; to miſs or
be wanting on a review: to give in charge, appoint, commit to another's care. פקדה charge,
overſight, viſitation, office. פקיד an overſeer.
פקודים precepts; appointments, charges given
us by God to be obſerved. פקדון a depoſite in
truſt, or charge. מפקד number or muſter, 2 *Sa.*
24.9. command, appointment, 2 *Chron.* 31. 13.
appointed place, *Ezek.*43.21.†

פקח to open the eyes or ears; the wife or feeing,
*Exod.*4.11: 23.8. פקה קוח opening of the pri-
ſon, *Iſai.*41.1. one word פקחקוח, according to the
70; opening or releaſe.

פקע (to cut, corrode, diſſect) פקעה the Coloquin-
tida or wild gourd, 2 *Kings* 4.39. פקעים artifi-
cial knops in the ſhape of wild gourds, 1 *Kings*
6.18: 7.24.

פר־ה to break, burſt out; to bear fruit; be fruitful, increaſe, to break, make void, diſſolve, abo-
liſh, diſannul. פורה a wine preſs, where grapes
are ſqueezed, *Iſai.* 43. 3. *Hag.* 2. 16. פּאֵר duſt,
aſhes; diſſolved by fire. פרי fruit. פרה, פר a
young bull or heifer, either from its horns burſt-
ing forth or being fit to breed. אפריון a nuptial

* Der. Pitch, fall head-long. Peccare. Peccant.   † Caput.

bed,

bed, not chariot, *Cant.*3.9. פור Chald. or Perſic
a lot. פרות moles, ſee חפר פרר to break or
divide intirely, *Pſal.*74.13. פרור a pan or pot,
*Num.*11.8. *Judg.*6.19. 1*Sam.*2.14. פרורים Pa-
rurim, a proper name of a place, rather than ſuburbs, 2 *Kings* 23. 11. פרפר to diſſolve utterly,
break in ſmall pieces, *Job* 16.12, פרא to be diſſolute, break free from reſtraint. פרה, פרא a
wild aſs. יפריא be diſſolute, *Hoſ.*13.15.*

פרבר Parbar (from פר to divide and בר without)
the outer diviſion, the name of a place, 1 *Chron.*
26.18.

פרד to ſeparate, part or ſcatter: a mule, *i.e.* ſeparated from their natural ſtock. פרדות ſeed or
grains ſcattered in ſowing, *Joel* 1.17.†

פרדס an orchard or garden, *Eccl.*2.5. *Cant.*4.13.
a foreſt, *Neh.*2.8.‡

פרז to diſperſe, ſcatter; ſcattered, *Eſth.*9.18. ראש
פרזו the head of him that ſcattereth him, *Hab.*3.
14. פרזי a village, 1*Sam.*6.18. villagers, *Deut.*
3.5. פרזון, פרזות villages, open country.‖

פרזל, פרזלא iron, Chal.. ſee ברזל

פרח to break forth, bud, bloſſom, flouriſh: a bud,
bloſſom or flower; to break out in ſores. פרחה
the youth, young buds or brood, *Job* 30.12. אפרח
the young of birds, לפרחות into the flower gar-
dens, *Ezek.*30.20. perhaps places conſecrated to
Aſhteroth and obſcenity.§

פרט to particulariſe; a particular grape left after

* Der. Ποξτις. Fera. Ferus. Aper. Boar. Pair. Pear. Pirum. Οπωρα, au-
tumn. Πυρ Fire. Fear. Pyre, and with Sin prefixed, Spire. Frio. Friable.
Φιξω Fero. Bear. Free. Farrow. Ferio. Fors. Ferrum. The Saxon god-
deſs Friga, Freya or Fria, whence Friday. W. Ffrwyth. † Part.
Parted. Præda. Veredus, a poſt-horſe. Παξδος Pardus, Leo-pard. Fret,
Fretum. Frith. Froth. Forth. W. Parthu. ‡ Παξαδεισος Paradiſſus,
Paradiſe. Foreſt. W. Paradwys. Spargo. Sparſum, Aſperſe.
§ Florio. Floralia. Freak. Spark.

gathering,

gathering, *Lev.*19.10. to particularife in mufic,
i.e. quaver, chant, *Amos* 6.5.*

פרך (feparate from the fight) rigor, cruelty: פרכת
the vail of the holy of holies, which feparated
the holy place from the moft holy.†

פרם to rend at the feam, to tear, rip, *Lev.*10.6:
13.45: 21.10.‡

פרם to divide, break; deal out bread; *Ifai.* 58.7.
*Jer.*16:7. to divide the hoof, or have the hoof
parted. פרסה an hoof. פרס the Offifrage, a
kind of eagle that breaks and fwallows the bones
of his prey.‖

פרע to throw off, fet free, difcharge, *Exod.*5.4. ex-
empt; ftrip, make naked, refufe, avoid, fet at
nought; apoftatize, *i.e.* throw off their religion,
*Prov.*29.18. locks of hair, growing freely, *Num.*
6.5. *Ezek.*44.20. מראש פרעות with blood, from
the *hairy head* of the enemy, *Deut.*32.42. בפרע
פרשת בישראל in the fad apoftafy in Ifrael, *Judg.*
5.2. הפריע to caufe to apoftatife. Thefe two
laft paffages are rendered to revenge.§

פרעש a flea (from פרע and רעש move, leap) 1 *Sa.*
24.15. 26.20.

פרץ to burft out, break forth, come abroad, increafe, break in upon, prefs, urge; a breach.
מפרץ the fame. פריץ, פריץ a robber, ravenous
beaft. נפרץ open, publifhed, 1 *Sam.*3.1.¶

פרק to break, rend, pull off; refcue, deliver; Chal.
break off, ceafe from, *Dan.*4.24, or 27. robbery,
*Na.*3.1. broth or torn pieces, *If.*45.4. a crofs way,

---

* Der. Part. Bard. W. Prydydd.   † Ferox. Ferocia, Fierce. to
Trick, Pierce. Break. Parcæ.   ‡ From.   ‖ Pars, Pait Φαρσος
Fruftrum, Cruft. Ofprey. Frefh.   § Παρεια cheek. Fro, Fray.
Frank. Frango. Prance, Prank, and with f prefixed, Spring.   ¶ Πε-
ρατης. Φωρ. Fur. Πειρατης Pirate, Prefs. Burft,

where

where the road breaks off, *Obad.*14. מפרקת the neck or vertebræ, 1 *Sam.*4.8.*

פרש to expand, fpread out, feparate; fpread a-broad, ftretch out, fcatter, difperfe: expound, de-clare, fpread out the mind, *Lev.*24.12. *Num.*15. 54. to diffufe, יפרש fhall diffufe (poifon) like a bafilifk, *Prov.*23.32. dung, excrement feparated from the body: to break or chop in pieces, *Lam.* 4.4. *Mic.*3.3. it may be here put for הרס. מפרש fomewhat expanded : plainly read or expounded, *Ezra* 4.18. *Neh.*8.8. פרשט a declaration, *Efth.* 4.7: 10.2. פרשים horfemen which overfpread a country. פרשי the threfhing inftrument.†

פרשגן a copy, declaration, *Ezra* 7. 11. from פרש expound, and גון Chald. form, *i.e.* a declarative form.

פרשדנה dung, excrement, *Judg.*3.22. from פרש and שדה to fhed.

פרשז to fpread, expand, *Job* 26.9. from פרש and זז motion.

פרת Euphrates, from פרי־ה

פרתמים nobles, princes, *Efth.*1.3: 6.9. *Dan.*1.3. from the Perfic פר Heb. פאר honourable, and תם perfect.‡

פש־ה to fpread or extend, as a fore, *Lev.*13, &c. to range at large, frifk as a calf, *Jer.*50.11. *Mal.* 4.2. others, grow corpulent: to fcatter, fpread abroad, *Nah.*3.18. *Hab.*1.8. פש extent, *Job* 35. 15. בפש מאד the full extent.---נפש to breathe; be refrefhed, *Exod.* 23. 12: 31. 17. 2 *Sam.* 16.14. breath, foul, life, perfon, one's felf, living crea-

---

* Der. Break; Brack. Fractum. Βϱαχω. Crack. Parco, deliver. ‡ Φϱαζω. Φϱασις Phrafe. Profa, Profe. Perfian, i. e. excellent horfe-men, Pharifee, i. e. feparated; or expounders of the law. † The *Phar* enters into feveral noble names of Perfea and Medea, as Phar-naces, Pharnafpes, Pharnuchus, Phraortes, Phraates, Phradates, &c.

ture, animal: alſo a dead body, a carcaſe. בתי
הנפש boxes of refreſhment; perfume boxes, which
ladies wore hanging to their neck.*

פשח to rend or tear in pieces, *Lam.* 3. 11.

פשט to ſpoil, plunder, ſtrip; put off; ruſh, invade; ruſh forth from ambuſh.†

פשע to paſs by, treſpaſs; tranſgreſs; tranſgreſſion:
to go, *Iſai.* 27. 4. a ſtep, 2 *Sam.* 20. 3. a tranſ-
greſſor. מפשעה the buttocks on which our ſteps
depend, 1 *Chron.* 19. 4. ‡

פשק to diſtend, open, *Prov.* 13. 3. *Ezek.* 16. 25.

פשר to expound, *Dan.* 5. 16. interpretation, *Eccl.*
8. 1. *Dan.* 4. 15, 16.

פשת flax, linen.

פת־ה to part, portion, divide: to entice, perſuade,
deceive. Chald. to be dilated. פתי breadth,
Dan. 3. 1. *Ezra* 6. 3. פת, פתות a piece, morſel
of bread or victuals. פות, פתות hinges, 1 *Kings*
7. 30. פת ſecret part, pudendum muliebre,
Iſai. 3. 17. פתת to divide minutely : to ſeduce
entirely. פתה, פתי, פתא ſimple, ſilly, *i. e.* eaſily ſeduced. יפת a prodigy, wonder, miracle,
ſign. ‖

פתאם ſudden, ſuddenly; from פת a ſmall portion of time, and תאם to join, *quaſi* in the ſuc-
ceeding moment.

פתבג a piece of meat, *Dan.* 1. 5, 13. from פת piece,
and בג cut off.

פתגם a word, ſentence, command, decree, *Eſther*
1. 20. *Eccl.* 8. 11. §

פתיגיל a ſwathe for the breaſt, a ſtomacher, *Iſai.*
3. 24. from פת a piece, and גל to roll.

---

* Der. Puſh. Piſcis, Fiſh, from their increaſe. Φυσις. Πας. † Vaſ-
to, Vaſt. Waſte. ‡ Paſs. Pace. It. Paſſio. W. Paſſio. ‖ Puto.
Fr. Petit. Petty. Bit. § Φθεγμα. Φθεγγομαι. Αποφθεγμα. Apothegm.

פתח to open, loofe, ungird: to make an opening; to engrave or carve: to draw a fword: plough the ground; declare, fet forth: a door. מפתח, פתחון a key, opening. פתוח an engraving. פתחות drawn fwords, *Pf.* 55. 21. פתחים entrances or openings, *Mic.*5.6.*

פתל to wreathe, intwift, intwine, wreftle, *Gen.*30. 8. נפתל intricate, *Job* 5.13. *Prov.*8.8. התפתל to fhew one's felf forward, or contend with, *Pf.* 18.26. תתפל for תתפתל the fame, 2*Sam.*22.27. פתיל a lace, line, ribband, wire, &c. twifted in its make. A covering wreathed about the mouth of a veffel, *Numb.*19.15. a twifted neck ornament, *Gen.*38.18,25. פתלתל very crooked or perverfe, *Deut.*32.5.

פתן (to difturb) an afp or adder. מפתן the thref-hold of a door, often difturbed.†

פתע (to break in pieces) a moment.

פתר to expound, explain, interpret. פתרון inter-pretation.‡

פתשגן a copy, exemplar, *Ef.*3.14: 4.8. from פתש Sarmar. and Arab. to examine, and גון Chald. a form.

צ

צדי the eighteenth letter; the form of this letter might have been originally taken from fome net or inftrument ufed by the huntfman in the cap-ture of his prey; Mr. Baxter fays, it feems to be the *eel-fpear* or *trident*, for ftriking fifh. Sidon might have been fo called from its fifhery; and צדה to hunt after, differs but little from ἑσσω and ζατεω. This letter is a fibillant, and is perhaps

---

* Der. Pateo. Patent. Path.   † Πυθων Python.   ‡ Inter-pretor. Interpret. Patareus.

the afpirate of ז, as ס is of ש; as a numeral צ
ſtands for 90, but the final ץ for 900.

צא or יצא to come or go out, to go, come, bring
or carry forth; this word is varioufly tranſlated,
and as varioufly applied, but the fenfe is for the
moſt part obvious.. תוצא, מוצא a going out, a
border, a ſpring, iſſue; a draught-houſe to receive excrements, 2 *Kings* 10. 27. a vein whence
ſilver is brought forth, *Job* 28.1. a bud or ſprout,
Job 38. 27. a courſe for bringing out waters,
2 *Chron.*32.30.   צאה, צא, צוא excrements, filth,
filthy.   צאצא offspring, produce.---נצא for נצה
to flee away, *Jer.*48.9. *

צאל to ſhade.   צאלים ſhady trees, *Job* 40.21. ſee
צל

צאן to be fruitful: ſheep, cattle; flock, flocks. צאנו
Zaanan, *Mic.*1.11. ſo named from its fertility.†

צאר to incline. צואר the neck, Chal. אור *Neh.*3.
5. the fame. צורן the neck, *Cant.*4.9.

צב־ה to ſwell, *Num.* 5.21,22,27. the toad or tor-
toiſe, from their ſwelling; the tilt of a waggon,
ſwelled out, *Num.*7.3. *Iſai.*46.20. צבא to ſwell
in number, aſſemble in troops, go to war, to fight:
attend on ſervice in troops, *Numb.*8.24. ſervice,
war, warfare, hoſt, army. צבי, צבא elation,
glory, pride; the deer, roebuck or antilope, from
its beauty, or aſſembling in troops. צבא Chald.
an appointed time, *Job* 14.14. *Dan.*10.1. alſo, to
will, lift, defire. כמצביה according to his will,
juxta velle ſuum, Dan.5.32,35. צביה fight againſt
her, *Iſai.*29.7. מצבה becauſe of the army, *Zech.*
9.8. in theſe two places the א is dropped.---יצב
end נצב to ſtand, place, erect, rear up, eſtabliſh.
התיצב to ſtand, preſent one's ſelf. מצב a ſtation,

* Der. Iſſue.   † Γενομαι. Γενναω. Γενος, Genus. Gens. Generate.

garriſon

garrifon. מצבה a pillar, ftanding image; ftabi-
lity, fubftance, *Ifai*.6.13. נצב, נציב a pillar, fta-
tue, garrifon, ftanding officer. נצב the hilt of a
dagger, *Judg*.3.22. יצב firm, certain, true, *Dan*.
2.45: 6.12. נצבתא firmnefs, 2.41.*

צבט to reach, ftretch forth, *Ruth* 2.14.

צבע to ftreak; a ftreak or ftripe, *Judges* 5.30. a
ftriped animal, the Hyæna, *Jer*.12.9. 1*Sam*.13.
18. אצבע a finger or a toe, from its long form.
Chal. צבע to wet, moiften, imbrue, &c. for the
Heb. שבע

צבא to collect, heap up: an heap, 2*Kings* 10.8.†
צבת a fheaf; handful of corn, *Ruth* 2.16.

צג, יצג, הציג to fet or place in any fituation.‡

צד the fide of any thing: to lie in wait, *Exod*.21.
13. 1*Sam*.24.11. צוד, צדה, to enfnare, come fide-
ways upon the game, to hunt. מצד,מצדה,מצודה
a fortrefs, narrow pafs that defends the fides, &c.
צדיה a lying in wait, *Numb*.35.20,22. ציד an
hunter; game, venifon. מצודה, מצוד an hunting net or fnare. צידה, ציד, צדה food procured
by hunting, victuals, provifion. התציד for הצטיד
to take for provifion, *Josh*.9.12. Chal. נצד to be
made defolate, *Zeph*.3.6. צדא whence הצדא it is
true, *Dan*.3.14. for the Heb הצדק ‖

צדק to be juft or righteous; righteoufnefs. צדקה
the fame. הצדיק to juftify or make juft. הצטדק
to clear one's felf, *Gen*.44.17. צדיק righteous or
juft. §

צה, נצה to attack, fly at; contend, ftrive with: to
flee away, *Lam*.4.15. נץ an hawk, darting on his
prey. נוצה, נצה wings, or plumage of birds.

* Der. Σιβω. σιβασος.   † W. Yfgubor.   ‡ Iςαω, ςηκω, ιςηκω.
Sto. Statuo. W. Gofud.   ‖ Side· ζητεω feek.   § Δικη Δικαιος.
Index. Judico. Judge.

נצה to flower: a flower. נצנים flowers, *Cant.*2. 12. fee in נ   נצתה deftroyed, *Jer.*2.15. תצינה fhall be laid wafte, *Jer.*4.7. מצה contention, de- bate, ftrife. נצא, ניץ to flee away, *Jer.*48.9. *Lam.* 4.15.

צהב to fhine; yellow, fhining, *Lev.*13.30,32,36. *Ezra* 8.27.

צהל to exprefs pleafure by a loud found, to fhout: to neigh, *Jer.*5.8. to bellow as a bull, *Jer.*50.11. הצהיל to make to fhine or rejoice, *Pfal.*104.15. מצהלות neighings, *Jer.*8.16: 13.27.*

צהר to fhine, give light; a window, *Gen.* 6. 16. צהרים noon, meridian fplendor.   יצהר oil of olives.   הצהיר to make oil, *Job* 24.11.†

צוה to command, order, charge, appoint; to for- bid, *Deut.*4.23.   צו, מצוה commandment.

צול, צות, צוד, צוא fee צא, &c. without the ו

צח to be vigorous, active; to fhine ftrongly, *Cant.* 5.10. to be clear, bare, dry: intenfe, *Ifai.*18.4. to be violently agitated; dried up, *Ifai.*5.13. vio- lent, vehement, *Jer.*4.11. to cry aloud, in joy or diftrefs; to fhout, *Ifai.*13.11. צחיח fummit, high bare place, *Neh.* 4. 13. *Ezek.* 24. 7, 8: 26. 4, 14. צחיחה bare, dry land, *Pf.*68.6.   צחצחות intenfe droughts, *Ifai.* 13. 11.   צחות perfpicuous, clear, plain, *Ifai.* 32. 4.   צוחה a cry, complaint, *Pfal.* 144.14. *Ifai.*24.11. *Jer.*14.2. מצח, מצחות front or forehead.   מצחת polifhed plates, 1 *Sam.*17.6. נצח to prefs forward; to urge on a work, to over- fee, 1*Chron.*23.4. 2*Chron.*34.12. *Ezra* 3. 8,9. to excel, prefide, 1*Chron.*15. 21. ftrength, 1*Sam.*15. 29. *Lam.* 3.18. blood or ftrength, *Ifai.* 53. 3, 6. victory, 1*Chron.*29.11. *Ifai.*25.8. time onward; perpetuity; for ever, perpetually.   עד נצח to the end, *Job* 34. 36.   נצחת perpetual perfevering,

---

* Der. Fr. Joli. Jolly.   † to Stare. Star. Cheer.

צל   צחן   169

Jer.8.5. לנצח for ever, always, conſtantly, perpetual end, *Pſ*.9.6. מנצח overſeer, or conqueror.
לנצח נצחים for ever and ever, *Iſai*.34.10.*

צחן to corrupt. צחנה ſtink, ſtench, *Joel* 2.20.†

צהק to move or ſhake the ſides, to laugh; wanton,
make ſport: laughter.‡

צחר white, bright, vivid, *Judg*.5.10. *Ezek*.17.18.

צי-ה drought, dry, deſert.   ציון dry deſert place,
Iſai.25.5: 32.2.   צי a decked veſſel that carries
goods dry.   ציים inhabitants or wild beaſts of the
deſert.   ציון a ſign, ſee צן ‖

ציי, ציין, &c. ſee צן, צץ without the י

צל to overſhadow: to cover with fire; to bake or
roaſt under the aſhes, 1*Sam*.2.15. *Iſai*.44.16. to
be deep, *i.e.* overſhadowed; to tingle, quiver (by
Onomatopœia from the ſound of the word).
צלל to begin to be dark, overſhadowed, *Neh*.13.
19. to be overflowed, *Exod*. 15.10. to quaver,
ſound, *Hab*.13.16.   צלצל to overſhadow exceedingly.   צלא Chald. to pray, ſupplicate, *Ezra* 6.
10.*Dan*.6.10: מצל ſhadowing,*Ezek*.31.3. צל, צלל
a ſhadow, ſhade, defence, *Num*.14.9: מצלה a bottom, ſhady place, *Zech*. 1.8.   צלצל ſhadowing,
Iſai.18.1. a locuſt, *Deut*.28.42. (their ſwarms often obſcure the ſun) a twig-ſnare, ſunk under water to catch fiſh, *Job* 41.7.   צלמות ſhadow of
death.   מצלתים צלצלים cymbals. מצלות bells,
Zech.14.20.   צלי roaſted, roaſting, *Exod*.12.8,9.
Iſai.44.16:   צליל a cake, baked or roaſted, *Judg*.
7.13.   מצולה צולה the deep, a deep. --- נצל to
take away; to deliver; to plunder, ſpoil.   מצל
pluckt, taken out of, *Amos* 4.11. *Zeph*.3.2: הצילה

* Der. Siccus. Σικχος. Sick. Choak.   † Stain. Stink, Stench.
‡ Joke. Jog.   ‖ W. Sychu.

U   deliverance,

deliverance, *Efth*.4.14. התנצל to ſtrip one's ſelf, *Excd*.33.6.§

צלח to paſs forward, advance, proſper, proceed. צלחת, צלחית, a diſh, which paſſes from gueſt to gueſt.¶

צלם to form: an image. צלמות ſhadow of death, from צל and מות *

צלע a ſide, rib, *i.e.* ſide bone, a ſide chamber: to lean or ſlip aſide: to halt or ſidle in walking, an halting or ſlipping aſide. צלעות boards, planks, beams, the ribs of an houſe.†

צם empty, hollow; to faſt, abſtain; a faſt, faſting. צמת, צמה hair of the head, conſiſting of hollow tubes, *Cant*.4.1,3: 6.7. *Iſai*.47.2. צמם, צמים a robber, who makes others deſtitute, *Job* 5.5: 18.9. צמא to thirſt, be thirſty; thirſt. צמאה the ſame. צמאון drought, *Deut*. 8.15. thirſty ground, *Pſal*.107.33. *Iſai*.35.7.‡

צמד to join, faſten or couple together; a yoke of oxen, a pair, couple: an acre of land, or as much as a yoke of oxen can plough in a day, *Iſai*.5.10. a bracelet faſtened to the arm. צמיד the ſame; alſo, bound, *Numb*.19.15. הצמיד to frame, or artfully connect together, *Pſ*.50.19. צמדים riding in pairs, two a breaſt, 2*Kings* 9.25.

צמח to ſhoot up, bud, ſpring, grow: a branch, bud; produce; any thing that ſpringeth up; the riſing ſun.‖

צמק to be dry, or without moiſture, *Hoſea* 9.14. צמוק a bunch of dried grapes or raiſins, 1 *Sam*. 25.18: 30.12. 2*Sam*.16.1. 1 *Chron*.12.4.

צמר to be ſoft, tender; wool. צמרת the top ſhoot

---

§ Der. Λισσομαι. Shell. Shelter. W. Tywyll.   ¶ Luck. Infilio. Sulcus. Skillet.   * Similis. Similar. W. Delw.   † Sling. Slink. ‡ Jejunus.   ‖ Semen. Snake.

of the cedar, of a foft wooly texture, *Ezek.*17.3, 22: 31.3,10,14.§

צמת to cut off, deſtroy. צמתת to deſtroy entirely: a total cutting off and alienating, *Lev.* 25. 23. צמיתת the fame, *Lev.*25.30.*

צנה pointed, ſharp-pointed, piercing, penetrative: a buckler, ſhield or target with a ſharp point in the middle. צן, צנים thorns, prickles. צנות hooks, fiſh ſpears, ſome pointed inſtrument, *Amos* 4.2. צנת the piercing cold of fnow, *Prov.*25.13. ציון, צין a monument, 2*Kings*23.17. a way-mark, *Jer.*21.21. a fign or mark, *Ezek.*39.15. meaning fuch pyramids or pillars as terminated in a point. צנינם, צנינים very ſharp thorns or darts. צנצנת an urn or pot with a wide belly and ſtrait mouth, *Exod.*16.33. (צאן, צון flock, cattle. צנה ſheep, flocks of ſheep, *Pſ.*8.7. צנא ſheep, *Num.* 32.34. fee צאן. ציון a dry place, fee ציה) †

צנה to alight or fink down, *Joſh.*15.18. *Judg.*1.14. faftened or funk it down, *Judg.*4.21. ‡

צנם, צנמת withered, fmall, flender, *Gen.*41.23.

צנע, צנוע modeſt, lowly, humble, *Prov.*11.2. הצנע to be humble, or humble one's felf.

צנף to roll, turn or wind round, *Iſai.*22.18. to be attired with a turband, *Lev.*16.4. צניף, מצנפת a turband which confiſts of a cap and a linen faſh wound round in wreaths and worn on the head: it is rendered mitre, diadem, hood. צנפה a toſing or turning about, *Iſai.*22.28.‖

צנק, צינק a place of confinement, ſtocks, dungeon, *Jer.*29.26.§

§ Der. Smear.   * Smite. Smith.   † Σαννιον, a Perſian dart. Σανναζω to pierce. Sting, Stang. a ſtake. Snout. Snite, now Snipe. ‡ Sink.   ‖ Jump. Στιφω. Στιφανος.   § Snug.

צנר, צנור (to fill) a canal or deep paffage for water, 2 *Sam.* 5.8. *Pf.* 42.7. ¶

צנת, צנתרות round hollow pipes or tubes, *Zech.*
14.12. from צן penetrate, and תר round.

צעה to return triumphing from a complete victory, *Ifai.* 63.1. the captive exile, one led in triumph
by a conqueror, *Ifai.* 51.14. to wander, rather triumph, acting with a haughty fpirit, *Jer.* 2.20.
Jer. 48.12. might be rendered thus; I will fend
him צעים *triumphant conquerors,* וצעהו and they
fhall make him captive, or triumph over him;
thus Dr. Taylor: others render it, to fpread, o-
verlay, ftretched out. --- יצע to fpread any thing,
in order to lie down upon it. יצוע, מצע a bed.
יציע, עציע a chamber, that part in an eaftern chamber where the bed is placed, 1 *Kings* 6. 5, 6, 10.
צעצעים image work, 2 *Chron.* 3.10. rather, two
Cherubims triumphant, in the act of drawing a
triumphal car.

צעד to proceed, walk with a fteady pace; to march.
הצעיד to bring, or make to go, *Job* 18.14. צעה,
צעדה, מצעד a moving, ftep, going. צעדות ornaments of the head drefs, defigned to give gracefulnefs by their motion, *Ifai.* 3.20. according to
others, fhackles or ornaments for the legs, which
might give grace to the gait. אצעדה a chain or
bracelet, perhaps for the above purpofes, *Numb.*
31.50. 2 *Sam.* 3.10. *

צען to be removed, taken or thrown down, *Ifai.*
33.20.

צעף, צעיף a fummer veil, umbrel, *Gen.* 24.65: 38,
14,19.

¶ Der. Ciftern. Affinaros, a name given by the Phœnicians to a
deep and rapid river in Sicily.   * Cedo. Incedo. Σταδιον Stadium.

צפר   צעק   173

צעק to cry out, call together. צעקה a cry.
צער to be little, ſmall, mean. מצעיר ,מצער, צעיר
little, ſmall, young, younger. צערה youth,
*Gen.*43.33. מצער a little while, *Iſai.*63.18.
צפ־ה to overſpread, overlay; to overlook, view a
proſpect, look, eſpy, behold: to overflow as water, glide along, flow, ſwim, *Deut.*11.4. 2 *Kings*
6.6. *Lam.*3.54. *Ezek.*32.6. honey ſpontaneouſly
flowing from the comb, *Pſal.*19.10. *Prov.*16.24.
צפת the chapiter of a pillar, 2 *Chron.* 3. 15.
צפוי a covering, overlaying. צפון the north.
צפית, מצפה a watching, watch-tower. צפצפה
circumſpectly, not a willow tree, *Ezek.* 17. 5.
צפצף to *chirp* like a young bird with a weak que-
rulous voice, *Iſai.*8.19: 10.14: 29.4: 38.14.*
צפד to adhere, ſtick cloſe to, *Lam.*4.8.†
צ ח to contain. צפחת a cruſe, a ſmall veſſel to
contain liquors, 1 *Sam.* 26.11,12,16. 1 *Kings* 17.
12,14,16: 19.6. צפיחת a thin cake, probably to
hold ſome liquid, *Exod.*16.31. rendered wafer.
צפן to hide, conceal, lay up, lurk privily: צפון the
north, becauſe concealed in darkneſs and by ſnows
and froſt, if not from צפ־ה צפונה northward :
צפוני northern, *Joel* 2.20. מצפנים hidden things,
*Ob.*6. צפנת פענח Zaphath-Paaneah, *i.e.* treaſure
of comfort, a name given to Joſeph by Pharaoh.
צפע (to eject) צפעות an iſſue, *Iſai.* 22. 24. צפועי
dung, excrement, caſt out of the belly. צפע,
צפעוני the Baſaliſk or Dart; the moſt poiſonous
of all ſerpents, *Prov.*23.32. *Iſai.*11.8: 14.29: 59.
5. *Jer.*8.17.
צפר to move quickly, ruſh haſtily, *Judg.*7.3. צפר,
צפור a bird which moves ſwiftly. צפרה, צפירת

* Der. Σαφης Safe. Σοφος. ζοφος. Spy. W. Yſpio. † Spot.
Speed. Sped. ‡ Spew. Ασπις; Aſp.

the

the morning dawn when birds begin to ſtir, *Ezek.*
7.7,10. צפיר an he goat, from its nimble motion. צפירת a crown or diadem, ſhining like the
rays of the morning, *Iſai.* 28. 5. צפרן a ſharp
point; the nail of a finger, *Deut.*21.12. the point
of a graving tool, *Jer.*17.1.*

צפרדע a frog, from צפר the ſun beam, and ידע to
feel.

צפת a ſpherical crown or chapiter of a pillar, 2
*Chron.*3.15. ſee צפ־ה

צץ, צוץ, ציץ to bloom, put forth flowers, bloſſom,
flouriſh; appear beautiful, or irradiate as a flower. *Cant.*2.9. a flower. ציצת a flower. ציץ the
plate, or perhaps crown, of gold on the forehead
of the high prieſt, *Exod.*28.36: 29.30. *Lev.*8.9.
wings or feathers of a bird, *Jer.* 48. 9. ציצת
fringes, &c. conſidered as the flowers of a garment, *Num.*15.38,39. the hair which irradiates
from the head, *Ezek.*8.3.

צק to preſs, oppreſs, diſtreſs, ſtraiten; מוצק צוק
ſtraitneſs, diſtreſs, hardneſs. מצוק צוקה anguiſh,
diſtreſs. מצקים pillars or compreſſors, 1*Sam.*2.
8.---יצק to pour out, fuſe metal, caſt in a mould.
יצוק molten, firm, hard. מצק ſtedfaſt, *Job.*11.15.
יצקה a caſting of metal, 1 *Kings* 7. 24. מוצקות
pipes through which oil was poured, *Zech.* 4. 2.
יצק ſet down or place, 2*Sam.*15.24. מצוק ſitu-
ate, 1*Sam.*14.5. from יצג the ג being changed for
ק †

צקל, צקלן the huſk of corn, rather a ſcrip, bag,
2*Kings* 4.22.*

צר to bind up, incloſe, fortify; environ, beſiege,
incloſe, diſtreſs: an enemy, diſtreſſer: a rock, as

---

* Paſſer, Sparrow. Spire. ζεφυγος Zephyr. Spur. Sport. Spirit.
Stick. Stake. † Scale. Ger. Secchel. Satchel. Lit. tr. Siliqua.

a place

a place of defence ; or compreſſed hard together:
the edge of the ſword, *i.e.* that which diſtreſſeth,
*Pſ.*89.43. a ſtone, *Job*22.24. a ſharp ſtone,*Exod.*
4.25. a flint, *Joſh.*5.2,3. *Iſai* 5.28. *Ezek.*3.9. as
being piece of a ſtone or rock: narrow, ſtrait, dif-
treſs: an adverſary. צרה adverſity, afflicTion,
trouble. צר, ציר girding pangs. צרי balm, maſ-
tic. צור, צורן the narrow neck, ſee צאר. מצור
a bulwark, fortified place. מצורה a fort. מצר
a ſtrait, trouble, pain. מצור a ſiege; a fortified
or beſieged place. ציר an hinge, *Prov.*26.14. an
ambaſſador, agent, meſſenger,*i.e.* a cardinal agent.
הצטיר for התציר to feign one's ſelf an ambaſſador, *Joſh.*9.4. צירים idols, *Iſai.*45.16. the dif-
treſſers of their worſhippers, or perhaps ſome
rocks or *ſtones* held ſacred. צרר to bind cloſely,
confine, compreſs, diſtreſs exceedingly: a bitter
perſecutor : a bundle; a ſtone, a grain.---יצר to
frame, form, faſhion: an imagination, thought
framed in the mind: frame, *Pſ.*103.14. a thing
framed,*Iſai.*29.16.*Hab.*2.18. mind, imagination,
*Iſai.*29.16. צורה the form, *Ezek.*43.11. יצר,
יוצר a former, potter.---נצר to keep, preſerve: a
branch, ſcion, a young ſucker, reſerved for planting, *Iſai.*11.1: 14.19: 50.21. *Dan.*11.7. נצרים
keepers,watchers, watchmen. נצורים incloſures,
ſacred places, rendered monuments, *Iſai.* 55.4.
נצרה ſubtile, *i.e.* reſerved,*Prov.*7.10. נצרות hidden things, *i.e.* kept cloſe, *Iſai.*48.6.*
צרב to burn, ſcorch, *Ezek* 20.47. צרבת a burning or inflammation,*Lev.*13.23,28.*Prov.*16.27.†
צרח to cry aloud as from an eminence, *Iſai.*42.13.

* Der. Fr. Serrer, to bind hard. Sure. Sore. Sorry ; and with Mem
prefixed Miſer, Miſery. W. Saer. In-ſtauro. Servare. Preſerve. Cirrus.
Cirrulus. Curl. † Σαξαβος, Σαξβατανα. Ital. Zarabanda.

Zeph.

Zeph. 1. 14. an eminence, high place, or hold.
צריח the fame, *Judg.*9.46,49. 1*Sam.*13.6. ‡
צרך neceſſity, need, want, 2*Chron.*2.16.‖
צורן the neck, *Cant.*4.9. fee צאר
צרע, צרוע צרע, מצרע a leper, leprous. צרעת leprofy.
צרעה the hornet, *Exod.*23.21. *Deut.*7.20. *Joſh.*
24.20. this root may be derived by tranfpofition
from רצע.§

צרף to melt, refine, purify, try: a refiner, founder, goldſmith. צורף, מצרף the fame. מצרף a
crucible, fining pot.

צת, יצת to fet on fire, kindle, burn.

ק

קוף the 19th letter is a confonant and a palatine;
its ancient form was, in all probability, the a-
bridged fymbol of a tailed monkey, which קיף
fignifies, and which the Ægyptians adored; and
it is remarkable that in all languages wherein
this letter is retained it ftill preferves its tail. As
a numeral this letter ftands for 100.
קא to vomit, fpue; קיא vomit. קיו for קאו *Jer.*
25.27. קאת a pelican, whofe food is fiſh, which
it heaps in an enormous pouch, and then ejeĉts
them to feed upon at its leafure. מקוא linen
yarn, for מקוה 2*Chron.* 1. 16. feé פרד ¶
קאם Chal. to arife, from the Heb. קם *Hof.*10.14.
קב־ה (to curfe or blafpheme) --- נקב to pierce,
perforate; to mark or note an accompt, *Gen.*30.
28. by piercing a piece of wood: to mark or no-
minate a number of perfons; to name by way of
honour, *Ifai.*62.2. *Amos*6.1. to ſtigmatize, to no-

‡ Dcr. Κραζω Shrick. ‖ Χρηζω. § Dcr. Ψωρα. Sore, Strow,
Stroke. ¶ Dcr. Κωτιη Κιττα. Ικτιν. Kyte, Keck.

tice

note with ignominy, blafpheme, *Lev*.24.11,16. יקב a wine fat. קב a Cab, the 18th part of an Epha, little more than three pints, 2 *Kings* 6.25. נקבי pipes or flutes, *Ezek*.28.13. מקבת an hammer, with one fide of its head fharp to pierce: an hole, pudendum fœmininum, *Ifai*.51.1. נקבה a female. קבה an hollow tent or ftew, fuch as whores dwell in, *Numb*.25.8. *Deut*.18.3.*

קבל to take hold of, to take, receive, accept. מקבל that takes hold, *Exod*.26.5: 36.12. קבל עם before the people; rather, the people confenting and accepting it, 2 *Kings* 15.10. מחי קבלי mural hooks, engines of war which lay hold of the walls to demolifh it, *Ezek*. 26.9. לקבל Chal. becaufe of, on account of, *Ezra* 4.16. *Dan*.5.10. entirely, on account, for as much, becaufe.†

קבע to deprefs, rob or fpoil, *Prov*.22.23. *Mal*.38. 9. קבעת dregs, which fubfide, *Ifai*.51.17, 22. קובע an helmet, for כובע *1 Sam*.17.38. *Ezek*.23. 24.‡

קבץ to collect, gather together, gather in; withdraw, *Joel* 2.6. *Nab*.2.10. קבצת a gathering, *Ezek*.22.10. קבצים companies, *Ifai*.57.13.‖

קבר to inter, bury; a burying-place, grave, fepulchre. קבורה burial.§

קד to bow, ftoop, bow the head. קדה Caffia, *Ex*. 30.24. *Ezek*. 2.7. it is the bark of a reed that grows with its head inclined. קדקד the crown of the head. --- יקד to kindle, burn. מוקד, יקוד an hearth, burning. יקדתא Chal. burning. --- נקד marked with fpots, fpeckled, *Gen*.30.32,33,

---

* Der. Cabus. Κυβ.βις. Κωβειρος. Ceveo. W. Cauo. Cavo. Nun-cupo. † Fr. Gabelle. Καπηλος. Carbaretier. Καπηλευω. Capula. Quibble. Cavillor, Cavil. Cable. W. Cyfyl. ‡ W. Cipio. ‖ Κιβισις. Fr. Gibeciere. § Lit. tr. Grave. Κηβουρη. Κιβωριον. Fr. Ciboire.

39:31.8,10,11. a fhepherd, herdfman who marks his cattle to diftinguifh them, 2 *Kings* 3.4. *Amos* 1.1. נקדים mouldy fpots, *Joſh*.9.5,12. cakes, cracknels, 1 *Kings* 14.3. נקדות ſtuds or fpots of filver, *Cant*.1.11.*

קדח to kindle a fire. קדחת a fever, burning ague, *Lev*.26.16. *Deut*.28.22. אקדח a carbuncle, a ſtone of a fiery colour, *Iſai*.54.12.†

קדם to be, come, or go before; to be beforehand with, prevent: ancient, of old, aforetime: the eaſt, which in the earth's rotation precedes the weſt, the *riſing* fun making the fore part of the day. קדמת afore, former ſtate, antiquity. קדומה, קדים eaſtward. קדום, קדומוני ancient, former. קדמון eaſtern. קדים the eaſt wind.‡

קדר to be black, dark; to mourn, be mournful : קדרות blacknefs, darknefs, *Iſai*. 50. 3. קדרנית mournfully, *Mal*.3.14.||

קדש to fet apart; to hallow, fanctify, devote, confecrate, prepare. in a bad fenfe, to be fet apart as defiled, *Deut*.22.9. a fodomite or male proſtitute. קדשה an harlot, whore, *Gen*. 38. 21, 22. *Deut*.23.17. *Hoſ*.4.14. in the laſt fenfe it means *devoted* to lewdnefs: in a good fenfe, holy, holinefs, devoted place or thing. קדוש the fame. מקדש fanctuary, holy place. §

קה־ה to be blunt, *Eccl*.10.10. blunted, fet on edge, *Jer*.31.29,30. *Ezek*.18.2.---יקה to fubmit, יקהה ready obedience, *Gen*.49.10. *Prov*.30.17.---נקה to be empty, void, clean, clear, quit, guiltlefs, hold guiltlefs, leave unpunifhed, cleanfe, acquit: void of inhabitants, defolate, *Iſai*.3.26. cut off,

---

* Der. Κοτις. Κοττη. Κωθια Head. Nicked.   † Candeo. In-cendo. ‡ Quondam. Καθμος an eaſtern man. || Κηδαξ. Δαιξος Ater. Dark. § Κινδz. Κιναιδος Cinædus. Κιδος.

cleared

cleared away, *Zech.* 5.3.   נקי clear, clean, innocent, blamelefs, guiltlefs.   נקיון cleannefs, innocency.   מנקית bowls, cups; rather, rods laid between the fhew bread to keep them from growing mouldy, *Exod.*25.29: 37.16. *Num.*4.7. *Jer.*
52.19.   נקא pure, clean, *Dan.*7.9.   נקיא innocent, *Joel* 3.19. *Jonah* 1.14.¶

קהל to collect, affemble, congregate: a congregation, company, affembly; קהלה the fame.   קהלת
the preacher, who affembles and difcourfes to people on important fubjects.*

קוה to ftretch out as a line, tend forwards in a
ftrait direction, *Gen.*1.9. *Jer.*3.17. to wait, look
for: a line, קו, תקוה the fame.   מקוה thread,
linen yarn, 1 *Kings* 10.28. alfo a collection of water flowing into a cavity, *Gen.*1.10. *Ex.*7.19. *Lev.*
11.36. a ditch, pond, *Ifai.*22.11.   מקוא thread,
linen yarn, 2 *Chron.*1.10.†

קוט, קול, קום &c. fee קט, קל &c. without the ו
קה fee לקה --- קוח prifon, *Ifai.*51.1. fee פקח
קט to loathe, be difgufted at, tired with: a loathing, difguft.   קטט to be exceedingly difgufted,
Job 8.14. fhould be, who loathes or is tired with
his hope.‡

קטב to cut off; deftruction; deftroying, *Deut.*22.
24. *Pf.*91.6. *Ifai.*28.2. *Hofea* 13.14.‖

קטל Chal. to kill, flay, *Job* 13.15: 24.14. *Pf.*139.
19. flaughter, *Obad.*9. §

קטן to be little, fmall, young; fmall, young.

קטף to crop, pluck off, *Deut.*23.25. *Job* 8.12: 30.
4. *Ezek.*17:4,22.*‖

¶ Der. Innocuus, Innocency. Κενος.   * Καλεω Call. Οχλος. Εκ-
κλησια Ecclefia. W. Eglwys.   † Queo, can which in Arabic it fignifies. W. Chwydu.   ‡ Κιττα. Κοτεω. Κοτος. Quott, full to loathing.
W. Cat. Gwthio. Yfgwyd.   ‖ Καπτω.   § Κτεινω Kill. Cattle.
*‖ Κοπτω.

קטר to fume, fumigate, burn incenfe: incenfe, fmoke, vapour, perfume; קטורה, קיטור, קטרת the fame. מקטת an incenfe pot, cenfer. מקטרות incenfe altars, 2 *Chron.* 30. 14. קטר Chal. to bind, bind together. קטרות joined or made with chimneys, *Ezek.* 46. 22. קטרי ligatures, *Dan.* 5. 6. קטרין knot, difficulties, knotty points, *Dan.* 5. 12,16.*

קיו for קאו fpue, *Jer.* 25.27.

קיט Chald. fummer, *Dan.* 2. 35. from the Heb. קיץ

קיק, קיקיון the Ricinus or Palma Chrifti, *Jon.* 4.6,7, 9,10.†

קיר a wall, fee קר

קיקלון vile, fhameful vomit, *Hab.* 2. 16. from קי vomit and קלון vilenefs.

קיתרס an harp, fome mufical ftringed inftrument, *Dan.* 3. 5,7,10,15. fo called from קיתרס the citron, of which wood it was made.

קל־ה to be light, in oppofition to heavy, flow, difficult, weighty, or important: to be light, trifling, nimble, fwift; to lighten, make lighter: a light thing: to be efteemed light, vile, contemptible: to be eafy, fwift: to whet, polifh, make bright, in oppofition to looking dull or heavy: to roaft, parch, fry, dry at the fire. קל, קול a voice, noife, found, thunder. קליא, קלי parched; vile, debafed. קלון fhame, ignominy. נקלה loathfome or parched, *Pf.* 38.7. מקל a light rod or ftaff. קלקל to make exceeding light; to revile, curfe; to burnifh. קלקל carries the fame meaning as קל in all its fignifications, but in a very intenfe degree. ‡

קלחת, קלח a cauldron, kettle, 1 *Sa.* 2.14. *Mic.* 3.1. ||

* Der. Καθαιρω. † Κικι. Κηκιω. Quick. ‡ Κιλως Καλιω Call. Γλοζω Glocito. Gluck or hifs. Κλαζω Clango. Κλαιω. Κιλω. Κιλικ. Καλαμος Calamus. Καλον. Κιλοω. Calco. Coal. Keel. Quell. Quail. || Skillet.

קלט to contract; קלוט contracted, lacking, *Lev.*
22. 23. מקלט refuge; retirement: the cities of
refuge were fo called, becaufe tho' the manflayer
was protected, yet he was abridged of his liberty.＊

קלם to mock, deride, fcoff, fcorn: derifion, mock-
ing.†

קלע to fling, fwing: a fling, a flinger. מקעלים
the hangings of the tabernacle, which hung down
in a fwinging ftate: to carve or figure like hangings or tapeftry, 1 *Kings* 6. 29, 35, 35. מקלעה a
carving or figuring.‡

קלש (to be fmall) קלשון the fpike of a fork. שלש
קלשון a three forked inftrument, a trident.

קם to rife, arife, ftand up, rife up againft, to be
eftablifhed or confirmed: the eyes are faid to
ftand, when blindnefs impedes their motion, 1 *Sa.*
4. 15. 1 *Kings* 14.4. קומה ftanding corn. קומה
height, ftature. יקום living fubftance, that
ftandeth or fubfifteth upon earth, *Gen.* 7. 4, 25.
Deut. 11. 6. מקום a ftation, ftanding, a place.
קים fubftance, eftate, *Job* 22.20. קימה a rifing
up, *Lam.* 3.63. קמם to raife onefelf up. קוממיות
upright, *Lev.*26.13. תקומה power to ftand, *Lev.*
26. 37. אל־קום no ftanding againft, *Prov.*30.
31.---נקם to avenge, revenge: vengeance, quarrel, *Lev.*26.25.‖

קמח meal, flour, corn reduced by grinding.
קמט to take hold of, arreft, punifh grievoufly, *Job*
16.8: 22.16.

קמל to wither, fade, *Ifai.*19.6: 32.9.§

קמץ to grafp, take an handful; an handful.¶

＊ Der. Κολουθεις of Κολουω. Claudus. Cold. W. Cloff.   † Κλεος.
Κλιναζω.   ‡ Cœlo, to carve. Cling.   ‖ Κυμα a furge. Εγκωμιον
Encomium. Calamus. Holm. Comb on the Head of a Cock.   § Lit.
tr. Qualm. Calm.   ¶ Κομιζω.

קמש

קמש to move. קימוש, קמוש, קמשון the thiftle or nettle, *Ifai.*34.13. *Hof.*9.6. *Prov.*24.31.

קנ־ה to hold, contain, poffefs, buy, get, acquire: an hollow pipe, ftalk of corn, branch of a candle-ftick made hollow to contain oil; reed or cane, an hollow bone, *Job*31.32. a beam of a balance, which perhaps at firft was a reed, *Ifai.*46.6. קנן to make a neft; to neftle; to lament, moan. קן a neft. מקנה poffeffion, property, cattle, purchafe, price. מקנת what is bought. קינה lamentation. קין a fpear, 2*Sam.*21.12. קנא to burn with zeal, be jealous; envy: Chal. to buy, *Ezra*7.17. קנאה zeal, jealoufy. הקניא provoke to jealoufy. מקנה for מקנא *Ezek.*8.3. provoking to jealoufy.*

קנם (to be fragrant) קנמון Cinnamon, *Exod.* 30. 23. *Cant.*4.14. *Prov.*7.17.†

קנץ; קנצי Chald. for קצי ends, *Job* 18.2.

קף, קסם to cut, pluck off, *Ezek.*17.9.‡

קסם to divine, prefage; divination: reward of di-vination, *Num.*22.7. a divine fentence, *Prov.*16. 10. prudent, fagacious, *Ifai.*3.2. מקסם the fame.||

קסת an ink-urn, rather a writing table, *Ezek.*9.2, 3,11.

קע to mark, ftigmatize. קעקע a ftigma or mark, *Lev.*19.28.---יקע and נקע to be out of joint, *Gen.* 32.25. disjointed, alienated, *Ezek.*23.17,18,22, 28. *Jer.*6.8. to hang up, perhaps on full ftretch, *Num.*25.4. 2*Sam.*21.6,9,13. §

קער, קערה a charger or difh.¶

קף, קפים, קופים apes, 1*Ki.*10.22. 2*Chron.*9.21. fo called from their antick geftures.--- יקף or נקף to

---

* Der Κτεομαι. Κανα Cane. Can. Canalis. Gain. Win. Kinc. Gnaw. W. Cawn. Cwyn. Cynnydd.   † Κιναμωμον Cinnamonium. Cinna-mon.   ‡ Quafh. || χρησμος. Dutch Ghiffen. Guefs, &c. § Fr. Coing. Coin, money ftamped.   ¶ Old Eng. Cowre. Char-ger.

furround, encompafs about, come round, cut
round, *Lev*.19.27. הקופה circuit, revolution.
נקף a compafs, circuit, *Ifai*.10.34. a girding, *Ifai.*
3.24. others, a rent: to tear in pieces; rendered
to deftroy, *Job* 19.26. cut down, *Ifai.*10.34. kill,
*Ifai.*29.1. fhaking, *Ifai.*17.6: 24.13. all the paffages where this root occurs might be better rendered, if the radical idea of *revolution* was preferved,viz.*Ifai.*29.1. add year to year. חגים ינקפו
let the feafts *come round*. *Job*1.5. and it came to
pafs when the days of feafting were *gone about*.
In *Job* 19.25,26. I know that my Redeemer liveth,
and hereafter my fkin *fhall inclofe* this, *i.e.* a body
like this.---קפא to be congealed,cruddled,thick-
ened as liquids, *Exod*.15.8. *Job* 10.10. *Zeph*.1.10.
יקפאון fhall be dark or foggy, *Zech.*14.6.*
קפד to pafs fwiftly, dart, fhoot away; others, cut
off, finifh focn. *Ifai*.34.11. I have *darted through*
life as a fhuttle. קפדה fwiftnefs, others deftruction, *Ezek*.7.25. קפד the bittern or cormorant,
Ifai.14.23: 34.11. *Zeph*.2.14.†
קפז the Jaculus or Dart, a poifonous ferpent that
darts fuddenly upon its prey, *Ifai*.34.15.‡
קפץ to contract, fhut, ftop, clofe up, *Deut*.15.7.
Job 5.16: 24.24. *Pf*.77.9: 107.42. *Ifai*.52.15. to
fkip, bound, leap, *Cant*.2.8.‖
קצ־ה to cut off the extremity of any thing, *Deut*.
25.12. *Prov*.26.6. to cut fhort, 2 *Kings* 10.32.
Hab.2.10. to fcrape,*Lev*.14.41,43. a thorn which
wounds the flefh. קוץ the fame: to grieve, vex,
fret, loathe, be weary of. קץ, מקצה end, extremity, border, outfide, uttermoft part, coaft, a

---

* Der· Παχυς, Πυκαζω. Πευκη, Παχιη. to Coop. old Eng. to Quappe,
fail or faint.   † Κοττω Chopt.   ‡ Κουρος.   ‖ Skip. Capfa,
Cafket.

part or fome of. קצוֹי ends. קצוֹת ends, extremities, parts, quarters, corners, edges. קיצוֹנה
outmoſt. קוֹצוֹתי locks of hair cut and trimmed,
*Cant.*5.2,11. קצץ to cut off through and through.
--- יקץ to awake. קיץ fummer, fummer fruit.
קיץ the awakening feafon includes fpring and
fummer, as חרף the ſtripping feafon, does autumn
and winter. קץ to fummer, fpend the fummer,
*Iſai.*18.6.*

קצב to act by rule and meafure; to cut down (a
ſtick) of proper length to be an helve, 2*Kings* 6.
6. fize, height, 1*Kings* 6.25: 7.37. קצובות ſhorn
even, rather of equal height, *Cant.*4.2. קצבי bot-
toms, or precife meafure, utmoſt depth, *Jonah* 2.
6.

קצה vetches or fennel flower, *Iſai.*28.25,27.

קצן, קצין a captain, commander in war; perhaps
from קץ extremity.

קצע to cut or fcrape off the extremity or furface,
*Lev.*14.41. מקצוע, מקצוע the extremity, corner,
end of a wall. מקצעות planes, *Iſai.* 44. 13.
קציעות corners, cornered, *Ezek.*46.22. מהקצעות
Caſſia, the bark ſtripped off the Caſſia plant, *Pſ.*
45.8.†

קצף to foam, froth with anger; to be wroth, be
provoked to wrath: foam, *Hoſ.*10.7. wrath, dif-
pleafure, indignation. קצפה foaming, fpoken of
figs which are of a frothy fubſtance, when they
don't ripen kindly.‡

קצר to cut ſhort, ſhorten; be ſhortened in fpirit,
i.e. vexed, grieved; vexed, difcouraged: anguiſh,
ſhortneſs, *Exod.* 6. 9. to reap, cut, mow. קציר
harveſt; a harveſt bough which bears fruit, and

---

* Der. Εσχατος. Εχιζω. Quaſh.   † Caſſia.   ‡ Spuma. Gaſp.

is

is ufually cut off, *Job* 14.9: 18.16: 29.19. *Pfal.*80.
11. *Ifai.*27.11.*

קק, קיק, קיקיון a gourd, the Ricinus or Palma
Chrifti, *Jonah* 4. 6, 7, 9, 10.---נק־ה to be empty,
void; to be empty of good, defolate, wafte, *Ifai.*
3.26. to make empty, free; cleanfe, *Joel* 3.26. to
free from guilt, make innocent. מנקיות large
cups, bowls or goblets. נקיון cleannefs, *Amos* 4.
6. clean, purge; cleannefs, innocence, *Gen.* 20.
5. נקי clean, pure, innocent. נקק, נקיק an hole,
hollow place, *Ifai.*7.19. *Jer.*13.4: 16.16. נקא
Chal. pure, clean, *Dan.*7.9. נקיא innocent, *Joel*
3.24. *Jonah* 1.14.

קיקלון fhameful fpuing, *Hab.*2.16. from קיא fpuing and קלון fhame.

קר־ה to meet, happen, occur, befall: to make
beams or rafters meet in a building: to make
beams, *Neb.*2.8. lay beams, *Neb.*3.3,6. *Pfal.*104.
3. to floor, rafter, 2 *Chron.*34.11. to meet with
water by digging, 2 *Kings* 19.24. *Ifai.*37.25. to
caft out water, *Jer.*6.7. הקרה to bring or caufe
to meet, *Gen.*27.20. fend good fpeed, *Gen.*24.12.
קרי meeting, oppofition, contrary, at all adven-
tures. קור, קרה cold. מקור a fountain or fpring.
מקרה an event, occurrence, chance; building or
roof: cooling, *Judg.*3.20,24. קורה, קרה a beam
or roof. קר, קיר a wall. קרית, קריה a city, from
being walled in, or from the concourfe of people.
Carthage, anciently Carthade קרתא הדתא the
new city. הקריתם ערים ye fhall appoint cities,
i. e. choofe out cities eafy to be met with, *Num.*
35.11. קרים the fpringing out of a fountain,
*Prov.*25.25. *Jer.*18.14. קורי threads of a fpi-
ders web joined together, *Ifai.* 59.5,6. קרקר to

* Der. Curto.

Y   deftroy,

deſtroy, break down, demoliſh, *Iſai*.22.5. *Num.*
24.17. קְרָא to meet, occur, happen, befall: to
call, proclaim, name, cry out; to read aloud, *i.e.*
call written ſigns by the names for which they
ſtand. קְרִיאָה preaching or proclaiming, *Jonah*
3.2. מִקְרָא a convocation, calling together; af-
ſembly, *Iſai*.4.5. reading, *Neh*.8.8. לִקְרַאת for
meeting, oppoſite, over againſt. קרא a partridge,
1 *Sam*.26.20. *Jer*.17.11. ſo named from the note
it utters in calling for its mate or brood. --- יקר
to be fine, ſplendid, bright, precious, dear, excellent, reputable, rare, ſcarce, coſtly; honour,
glory, precious things: brightneſs, precious luſ-
tre, *Job* 31.26. to prize, a price or value, *Zech.*
11.13. יקרות clear, or in full brightneſs, *Zech.*
14.6. הקר withdraw, *viz.* thy foot; make it
precious or rare, *Prov*.25.17.---נקר to bore out,
put out; to dig out, cut out: to be perforated,
rot; to be pierced, *Job* 30.17. to pick, dig out.
נקרה a clift or cavity, *Exod*.33.22. מְקוֹר a fountain, ſee above.*

קרב to approach, come, bring, draw, or go near;
to approach, offer: to aſſault, attack, *Pſal*.27.2:
119.150. battle, war: what is neareſt, inward,
inwards, amidſt, among, within, inward part or
thought: near, neighbour, near of kin. קרוב
the ſame. קרבת an approaching, *Pſal.* 73. 28.
Iſai.58.2. קרבן an oblation offering.†

קרדם an hatchet or ax, from קר to meet, and דם
ſubdue.

* Der. Κρυος. Frigus. Ριγω. Curia. Court. Carus. Μακαρ. Μακαριζς.
It. Macaroni. Carcer. Cry. Crow as a Cock. The Welſh Caer, a walled
town, whence Carliſle, Caermarthen. The Mahometan Koran, i.e. the
lecture or reading. Κυρω. Occurro, Occur. W. Catchar. Creu. Crio.
Cwyr. Gawri. Gocr.   † Χριπτω, Χριμπτω.

קרח

קרח to make fmooth or bald: froſt, *Gen.* 31. 40.
fmooth ice; chryſtal, fmooth like ice, *Ezek.* 1.20.
קרחה baldnefs, baldhead.*

קרם to extend, cover over with, *Ezek.* 37.6,8.†

קרן to fhine forth, emit rays, *Exod.* 34.29,30,35.
an horn, perhaps becaufe horns fhoot forth like
rays. קרנים rays or beams of light, *Hab.* 3. 4.
מקרן horned, *Pf.* 69. 31. קרנא Chald. a cornet or
wind inſtrument.‡

קרם to ſtoop or bend, *Ifai.* 46.1,2. קרסים tatches,
rings, or little hooks of a curved form.||

קרסל the foles of the feet, 2 *Sam.* 22.37. *Pf.* 18.36.
from קר־ה to meet, and סל־ה to level a road.

קרע to rend, rent, tear; cut or tear out, *Jer.* 22.
14. קרעים rags, pieces rent off.§

קרץ to twitch or nip; to move, agitate, be formed,
nipped, as a potter nippeth a piece of clay to form
it into a veſſel, *Job* 33.6. to taunt, wink with the
eye, *Prov.* 6.13: 10.10. *Pfal.* 35.19. to agitate the
lips, *Prov.* 16.30. agitation, deſtruction; rather
the gad fly, which agitates the cattle, *Jer.* 46.20.
קרצי Chal. accufations.

קרקע the floor; bottom (of the fea) *Amos* 9.3. from
קר־ה to join, and רקע expand, a pavement.

קרש to join: a board.¶

קש־ה to collect, be collected, gathered together,
Zeph. 2.1. to have hard labour, *Gen.* 35.16,17. to
be ſtiff, obſtinate, cruel: churlifh, 1 *Sam.* 25. 3,
נקשה hardly beſtead, *Ifai.* 8.21. הקשה done hard.
קש ſtubble. קשי ſtubbornnefs, *Deut.* 9.27. מקהה
beaten or hammered hard, beaten work: upright,

---

* Der. Κουρευω. Καρα. Κϱιοϛ.   † Χροα. Χρυμα. Κϱιμαω. Cream.
Cremor.   ‡ Κιϛαϛ. Cornu. Corona, Crown. Cornet. Corner. Ker-
nel. Cornwall. W. Corn. Coron. || Καϛϭιοϛ. Crux. Crofs.   § E-
ϛικω. Crack. Fr. Grever. Crevice. W. Rhwygo.   ¶ Craſſus. Crafs.
Coarfe. Grafs.

i.e. rigid, firm, *Jer.* 10. 5. a curling tool giving
shape and rigidity to the hair, *Isai.*3.24. קשׁות
veffels, cups of beaten gold, *Exod.*25.29: 37.16.
Num. 4. 7. 1 *Chron.* 28. 17. קשׁשׁ to gather up
sticks or straws, *Exod.*5.7,12. *Num.*15.32,33. 1
Kings 17. 10, 12. קשׂקשׂת the scales of a fish.
קשׂקשׂים the scales of a coat of mail, 1 *Sam.*18.5.
קשׁא a cucumber, *Num.*11.5. מקשׁה a garden of
cucumbers,*Isai.*1.8.---יקשׁ to infnare, lay fnares.
מורשׁ a fnare.---נקשׁ to infnare, catch in a fnare.
Chald. to dash, clash together.*

קשׁב to hearken, attend to, liften to, mark well:
attention.

קשׁה, הקשׁיח to harden, *Isai.*43.17. be hardened,
Job 39.16.†

קשׁט truth, rectitude, purity, *Pf.*60.4.*Prov.*22.21.
קשׁיטה a lamb or sheep, a type of purity: a piece
of money stamped with the figure of a lamb,*Gen.*
33.19. *Josh.*24.32. *Job* 42.11.‡

קשׁר to bind, band together, confpire: treafon,
confpiracy, confederacy. קשׁרים ornamental
bandages, *Isai.*3.20. *Jer.*2.32. מקשׁרות, קשׁרים
stronger, more firm and compact, *Gen.*30.41,42.

קשׁת (perhaps from קשׁה to be stiff) a bow, the
rain-bow.

ר

ריש the twentieth letter, is a confonant, and one
of the liquid dentals; its ancient form was taken
from the hawk's head, which was among the
fymbols of the Egyptians, and reprefented the

---

* Der. Σιχπος Cheefe, and with Sin prefixed Squeeze. W. Ceifio.
Caffis. It. Caccia, Sp. Capa. Fr. Chaffe. Chafe. † Sævus.
‡ Caftus, Chafte.

blowing

blowing of the northern monſoons, as the Ibis did ḟhe ſouthern. The form of this letter, as it appears in ſome of the Samaritan alphabets, is ſtill extant on ſome of the ancient monuments of Egypt. This letter as a numeral ſtands for 200. רא־ה to ſee, look, look at, regard, underſtand, perceive, be ſeen, appear: a ſeer: viſion. הראיה to cauſe to ſee, to ſhew. ראי a gazing ſtock, Nah. 3.6. appearance, aſpect. fem. plu. ראיות comely, of a good aſpect, Eſth.2.9. ראות a beholding, Eccl.5.11. מראה appearance, aſpect, look, viſion. מראה, ראי ſpeculum or mirror, Exod. 38.8. Job 37.18. ראה a crow, glede or kite, a bird of ſharp ſight, Deut. 14. 13. מוראה filthy, provoking, Zeph.3.1. and מראה gall, Lev.16. ſee in מר --- ירא to fear, venerate, reverence. נורא to be feared, fearful, dreadful. מורא, יראה fear, dread, terror. מורה in fear, Pſ.9.20. ירא Chald. to caſt; ſhoot, 2Chron.26.15. 2Sam.11.24. יורא ſhall be watered, Prov.11.25. from ירה in רה* ראם to be raiſed, exalted, Zech.14.10. רים, ראם the Oryx, ſome animal of the deer kind; ſomē think the Rinoceros, though rendered unicorn. ראמות coral, a marine production, branching like the horns of a deer, Job28.18. Ezek.27.16.† ראש head, top, principal, chief, captain, chief in place, beginning, firſt, chief thing, ſum total: a troop, military band under one leader: a capital poiſon whether animal or vegitable, it is rendered, gall, venom, or hemlock. ראש for רש or ריש poor, poverty, 2Sam.12.1,4. Prov.6.11:10.4:13. 23:30.8. ראשן, ראשון firſt, former, anceſtor, chief, foremoſt, before time, at firſt. ראשית

* Der. Ọ;αω Mirrour. Μαιξω. Miror, Admire. Ray. Radius. W. Rhaith. Athraw. Cyfraith. † Ramus. Ram.

firſt,

firſt, *Jer.* 25. 1. ראשית beginning, principal, chief, firſt, firſt fruit. מראשת, ראשת a pillow or bolſter for the head: head tire, or principality, *Jer.* 13.18.*

רב־ה to be or become great, or many; increaſe, multiply: to nouriſh or bring up, *i.e.* make great, *Lam.*2.22. *Ezek.*19.2. to multiply words in diſpute, to contend, ſtrive, plead, debate, elude: to fight, 1*Sam.*15.5. הרבה, רבה, רב much, more, many, enough, great, ſufficient, abound, abundantly, multitude, *&c.* מרבית increaſe, greatneſs. תרבית, תרבות increaſe, increment, progeny. רבות, רבו, רבא, רבוא ten thouſand. מררה much, *Ezek.*23.32. great, *Iſai.*33.23. רב, ריב ſuit or cauſe, controverſy, contention. מריבה יריב he that contendeth or ſtriveth, *Pſ.*35.1.*Iſai.* 49.25. *Jer.* 18. 19. ארבה the locuſt, an inſect which increaſes prodigiouſly. The idea of ſhooting or darting has been given to this root in the following paſſages, but they may be better rendered thus, *Gen.*21.10. powerful with his bow. *Gen.*49.23. contended with him; not ſhot at him. *Job*16.13. his great men; not archers. *Pſ.*18.14. he multiplied lightenings. *Jer.*50.29. many, not archers. רבו Chal. ten thouſand. רבות tens of thouſands. רבבה an indefinitely great number. רבבים,רביבים ſhowers, *i. e.* numberleſs drops of water. רברבין,רברבן Chal. very great, *Dan.* 2. 48: 3. 33. very great men. רבוא, רבא ten thouſand, *Ezra* 2.64: רבאות tens of thouſands, *Ezra* 2.69. *Dan.*11.12.*

רבד to deck, adorn, *Prov.* 7. 16. an ornamental

* Der. Raſh. a Ruſh, from its head.   † Βραβευω, Βραβευς. Brave; and with Tau prefixed Θορυβος Turba. Troop. Ομβρος Imber. Rabbet, from their Increaſe. Rabula. Αγαθευω. Αγαθος.

chain

chain or wreath for the neck. רביד the fame,
*Gen.*41.42. *Ezek.*16.11. מרבדים ornamental co-
verings of tapeftry, *Prov.*7.16: 31.32.†
רבך to fry, roaft, &c. מרבכת fried or baken,*Lev.*
6.21: 7.12. 1*Chron.*23.29.‡
רבע put for רבץ, to lie down, engender, *Lev.*18.
23:19.19:20.16. a lying down, *Pf.*139.3. fquare,
a fquare, fourth part; רבעי, רביעי fourth; fem.
ארבעתים forty. ארבעים four. ארבע, רביעית
fourfold.||
רבץ to lie down, couch, perch, fit, reft: a refting
or couching place. מרבץ the fame.
רבק (Arabic to tie up) מרבק a ftall for fattening
cattle, 1*Sa.*28.24. *Jer.*46.21. *Amos*6.4. *Mal.*4.2.
רגב to clod; a moift clod, *Job* 21.33: 38.38.
רגז to move, be moved, fhaken violently, be troubled, fhake, quake, tremble, hurried, difquieted:
to fall out, be ruffled, *Gen.*45.24. to fear, ftand
in awe, *Pfal.*4.4. to rage, *Prov.*29.9. fret, *Ezek.*
16.43. be wroth, *Ifai.*28.21. provoke, *Job* 12.6.
trouble, trembling, rage, fear, wrath: noife, con-
cuffion, *Job* 37.2. רגזה trembling, *Ezek.*12.18.
ארגז a fmall cheft which can be moved from place
to place.§
רגל to ftrike, imprefs as the feet againft the ground,
*Ifai.*32.20. the foot; footman; to foot it about,
to fpy out and report what is difcovered: to act
the fpy: to flander, 2*Sam.*19.27. *Pf.*15.3. רגלים
footings, turns, or times, *Exod.*23.14. *Numb.*22.
28,32,33. מרגלים fpies. מרגלת feet, *Ruth* 3.
4,7,8,14. *Dan.*10.6. הרגלתי I taught to go, rather, I intended; or as a noun, my footing was
for Ephraim, *Hof.*11.3.*

---

† Der. Drab. Drapery. Ραππω. Wreath.   ‡ Lit. tr. Parch.
|| Ρομβος.   § W. Rhegain.   * W. Celwydd.

רגם to heap: to ftone, the capital punifhment a-
mong the Ifraelites. מרגמה a fling or heap of
ftones, *Prov.* 26. 8.   רגמתם their affembly or
counfel, *Pfal.* 68. 27. affemblies were anciently
held in open air at fome heap of ftones.† ארגמן
the Purpura or purple fifh; purple. ארגון, ארגונא
Chald. the fame.

רגן to mutter, murmur, *Deut.* 1.27. *Pfal.* 106.25.
Ifai. 29. 24.   נרגן a tale-bearer, *Prov.* 18.8: 26.
20,22. a whifperer, *Prov.* 16.28.‡

רגע to ftill, ftop; make quiet; to reft, caufe to reft:
to be dry, fixed, ftiff, *Job* 7.5. In *Job* 26.12. *Ifai.*
51.15. *Jer.* 31.35. it fhould be *ftill* the fea, not
divide: a reft, ftop, moment, paufe, inftant of
time, fuddenly. ארגעיה the fame. מרגוע reft,
Jer. 6.16. מרגעה reft, quiet, refrefhing, *Ifai.* 28.
12. רגעים quiet, *Pf.* 35.20.‖

רגש to affemble, to join friendly together in mu-
tual confent, *Pf.* 55.14. in an hoftile manner, to
rage, mutiny, confpire, *Pfal.* 2.1. Chal. *Dan.* 6.
6. a confufed multitude. מרגשה an infurrection,
Pf. 64.2.§

רד־ה to defcend, come down, *Judg.* 14.9. to caft
down, fubdue, hold in a low eftate, fubject, to
rule, have dominion over: fpread or lay down,
1 *Kings* 6. 22. אריד I mourn, or come down,
Pf. 55.2. רדד to fubdue entirely, *Pfalm* 144.2.
רדיד a kind of veil reaching down to the feet,
Cant. 5.7. *Ifai.* 3.23.----ירד to defcend, come, go,
fink, run, take or caft down, &c. מורד declivi-
ty, going down, defcent: thin, beaten down,
1 *Kings* 7.29. מרוד caft out, reduced, *Ifai.* 58.7.

---

† Der. Our Stone-henge on Salifbury plain was perhaps a place for
holding affemblies.   ‡ Jargon.   ‖ Ρηγω. Ρηγνυμι. Ριγεω. Ριγος.
Rigeo. Rigor. Frigus. Rigid. Frigid.   ∥ Rage. W. Rhegu.

mifery,

mifery, dejection, *Lam*.1.7: 3.19.   ירדן a torrent, or ftream, rapid in its defcent, *Job* 40.18. the river Jordan. --- נרד fpike-nard, *Cant*.1.12: 4.13, 14.*

רדם to be in a deep fleep,   תרדמה a deep fleep.†
רדף to follow after, feek, purfue, perfecute, chafe. נרדף what is paft or driven away, *Eccl*.3.15.‡
רהה to be afraid, *Ifai*.44.8.   מורה in fear, *Pfal*. 9.20.   רוה fee below.---ירה to caft, throw, fhoot at: to lay, place right or true, *Gen*. 31. 51. *Job* 38.6.   הורה to fhower down as rain, *Hof*.10.12. הורה to caft into the mind, to fhew, teach. מרים, מורים, יורים archers, fhooters.   יורה the former rain which fell about the middle of November.   מורה the fame, *Joel* 2. 23. a plentiful rain, *Pf*.84.6.   יורא fhall be watered, *Prov*. 11. 25.   מורה a teacher.   תורה a doctrine or law. מורה a razor which cuts and cafts off what is oppofed to it.   מורה a rebel, fee מרה.   ירא &c. fee above in רא

רהב to be firm, couragious, *Pfal*. 60. 5. to make fure or firm, *Prov* 6.3. to behave couragioufly or proudly, *Ifai*. 3. 5. to ftrengthen, make couragious, *Pfal*. 138. 3. turn thine eyes that they may *comfort* me, *Cant*. 6. 5. ftrength, courage, firmnefs, *Job* 9. 13: 26. 12. *Pfal*. 90. 10. *Ifai*. 30. 7. רהבים the ftout or proud, *Pfal*.40.4. ‖
רהט to run, flow: רהיט a gutter, trough, gallery, *Gen*.30.38,41. *Exod*.2.16. *Cant*.1.17.   רהטים in *Cant*. 7. 5. feems fome flowing ornament of the head. The hair of thine head is like the purple of a king bound with *flowing ornaments*, ribbands.§

---

* Der. Road. Rudis Rude. W. Cerydd. Fr. Rideau. Erudio Read. Rod. W. Gwaered. Ναρδος.   † Lit tr. Δαρθανω Dormio, Dream.   ‡ W. Rhodio.   ‖ Robur. Robuft. Rio.   § Rout, Riot,

רו־ה to be wet, foaked, faturated with liquor, drunkennefs, *Deut.* 29. 19. רויה well watered, *Pf.*66.12. plentifully fupplied, *Pf.*23.5. ברי by watering, *Job* 37.11. perhaps this laft word may be from בר־ה and mean the purity or pure æther.*

רוב, רוד, &c. fee רב, רד, &c. without the ו

רז־ה to wafte, diminifh, make lean. רזי, רזון lean-nefs. תרזה the *(flender)* pine. רז, רזא Chald. a fecret, a myftery.†

רוח to fhriek: a mourning feaft, *Jer.* 16.5. a ban-quet, *Amos* 6.7.‡

רום to ftare, wink at, *Job* 15.12.

רזן (Arab. to weigh, ponder) רזון a weigher of coun-fel, a counfellor, or prince.‖

רח־ה fpirit, air, wind, breath: fpace, diftance, *Gen.* 22.16. to take breath, be refrefhed, 1*Sam.*16.23. *Job* 32.20. refpiration, enlargement, *Efth.*4.14. ריה to infpire, fmell; a fmell, favoury fcent, fteam, exhalation. רחת a fan for winnowing corn, *Ifai.*30.24. ריה a wind-mill, *Exod.*11.5. *Num.*11.8. רחים mill-ftones, *Deut.*24.6. *Ifai.* 47. 2. *Jer.* 25. 10. רוחה refpite, or breathing time, *Exod.*8.15. breathing, *Lam.*3.56. מרוחים large, airy, *Jer.*22.14.---ירה the lunar light, re-flected from the moon's orb: the moon: a luna-tion, or month.§

רחב to be dilated, broad, large, wide; proud, *i.e.* dilated in heart, enlarge, be enlarged: breadth. רחר, רחוב a ftreet, broad way. מרחב breadth; a large broad place.

רחל (Arab. to remove from place to place) a fheep, *Gen.*31.38: 32.14. *Cant.*6.6. *Ifai.*53.7.¶

* Der. Ρεω. Ρευμα. Ρω. Irrigo. Ebrius.   Fr. Ivre. Rheum.
† Reazy. Ruft. Rufty.   ‡ Ραζω, Ροζω, Ρυζω. Αραζω.   ‖ Ratio.
Reafon.   § Ρογχος, Ριγχω. Raucus. to Rack, *i.e.* ftream as Clouds before the wind. Reek, Reeky.   ¶ Rachel.

נהם

רחם to inclofe: the matrix, womb or bowels; the feat of the tendereft feelings, hence to love, compaffionate, find, obtain mercy: a dam-fel, a girl of ˙tender age, *Judg.* 5. 5. the Gier eagle, a kind of vulture remarkably tender to its young, *Lev.* 11.18. *Deut.* 16.17. רחים the lower mill-ftone, inclofed on all fides. רחמים tender mercies, bowels. רחמיות tender, pitiful, *Lam.* 4.10.*

רחף to move tremuloufly, to fhiver or flutter, *Deut.* 32.11. *Jer.* 23.9. מרחפת moving or caufing a tremulous motion, *Gen.* 1.2.

רחץ to rinfe, wafh: a wafhing, *Pfal.* 60.8: 108.9. *Cant.* 4.2: 6.6. Chal. to confide, truft, depend upon, *Dan.* 3.28.†

רחק to be, go, flee, remove, put far away: to be diffolved or loofed, *Eccl.* 12.10. רחוק a large fpace or diftance, *Jofh.* 3.4. far off; long ago; a great while to come. מרחק, רקוקה, רחקה far off, diftant.‡

רחש to bubble or throw up: to indite, *Pfal.* 45.1. מרחשת a frying pan, *Lev.* 2.7: 7.9.

רחת a van, fee רוח˙

רט, רטט Chal. to tremble exceedingly: great or exceffive tremor or horror, *Jer.* 49.24. --- ירט to turn afide, or be perverfe, *Num.* 22.32. turn over, *Job* 16.11.‖

רטב to be wet, or moift, *Job* 24.8. moift, full of fap, *Job* 8.16.§

רטפש frefh, fucculent, *Job* 33.25. from רטב and פש to fpread.

רטש to dafh, or be dafhed in pieces.¶

רי watering, *Job* 37.11. fee in רויה

* Der. Rim.   † Renfe or Rinfe.   ‡ Εξυκω. Ειργω. Arceo. ‖ Ταξαττω. Tartarus. Dread.   § W. Tirf.   ¶ Ραθασσω.

ריח, ריק &c. fee רח, רק without the י

רך to be foft, tender, delicate: faintnefs, tender-nefs, *Lev.* 26. 36.   מרך the fame, *Deut.* 27. 56. רכך to be mollified or fupplied repeatedly, *Ifai.*1. 6. --- יכך (to extend) the thigh: a fide of any thing; the branch of a chandelier; the coaft or border of a country.*

רכב to ride, a rider, horfeman, charioteer: a cha-riot; the upper mill-ftone which rides the lower, *Deut.* 24.6. *Judg.* 9. 53. 2*Sam.* 11. 21. מרכבה, רכוב a chariot.   מרכב a faddle, *Lev.* 15.9. cover-ing or tilt of a chariot, or perhaps the feat of the chariot, *Cant.* 3, 10.   ארכבת Chal. the knees (the letters in רכב being tranfpofed from the Heb. ברך) *Dan.* 5.6.†

רכל to trade; a merchant; merchandife, traffic. מרכלה a market, *Ezek.* 27.24.   רכיל a trader in flander, a tale bearer.

רכס to bind hard; to knot, bind faft with a knot, *Exod.* 28.28: 39.21. to lift up.   מרכסי combina-tions, confpiracies, *Pfal.* 31.21.   רכסים knotty, rugged places, *Ifai.* 40.4. pride, rather vexatious tempers or actions which are like rugged places in a road, *Pfal.* 31.20.‡

רכש to earn, acquire by labour or induftry; work-ing cattle; horfes, mules, oxen, &c. 1*Kings* 4.28. *Efth.* 8.10,14. *Mic.* 1.13.   רכוש fubftance, wealth acquired.||

רמ׳׳ה to be lifted up, exalted, elevated: to lift up: be high, tall, lofty: to project, dart, fhoot; to hurt in an unexpected way, *Exod.* 15.3,21. *Pfal.* 78.9. *Jer.* 4. 29. to deceive, beguile, betray; impofe: high place.   רים, רם highnefs, height, haugh-

* Der. Old Eng. Ragg, a drizzling rain or mift. Μηεαξ.   † Ca-ravan.   ‡ Αεριχαθαι. || Riches.

tinefs.

tinefs. רומה haughtily, *Mic.*2.3. רמות height,
Ezek. 32.5. מרום high, on high, upwards, a-
bove, height, high place. תרומה an oblation or
offering, an heave offering. תרומיה the fame,
*Ezek.*48.12. רים an unicorn, *Job* 30.9.10. fee
in ראם. רמיה deceit, deceitfully. מרמה,
תרמית, תרמה, מרמית, מרמת treachery, deceit,
guile, falfe, deceitful. רמה a worm, which in
its motion darts out the fore part of its body: to
produce worms, *Exod.*16.20. ארמון, plu. fem.
ארמנות a lofty palace, caftle, &c. הרם *Jofh.*13.
27. the Projector, an idol of the Canaanites. רמון
the Pomegranate tree and fruit: Rimnon, a Syri-
an idol, 2*Kings* 5.18. רמן the fame. רמה,רמע
Chald. to caft, or be caft, caft down, *Dan.*3.20,
21. רמם to raife or lift on high, to extol very
much. רממת,רומם exaltation, praife. רוממות
exaltations, high praifes, *Pfal.*149.6.*

רמח (Arab. to ftab) a fpear, javelin, lance.†

רמך (to rufh forward) a mare, dromedary, *Efther*
8.10.‡

ארמון, רמון, רמן in *Amos* 4.3. written. הרמון fee
above in רמ־ה

רמם to tread, trample. מרמם a treading, trampling.

רמש to creep, crawl, move along: a reptile.‖

רן to vibrate, found aloud, exert the voice, to
fhout, fing aloud, rejoice, cry out, triumph.
רנה fhouting, proclamation, cry: rattleth, *Job*
39.23. ארן the pine tree, which vibrates with
the wind, *Ifai.*44.14. ארון an ark or cheft, rather a *triumphant chariot*, for fuch the figure of
that in the holy of holies feems to be from the

---

* Der. Sp. Armar. Room. Rooms.   † Rumex.   ‡ Μαγκας.
Mare. March. Marefchal. Marfhal.   ‖ Vermis, Worm.

vifion

vifion Ezekiel had of it, chap. i. a bier or coffin,
Gen. 1. 26. a cheft in general, 2 Kings 12. 9, 10.
2 Chron. 24. 8. רנן to vibrate brifkly, to palpitate
for joy, Job 29. 13. to wave to and fro, Pf. 96. 12.
to fhout intenfely. רננה finging, joy: vibra-
tion of light, Job 3. 7. רננים oftriches, Job 39.
13. thefe birds being too heavy to fly aflift their
running with fluttering their wings: rendered
goodly.*

רנב, ארנבת the hare, Lev. 11. 6. Deut. 14. 7. fee
in א

רס to moiften, temper, Ezek. 46. 14. רסים continual moifture, a drop, Cant. 5. 2. a breach which
lets in moifture, Amos 6. 11.†

רסן (Arab. to bind) a bridle, Job 30. 11: 41. 13. Pf.
32. 9. Ifai. 30. 21.‡

רע־ה to break off or in pieces, deftroy; to be broken in mind, terrified, afflicted: to break food, to
feed, eat; to feed cattle, to give pafture: to break
order, to do evil, be evil, wrong, difordered: to
found, fhout, triumph, make a joyful noife, cry
aloud, found an alarm, ring: a feeder, fhepherd,
paftor, herdfman. רעע to break or be broken in
pieces: to make a loud and repeated noife, to
ring again: to do harm; be grievous, be grieved.
רע, מרעה, מרעית, מרעית pafture. רע thought, care, Pf.
139. 2, 17. רעיון, רעות vexation, which devours
the heart, Ecclef. paffim. מרע רעות, רע companion, friend; fellow, neighbour, one as it were
of the fame flock, feeding together. רעיתי my
love, Cant. . רעה to ufe as a friend, Judg. 14. 20.
התרע make friendfhip with, Pro. 18. 24. התרועע
fhew one's felf friendly. רעע, הריע, ריע, רוע,

---

* Der. Rant. Run. Reins. Old Eng. Rane, a fong.   † From Ros.
‡ Refne or Rein.

התרועע

התרועע to found, fhout, &c. as above. תרועה a fhout, fhouting, blowing of trumpets, joyful found, rejoicing, alarm. --- ירע the fame as רעע above. חרע to hurt, do ill or wickedly, afflict, bring evil upon, harm. מרע an evil doer. רע evil, bad, wicked, grievous: wickednefs, fadnefs, badnefs, hurt, evil, harm, affliction, wrong, mifchief and the like. יריעה a curtain affociated to another by loops and taches. רעות Chald. will, pleafure, *Ezra* 5.17:7.18. רעיון Chal. a thought, conception, imagination. plu. רעים thoughts, *Pfal.* 139. 2,17. ארע Chal. below, *Dan.* 2. 39. ארעית the bottom, *Dan.*6.25.*

רעב to fuffer hunger; hungry; famine, hunger, dearth. רעבון the fame.†

רעד to tremble, fhake, *Pfal.*104.32. tremor, trembling. מרעיד, *Ezra* 10.9. *Dan.*10.11.‡

רעל to be violently agitated, *Num.*2.3. trembling, *Zech.*12.2. תרעלה aftonifhment, confufion,*Pf.* 60.3. *Ifai.*51.17,22. רעלות fpangles, fpangled ornaments, *Ifai.*3.19.||

רעם violent commotion: to trouble, be troubled, 1*Sa.*1.6. *Ezek.*27.35. to thunder, roar like thunder, be violently agitated: thunder.§

רען to flourifh. רענן to be green or flourifhing : fruitful, green,*Cant.*1.16. frefh, verdant, blooming, *Pfal.*92.10.¶

רעף to diftill, drop, *Job*36.28. *Pf.*65.11,12. *Prov.* 3.20. *Ifai.*45.8.**

רעץ to crufh, ruin, break, *Exod.*5.6. *Judg.*10.8.||§

---

* Der. Παιω. Ρυω. Εραω. Ερος. Εταιρος. Ring. Wrong. Wrangle. Wring. Wrench. Range. Rough. Ruffle. Rogue. Rag. W. Rhwygo. Drwg. Rhŷ. † Rabies. Rabidus. ‡ Rid. Riddle, a fieve. || Reel. Roll. Hirl. Whirl. Wriggle. § Βρωμος. Βροντη. Roam. Rumor. Rumble. W. Taran. ¶ Ραμνος. Ερνον. Lit. tr. Green. ** Ropy. Rivus. De-rivo. River. ||§ Crufh.

רעש

רעש to fhake, tremble, quake: a fhaking; an earthquake; a bounding, rufhing.††

רפ־ה to yield, give way, remit, be flack, loofen, flacken, relax, abate, wax faint, be feeble; to weaken; to confume or loofen the parts, *Ifai.* 5. 24. to difmifs, let go, let alone, leave, ceafe from: let down, or flacken, *Ezek.*1.24,25. ftay, remit, flacken, 1*Sam.*15.16. 2*Sam.*24.16. 1*Chron.*21.15. be ftill, fubmit, yield, *Pf.*46.10. to tremble, be exceedingly fhaken. רפף the fame, *Job* 26. 11. רפא to repair, heal, be healed: alfo to weaken, *Jer.*38.4. a phyfician, נרפים idle, remifs, *Ex.* 5.8,17. מרפה flothful,*Prov.*18.9. מתרפים flack, *Jofh.*18.3. *i.e.* remifs. מרפיון feeblenefs, relaxation, *Jer.*47.3. מרפא yielding, *i.e.* relaxing or abating of fpirit, *Ecclef.* 10. 4. weakening, *Jer.* 38.4. ריפות, רפות grains of corn pounded in a mortar, 2*Sam.*17.19. *Prov.*17.22. רפאות medicines. מרפא health, healing, cure, healthy, found. ירפו they have healed, *Jer.*8.11. תרופה medicine, *Ezek.* 47. 12. רפה, רפא a giant. רפאים the dead, *i.e.* loofened into duft. תרפים Teraphim, fmall idols or Penates, objects of religious fear.*

רפד to ftrew, fpread under one, *Job*27.13: 41.30. *Cant.*2.5. רפידה the bottom, *Cant.*3.10.†

רפס to move nimbly, fkip, trip, exult, *Pf.*68.30. *Prov.*6.3. others render התרפס to humble one's felf, *i.e.* to trample on one's felf. Chal. to ftamp, trample, *Dan.*7.7,9.‡

רפסד, רפסדות rafts, floats, 2*Chron.*2.16. perhaps from רפא repair, and סד faften.

†† Der. Ρασσω. Ρησσω. Bruife. Rufh. Rafh.   * Θεςα πιυω. Ραπτω. Ραπις. Rip, Rive, Rift, Be-reave. Cor-rupt. Raft.   † Ιραββατος. ‡ Ερπυζω. Ερπω. Repo. Creep.

רפש to foul water by trampling in it, to trouble, difturb, *Prov.*25.26. *Ezek.*32.2: 34.18,19. mire, filth, mud of troubled water, *Ifai.*47.20.

רפת ftall for oxen, *Hab.*3.17. from רפה to un-loofe.*

רצד to run, move fwiftly, to caufe to run; run through, fulfil, accomplifh: to drive, force, dafh, bruife, crufh, break, opprefs, difcourage: to let the thought run upon, to pleafe, take pleafure in, accept, delight in, enjoy, treat with favour, be favourable to. רצץ to run or dafh one againft another; dafh, bruife, break, opprefs. התרצץ ftruggle together, bruife one another, *Gen.*25.22. רצים fhattered pieces, *Pfal.*68.30. רצון favour, pleafure, voluntary will, goodwill, delight, acceptance. רצים runners, pofts, footmen, guard, attendants. תריץ fhall ftretch out foon, act with expedition, *Pfal.* 68. 31. מרוץ a running, race, courfe; violence, incurfion, *Jer.* 22. 17. רצא Chal. to run, *Ezek.*1.14. to be kindly affected towards, *Ezek.*43.27.†

רצד to leap, exult, *Pfal.*68.19. rather as in Arab. to fee, view attentively. *Why* (O ye people) *look ye on the high hills*, and worfhip their idols, &c.

רצח to kill, flay, murder: fword, &c. *Pfal.*42.11. murder, killing, flaughter, murderer.‡

רצע to perforate, bore, *Exod.*21.6. מרצע an awl, *Exod.*21.6. *Deut.*15.17.

רצף to pave; an heart, coal, 1 *Kings* 19.6. *Ifai.*6. 6. the hearth was the only place paved. רצפה, מרצפה a pavement.

רק to evacuate, empty, draw out, pour, extenuate, attenuate: a particle of extenuation, fave,

* Der. Φατνη.   † Ρησσω. Ευαρισεω. Αρεσκω. Ριζω.   ‡ With mem prefixed, Maff-acre.

only, neverthelefs, in any wife, &c. רקות lean,
Gen. 41. 19, 20, 27. רקת the temple, the thin
bone of the temples, Judg.4.21,22,26. Cant.4.
3: 6.7. אריקם I caft them out or fpread them
thin, Pfal.18.42. רק, ריק empty, vain. ריקם
empty, void, vain, without caufe. רק armed,
drawn out, Gen.14.14. רקיק, רקק a thin cake or
wafer. --- ירק to fpit, fpit out, throw out moifture: the moift tender fhoot of a plant, herb or
grafs. רק moifture of the mouth, fpitting, fpittle. ירקון a difeafe of the corn from too much
moifture, mildew: alfo a livid palenefs, Jer.30.
6. ירקרק a bright yellow, green, Lev.13.49:14.
37. Pfal.68.13.*

רקב to rot, become putrid: rottennefs. רקבון the
fame.

רקד to leap, bound, fkip, dance, jump.†

רקח to compound drugs, fpices or perfumes: to
feafon: an apothecary, confectioner; perfume,
compofition of aromatics; perfumed unguent.
מקדה the fame. מקדחה a confectioner's pot,
Job 41.31.‡

רקם to raife figures upon a ground, to embroider:
an embroiderer: needlework, embroidered work
of divers colours: curioufly wrought, Pfal.139.
15. ריקם vain, empty, without caufe, from רק||
רקע to ftretch forth, extend, expand; to fpread by
beating or ftamping upon. רקעים broad plates,
Numb. 6. 28. רקיע the firmament, air, atmofphere, which is capable of expanfion, Gen.1.6,7.§

רר to trickle down, Lev.15.3. ריר flaver, fpittle,
1Sam.21.13. the white of an egg; rather the flaver, i.e. the infipid talk, Job 6.6.

---

* Der. Jerk. Κροτοφος. Wreck. Rack. Rake. Rickets.   † Rack-
et.   ‡ Ταραχος. Ταχια. || Sp. Recamer.   § Brachia.

רש to lack, be in want, be poor; poor. ריש poverty. רשה Chal. to have licence. רשיון Chal.
a grant, licence, permiſſion, *Ezra* 7.3. רשש to
be reduced to extreme poverty, *Jer.* 5.11. *Mal.* 1.
4. התרישש to make himſelf poor, *Prov.* 13.7.
ראש is ſometimes uſed for רש. רוש for ראש
gall, *Deut.* 32.32. רישון for ראשון former, *Job*
8.8. מרשית for מראשית from the beginning,
Deut. 11.12.---ירש׳ to drive out, expel; to poſſeſs
by violence, gift or inheritance, what belongs to
others : to inherit, ſucceed, take poſſeſſion of.
נורש to be diſpoſſeſſed, come to poverty. הוריש
to drive out, diſpoſſeſs, diſinherit; cauſe to poſſeſs. מורש, ירושה poſſeſſion, heritage. מורשים
thoughts or poſſeſſions, *Job* 17.11. תירש new
wine; expreſſed juice of the grape: juice of the
grape not yet expreſſed, *Iſai.* 65.8.*

רשם Chal. to impreſs, mark, note, *Dan.* 5.24: 6.
8: 10.21.

רשע to be reſtleſs, turbulent, unjuſt; diſturb,
throw into confuſion, 1 *Sam.* 12.47. *Job* 34.29.
to be wicked, act wickedly: wicked: wickedneſs.
הרשיע to condemn as wicked. מרשעת wicked
woman, 2 *Chron.* 24.7.

רשף to inflame: a red hot coal, *Job* 5.7. *Cant.* 8.
6. *Hab.* 3.5. burning heat, *Deut.* 32.24. a flaſh
of lightening, *Pſ.* 78.48. a glittering, flaſhing arrow, *Pſal.* 74.3.†

רשת a net, net work, a ſieve.‡

רת, רתת Chal. to tremble : horror, trembling,
Hoſ. 13.1.

רתח to boil, cauſe to boil, *Job* 30.27: 41.31. *Ezek.*
24.5. רתחים boilings, bubbles, ebullitions,
Ezek. 24.5. §

* Der. Wretch. Irus.   † W. Rhyſod.   ‡ Rete. Reſtis.
§ Rot, Rotten.

רתם to bind, tie, faſten, *Mic.*1.13. the juniper,
broom or birch tree, whoſe flexible twigs ſerved
for binding, 1*Kings* 19.4,5. *Job* 30.4. *Pſ.*120.4.
רתק to bind, confine with chains, *Nahum* 3. 10.
bound too much, contracted, rather than looſed,
*Eccl.*12.6. רתוק a chain, 1*Kings* 6.21. *Iſai.*40.
19. *Ezek.*7.23.†

ש

שׁן the twenty-firſt letter ſignifies a tooth, and anciently bore a form nearly reſembling a jaw bone
with teeth in it: in ſound it is a ſibilant, it is alſo a ſervile, and prefixed only where it is an a-
bridgment of the word אשׁר who, or of ישׁ is,
whence it ſignifies (1.) who, which, *Pſal.*124.6.
*Lam.*2.16. *Eccleſ.*2.8. the *perſon* or thing that,
*Cant.*1.7. *Eccleſ.*1.9. (2.) the conjunction *that*,
*Eccleſ.*1.17: 3.7. (3.) for, becauſe, *Cant.* 1.7.
*Lam.*4.9. (4.) the time *that*, *when*, *Judg.* 5.7.
*Eccleſ.*4.10.

ישׁ-ה, ישׁ, אשׁ to be, is, are, *Gen.* 18. 24: 24. 23.
Deut. 29. 17. it ſeems to have the nature of a
noun from its affixes, as ישׁך thou art, ישׁכם you
are, &c. intimating exiſtence, reality and ſubſtance. אישׁ fem. אשׁה a being, thing, each, every one; man, woman. אישׁים men, perſons.
אשׁ ſee in א. תשׁיה, תושׁיה thing, being, ſubſtance, reality; enterpriſe, ſubſtance, wealth, *Job*
5.12. *Prov.*2.7. firmneſs, wiſdom, ſolidity, *Job*
6.13: 12.16. *Prov.*18.1. *Mic.*6.9. ſound wiſdom,
*Prov.*3.21: 8.14. ſubſtance, firmneſs, *Job* 30.22,
in working, *i.e.* in perfecting his deſigns, *Iſai.*28.
29. the thing as it is, *i.e.* the ſolidity of reaſon,

† Der. Reticulum. Retinaculum.

Job

Job 26. 3. that which is, *i.e.* the total fum. יָשִׁישׁ,
יָשִׁישׁ very old, ancient.*

שָׁאָה־ר to tumultuate, be tumultuous, rush, make
a rushing noife, *Ifai.* 17. 12, 13. to confound, con-
fufe, lay wait, make defolate; to be aftonifhed.
מַשּׁוּאָה, מְשׁוֹאָה, מַשָּׁאוֹן, שְׁאֵת, שָׁאָן, שָׁאוֹן, שׁוֹאָה, שְׁאִיָּה,
defolate, defolation, tumultuous, tumult, rufh-
ing noife. שָׁאוֹן noify pomp, *Ifai.* 5. 14. תְּשֻׁאוֹת
noife, *Job* 36. 29. crying, 39. 7. ftirs, *Ifai.* 22. 2.
fhouting, *Zech.* 4. 7. מִשְׁתָּאֵה wondering or aftonifhed in mind, *Gen.* 24. 21. שׁוֹא written שׁוֹ *Job*
15. 31. fee in שָׁוָה --- נָשָׁה and נָשָׁא fee in שָׁה †
שָׁאַב to draw water. מַשְׁאַבִּים places of drawing
water, *Judg.* 5. 11. ‡

שָׁאַג to roar: שְׁאָגָה a roaring. ||

שָׁאַט to defpife, infult, *Ezek.* 16. 57: 28. 24, 26. contempt, infult, *Ezek.* 26. 6, 15: 36. 5. §

שָׁאַל to afk, enquire, require; defire, requeft, borrow, lend. מִשְׁאָלָה, שְׁאֵלָה petition, requeft, loan,
defire. שָׁאַל, שְׁאוֹל the receptacle or region of
the dead; the grave, fo called from its infatiabi-
lity, which is as it were always craving and never fatisfied. ¶

שָׁאָן, שָׁאַן to be in profound eafe and tranquility:
quiet, fecurity, infolent fecurity, confidence, 2
Kings 19. 28. *Ifai.* 37. 29. in *Job* 21. 23. it is written שַׁלְאָן **

שָׁאַס *Jer.* 30. 16. written for שׁׁׁ to fpoil, plunder.

שָׁאַף to abforb, fwallow up, devour, *Job* 5. 6. *Pfal.*
56. 1: 57. 3. *Ifai.* 42. 14. *Ezek.* 36. 3. *Amos* 8. 4. to
fnuff or draw in the breath or grofs air, *Jer.* 2. 24:
14. 6. hafteth or draweth in the air, *Eccl.* 1. 5. to

* Der. Εις. Ος. Ις. Vis. † W. Sio. Sonus, Sound. ‡ Αφύσσω.
Sap. || Singultus. § Sot. ¶ Con-fulo, Confult. Σελλος.
Hell. ** Sonus, Sound.

pant,

pant, afpire after, defire; gape as it were after,
Job 7.2: 36.20. *Pfal.* 119.131. *Amos* 2.4.*

שאר to remain as a refidue, to leave, be left; refidue, remainder : food, part referved, *Exod* 21.
10. flefh, *i.e.* the part of an animal which is referved for food, after life is extinguifhed : a relation by confanguinity, *i. e.* a remainder of the
fame flefh and blood: confanguinity, family, *Pro.*
5.11. leaven, a piece of dough left in the kneading trough, which by growing four contracts a
fermenting quality, *Exod.* 12.15,19: 13.7. *Lev.* 2.
21. *Deut.* 16.14. שארית the reft, a refidue, remnant, remainder. משארה a kneading trough,
Exod. 8.3: 12.34. *Deut.* 28.5,17.†

שארת fee in נשא under שה

שב־ה to turn, turn back, turn away, return; go,
come, bring again : return an anfwer, transfer,
remove, carry or be carried away captive; con-
vert, reftore, requite, recompence, and the like.
שובה returning. תשובה a return, anfwer. שב
to be grey-headed; 1 *Sam.* 12.2. *Job* 15. 10. *i. e.*
when a man is returning to duft from whence he
was taken. שב, שיבה old age, hoary head; grey,
hoary head. שבי a captive; captivity. שבית,
שיבת, שבות captivity. שבו an agate, *Exod.* 28.
19: 39.12. perhaps from its reflecting a variety of
colours. שבב to turn intenfely, to pervert, be
perverted; to bring back, caufe to return, reftore, return. שובב flidden back, pervert; froward, backfliding. שביבא, שביב Chal. a fpark,
bright flame, a blaft of ignited air returned from
the fire, *Job* 18. 5. *Dan.* 3. 2: 7. 9. plu. שביבין
שבבים violent flames, *Hofea* 8.5. ---- ישב to fit,

* Der. Sup. Sip. Fr. Soupe. Soop. Supper.   † Cæterus. Reft.
Sour. Σαϛξ, Fr. Chair. Soror. Caro. Carnage. W. Sarritt. Sûr.

dwell,

dwell, inhabit, abide. הושיב to caufe to dwell, to fet, place, and the like. שיבה abode or ftay, 2 *Sam.* 19. 32. מושב a feat, habitation. תושב a fojourner, foreigner, ftranger permitted to dwell among the Ifraelites; as profelytes of the gate. נשב--- to breathe, blow, blaft, diffipate by blowing, *Pfal.*147.18. *Ifai.*4.7. to drive away, *Gen.* 15.11.*

שבח to footh, pleafe, praife, commend: appeafe, calm, *Pfal.*65.7: 89.9. to keep in, reprefs, footh refentment, *Prov.* 29. 11. השתבח to triumph, glory; rather footh, or folace one's felf, 1 *Chron.* 16.35. *Pfal.*106.47.

שבט (Syr. to extend) a rod, fhoot, ftaff: a fceptre or rod, the enfign of authority: a tribe, the fhoot or branch of a family: a pen, or ftyle, *i.e.* a fmall rod, *Judg.* 5.14. a dart, fhaft of a dart, 2*Sam.*18.14. Sebat, *Zech.* 1. 7. the month when the trees and plants begin to fhoot out, it anfwers to our January or February.†

שבך the fame as סבך to be intangled. שובך thick intangled bough, 2 *Sam.* 18. 9. שבכים nets, 1 *Kings* 7.17. שבכה chequer work, net work, a wreath, wreathen work: a lattefs, 2*Kings* 1.2.

שבל to ftretch forward: an ear of corn fhot forth from the ftalk: a branch or fhoot of the olive, *Zech.*4.12. the leg which is extended forward in walking. שביל a path, ftretching on forward, *Pfal.*77.19. *Jer.*18.15. שבלת ears of corn, *Job* 24.24. ftreams of water, *Pf.*69.2,15. a current, channel, *Ifai.*27.12.‡

שבלל a fnail, *Pf.*58.8. if this word is not from the former root becaufe the fnail marks out his *path*,

* Der. Σεβεω. Shove. Shift. Πρεσβευς.   † Σκηπτρον Sceptre. Scipio. Fr. Baton. Bat. Shaft.   ‡ Shovel.

it

it may be derived from ישב to dwell, ב in, לול a winding fhell.

שבם, שביסים cauls or twifted fillets, *Ifai.* 3. 18. perhaps by change of letters, from שבץ or שבש שבע to be fatisfied, have enough; to fatisfy, fill, be filled: full, fulnefs, plenty; feven, the number of days in which God fulfilled the works of creation; a week. שבוע a week. נשבע to give fufficient affurance, to fwear. השביע to adjure or charge, to fwear, caufe to fwear. שבעה, שבועה an oath. שבעי, שביעי feventh, שבעים feventy, שבעתים feventy times, fevenfold.*

שבץ to inclofe, be ftraitly inclofed, *Exod.*28.20. to tie clofe, *Exod.*28.39. השבץ anguifh; rather an inclofing party, *i.e.* a party of the enemy, 2 *Sam.* 1.9. משבצות Ouches, pieces of gold made to inclofe firmly the onyx ftone, *Exod.*28.11,13,14, 25: 39.6,13,16. *Pf.*45.13. תשבץ, כתנת a coat of inclofing, *i.e.* a clofe ftrait coat, *Exod.*28.4.

שבק Chal. to leave, let alone, *Ezra* 6. 7. *Dan.* 4. 12, 20, 23. to be left, *Dan.* 2. 44. hence Sabac-thani שבקתני haft thou left me, *Mat.*26.46.

שבר to break, hurt, deftroy: to feparate into portions, to buy or fell food thus diftributed; to break, *i. e.* quench thirft, *Pfal.*104.11. to break the heart, *i.e.* make forrowful; breach, breaking, bruife, deftruction; interpretation, breaking open, *Judg.*7.15. Chal. to view attentively, wait for, hope, expect; expectation, hope, *Ruth* 1.13. *Neh.*2.13,15. *Efth.*9.1. *Pf.*104.27:119.116,166: 145.15: 146.5. *Ifai.*38.18. אשביר fhall I caufe to break forth, *i. e.* be born, *Ifai.* 46.9. שברון deftruction, breaking, *Jer.* 17. 18. *Ezek.* 21. 6.

* Der. Septem, Seven,

משבר

מִשְׁבָּר birth, breaking forth. מִשְׁבָּרִים waves, breakers.*

שְׁבַשׁ Chald. to intangle, perplex, confound, *Dan.* 5.9.

שָׁבַת to ceafe, leave off, ceafe to work: fabbath, reft. מִשְׁבָּת, שַׁבָּתוֹן fabbath, reft. שַׁבָּת is often the infinitive of יָשַׁב †

שָׁגָה to err, be deceived; go aftray, wander thro' ignorance or miftake, to be ravifhed or carried away by violent affection, *Prov.* 5.19,20. Chal. to grow, increafe, *Job* 8.7,11. *Pfal.* 92.13. מְשַׁגֶּה, מְשׁוּגָה ignorance, error. יָשִׁיגוּ remove, for יָשִׁיגוּ *Job* 24.2. נָשׁוּג for נָסוֹג turned back, 2 *Sam.* 1.22. fee סג. שִׁגָּיוֹן a wandering fong. *Pfal.* 7. title. שִׁגְיוֹנוֹת wanderings, *Hab.* 3. 1. שִׁיג a purfuit, 1 *Kings* 18.27. שָׁגַג to err, offend, &c. through mere miftake. שְׁגָגָה miftake, inadvertency. שַׂגְשֵׂג Chal. to grow repeatedly, to caufe growth, *Ifai.* 17.11. שָׁגָא err, miftake. שְׁגִיאָה error, deviation: Chal. to grow, increafe, be increafed; to multiply, magnify. שַׂגִּיא very much, exceedingly; very many, very great, magnificent, *Job* 36.26: 37.23. --- נָשַׂג to overtake, reach, attain to, take hold of. תַּסֵּג thou fhalt take hold, *Mic.* 6. 14. for תַּשֵּׂג

שָׂגַב to be raifed high, as fortreffes inacceffible and impregnable are; to be fafe, exalted, lofty; to fet on high out of the reach of danger. מִשְׂגָּב refuge, defence, high tower.

שֶׁגָה to wander, ftray; contemplate: to look attentively or narrowly, *Pf.* 34.14. *Cant.* 2.9. *Ifai.* 14.16.

שָׁגַל to lie with a woman; to be ravifhed, violated, *Deut.* 28. 30. *Jer.* 3. 2. *Ifai.* 13. 16. *Zech.* 14. 2.

---

* Der. Bruife. Shiver. Cibare. Spero. Sabre. Sever.   † Sab-bath.

Chal. a queen, wife, *Neh*.2.6. *Pſal*.45.9. שגלת
wives, *Dan*.5.2: 3.23.*

שגע to be mad, diſtracted. השתגע to act the madman, 1 *Sam*.21.14,15. שגעון madneſs.†

שגר Chal. to ſend forth, break forth: Heb. fruit
of the womb, iſſue or increaſe of cattle, *Exod*.13.
12. *Deut*.7.13: 28.4,18,51.‡

שד־ה to put forth, ſhed: a breaſt or teat which
ſheds forth milk: to ſhed, ſcatter, ſpoil, lay waſte:
to plaiſter with lime, *Deut*. 27. 2, 4.   אשד plu.
אשדות an effuſion of water, a ſtream, brook.
שדה plu. fem. שדות a cup-bearer who pours out
wine at feaſts, rendered muſical inſtruments, *Ecclef*.2.8. a field, land, the country, ground.   שיד
lime, *Iſai*.33.12. *Amos* 2.1. plaiſter of lime,*Deut*.
27.2,4.   שדי the Almighty, *i.e.* the ſhedder forth
of bleſſings, unleſs derived from ש who is, and די
ſufficiency.   שדים idols ¶ of the Canaanites,
from whence the vale of Siddim, *Gen*. 3. 8, 10.
was probably denominated.   devils, deſtroyers,
Deut.32.17. *Pſal*.106.37.   שד, שוד ſpoil, ſpoil-
ing, robbery, waſte, deſolation, deſtruction.   שד
a ſpoiler,*Iſai*.16.4.   שדד to harrow or break the
clods, *Job* 39. 10. *Iſai*. 28. 24. *Hoſea* 10. 11. to
waſte, deſtroy, be waſted, laid waſte.||

שדם a field.   שדמה corn blaſted, *Iſai*.37.27. here
שדם is put for שדף unleſs the paſſage be rendered thus; as a field before the corn is ſown.

שדף to blaſt, blight; שדפון a blaſt, blight. §

---

* Der. Σαλαγω, Γαλιαω. Ασιλγη; Salax, Salacious.   † Skew.
Aſkew.   ‡ Iſlandic Skara. Old Eng. Skere, a multitude. W. Yſ-
gar. || Σκεδαω. Shed. Shatter.   ¶ The Siddim were perhaps the
Multimammiæ, or many breaſted idols, of the heathen, which they
worſhipped as the genial powers of nature ; of which ſort, in particu-
lar, was the Diana of the Epheſians.   § Tabes. Στυφω Stop: Stiff.
Stiffle.

שׁדּר to arrange, a range or rank of armed men, 2 *Kings* 11.8,15. 2 *Chron.* 23.14. ranges of boards placed parallel, 1 *Kings* 6.9. Chal. to exert one's felf, take pains, labour, ftrive, *Dan.* 6.14. אשתדור fedition, commotion.*

שֶׂה (to be chill or cold) a lamb or kid, one of the fmaller kind of cattle; it is written שֵׂי *Deut.* 22. 1. 1 *Sam.* 14. 34.   שֵׁיִני urine, by the paffing of which the body is cooled.   שׁוה fee below.---יֵשׁ־ה; fee above the firft root in the letter שׁ --- נשׁ־ה to bear, lift, remove, carry, carry away; to be in a loofe relaxed ftate as a finew ftrained, *Gen.* 32.32. to lay wafte, *i. e.* relax the ftrength of a nation, *Num.* 21.30. to fail, be relaxed, *Jer.* 51.30. to forget, *i.e.* when the mind is in a relaxed ftate: to lend; to lend upon ufury and exact it to the utmoft.   נשׁים women, wives, who bear children. נשׁיה forgetfulnefs, *Pf.* 88.12. נשׁני made me forget, *Gen.* 41.51. השׁה hath deprived her, made her heedlefs about, *viz.* wifdom, *Job* 39.17. נשׁה, משׁה a creditor, ufurer. ----- נשׁא in fenfe the fame as the above, but of more intenfe fignification: to bear, take, take up, carry, accept, lift up, take away, bring forth, bear up, bring, give, prefent: to lift up, exalt, elate, deceive, puff up, feduce by elation: to bear, fpare, forgive, take away fin. lade, to lay upon, make to bear. taken away by burning, *Nah.* 1.5. to contain, take in, *Ezek.* 45.11. obtain, receive, *Efth.* 2.9,15,17. to lend, exact, *Neh.* 5.7. *Pfal.* 89.22. a creditor, ufurer.   משׁא ufury, *Neh.* 5.7. exaction, *Neh.* 10. 31.   משׁאת loan, *Deut.* 24. 10. משׁאות debts, *Prov.* 22.26.   נשׁאת carriages, *Ifai.* 46.1.   משׁא a burden; a collection, 2*Chron.* 24.

* Der. Stir. Start. W. Yftyr.

6,9. refpect, acceptance, 2 *Chron.*19. 7.   מִשְׂאֵת
a mefs, gift or reward taken : an oblation, *Ezek.*
20. 40.   שְׂאֵת dignity, highnefs, excellency, a
rifing.   שִׂיא excellency, *Job* 20.6.   מַשְׂאֵת an elevated fign, *Jer.*6.1.   a flame or elevation, *Judg.*
20.38,40.   נָשִׂיא a prince, ruler or captain, one
in an elevated ftation.   נְשִׂאִים or נְשִׂיאִים vapours
raifed from the earth, *Pfal.*135.7. *Prov.*25.14.
*Jer.*10.13: 51.16.   נְשׂוּי forgiven or taken away,
*Pfal.*32.1.   מַשְׂאוֹן deceit, *Prov.*26.26.

שָׂהֵד a witnefs, *Job* 16.19.

שָׂהֲדוּתָא witnefs of appointment, from שְׂהַד and
רוּתָא an appointment.

שֹׁהַם an onyx.

שְׂהַר, שַׂהֲרֹנִים round ornaments like the moon,
*Judg.*8.21,26. *Ifai.*3.18.

שׁוה to make level, *Ifai.*28.25. to put upon a level, compare, be equal; to profit, or countervail,
i.e. to be an equivalent, *Efther* 3.8: 5.13: 7.4. *Job*
33.27. to place oppofite in full view, *Pfal.*16.8:
119.30. to make equal, make like, 2*Sam.*22.34.
*Pfal.*18.33. to put even, firm, not tottering or
declining, *Pfal.*21.5: 89.19. to reckon, accompt;
behave, compofe one's felf, *Ifai.*38.13. *Pf.*131.2.
to lay in an orderly manner as grapes were ufually ftored, *Hof.* 10. 1.   נִשְׁתַּוָה to be alike, equal,
*Prov.*27.15. שָׁו even, equal, right, *Job* 15.31.
שָׁי gift for benefits received, *Pfal.*68.29: 76. 11.
*Ifai.*18.7. שָׁוא the contrary in fenfe to the above:
vanity, a vain thing, a lie; in vain; a vain idol,
a falfe god.   It is written שׁו *Job* 15.31.*

שׁוא, שׁוב, שׁוד, שׁוח &c. fee שׂא, שׂב &c. without
the ו

שׁוב Chal. to refcue, deliver, fet free.

* Der. Ισοω. Ισος. Αξιος.

שׁוּף to gaze, look full upon, *Job* 23.9: 28.7. look or ſhine full upon, *Cant.*1.6.*

שׁזר to twiſt, twine; מִשְׁזר twiſted, twined.

שׁחה־ה to incline, bow down, ſtoop, be bowed down, bring low; to couch, crouch: to ſwim, in which action the body is proſtrated, *Pſ.*6.6. *Iſai.*25.11. שׁחו ſwimming, *Ezek.* 47. 5. but theſe three laſt paſſages might be rendered thus : I have been depreſſed, *Pſal.* 6.6. as a man proſtrating himſelf, extendeth his hands in his proſtration, *Iſai.*25.11. waters of depth, *Ezek.*47.5. שׁוח, שׁיח to be deep in thought, to meditate, think, talk, complain, pray freely; to meditate in walking. שׁח humble, *Job* 22.29. ישׁח a caſting down, *Mic.*6.14. שׁחית, שׁחות, שׁחת, שׁחת, שׁיחה, שׁוחה, שׁוח a pit, hole, ſlough. שׁיח, שׁח thought, meditation, talk, complaint, prayer: a ſhrub or lowly plant. שׁחה to bow, ſtoop, bend much. השׁתחה caſt down, *Pſal.*52.6. to bow down, proſtrate one's ſelf, to do obeiſance, worſhip, reverence. בהשׁתחויתי in my proſtrating myſelf, 2 *Kings* 5.18. --- ישׁח ſee above.

שׁחד to preſent, to bribe; a bribe, preſent, reward, gift, bribery.

שׁחט to drain off the blood of men and animals ; rendered to kill, ſlay: to offer, drain the blood in ſacrifice, *Exod.* 24. 25. to preſs out, drain, *Gen.* 40.11. שׁוחט killing, murdering, *Jer.*9.8. שׁחוט drained, purified, cleared of its droſs, 1 *Kings* 10. 16,17. 2 *Chron.*9.15,16. rendered beaten. שׁחיטה a killing, 2 *Chron.*30.17.

שׁחל to be black; a lion of a dark colour. שׁחלת the black Babilonian onyx, an odoriferous ſhell, *Exod.*30.34.

* Der. Specio. Aſpicio, &c. Species. Aſpect. Deſpiſe. Reſpect. Specto, Spectre, &c.

שחן (to be warm, hot) שחין an inflammatory fwelling, a boil, tumour, botch, leprofy.*

שהם to. fpring up: שחים that which fpringeth up of its own accord, *Ifai.*37.30. the fame as סחיש

שחף to wafte away. the fea mew, or lean flender cuckow, *Lev.* 11. 16. *Deut.* 14. 15. שחפת the confumption, atrophe, *Lev.*26.16. *Deut.*28.22. שחיף cieling, or flender planks of wood, *Ezek.*41. 16.†

שחץ to be fiercely wild, undaunted: pride, *Job* 41. 34. lion, 28.8.

שחק tò conflict; beat or wear to pieces by collifion: to laugh, deride, mock, make fport of by reciprocal motions: fmall duft, *Ifai.* 40. 15. שחק, שחקים the fkies or æthers in conflict. שחוק,שחק fport, laughter. משחק ·a fcorn, *Hab.*1.10. שחקת rejoicing, *Prov.*8.30,31.‡

שחר to be dark-coloured, dufky, fwarthy, *Job* 30. 30. to feek early in the morning, *i.e.* diligently; to.do a thing betimes or· with diligence: to rife betimes, *Job* 24.5. the grey or dufk of the morning, day-break: light, or dawn of light, *Ifai.* 8. 20. black, darkifh, dufky. שחור blacknefs, *Lam.* 4.8. משחר morning dawn. שחרות the dawn of life, youth, *Ecclef.* 11. 10. שחרחרת very dark, *Cant.*1.6.‖

שהת to corrupt, mar, deftroy : corruption, deftruction. משחת ,שחית the fame. שחת a pit, fee שח־ה §

שט־ה to. decline, turn afide, to go or move to and fro; to row. שוט ,שיט a whip, fcourge. שטים revolters, them that turn afide, *Hof.*5.2. in *Pfal.*

---

* Der. Iflandic Skin. Shine. Sun.   † Κινφος.   ‡ Σκοπτω.
Σωγαζομαι. Shake, Shock, Shog. Jog. Skies.   ‖ Scrutor. Swart.
Swarthy. Ob-fcurus, Obfcure.   § Scath, hurt, wafte.

101.3. סטים is used. שיט, משוט an oar, *Isai*.33.
21. *Ezek*.27.6,29. שטים mariners, *Ezek*.27.8,
26. בית השטה mentioned *Judges* 7.22. might be
so called from having its temple dedicated to the
sun. שטט to run, or move hither and thither
repeatedly: a whip.---ישט to extend, shoot out,
Esth.4.11: 5.2: 8.4. שטה, שטים the Shittah tree
Cedar, Shittim wood, a tall extended tree, *Isai*.
41.19. thought to be the Acacia or Spina Egyp-
tiaca, though perhaps it may mean any foreign
wood they were forced to make a voyage for.*

שטה to spread abroad. משטח a place for spreading.
שטם to hate, set one's self against, infest, molest.
משטמה hatred.†

שטן to oppose, be an adversary against: Satan, an
adversary. שטנה an accusation, *Ezra* 4.6.‡

שטף to overflow, rush forth upon like water; to
rinse, wash by immersion: overflowing, outrage-
ous, *Prov*.27.4. an inundation, flood.||

שטר an inferior officer, an overseer, ruler. משטר
ministerial power, *Job* 38.33. Chal. a side or part,
Dan.7.5.§

שי presents, see in שורה. sheep, see in שה
שית, שיש, שיר, שין, שיל, שיח, שיג fee שג &c. without the י

שיצי Chal. to finish : שיציא finished, compleated,
Ezra 6.15.

שכה to settle, subside; assuage, appease: to fix,
set: to hedge round, fence, *Job* 1.10. *Hos*.26.8.
cause to subside, *Num*.17.5. assuaged, *Gen*. 8.1.
כשך as he that setteth, *Jer*.5.26. rather, as fow-
lers *stoop down*. שך *Exod*. 33.22. for סך cover.

* Der. Shoot, Shot. Swedish Skutta. Scad. Scuddle. † Stem.
‡ Σαταια; Satan. || to Steep. a Stoop for liquids. § Saturnus.
Sax. Scatur, and with Mem prefixed, Master, Mister, Magister. W.
Swyddwr.

שכן

שכו for סכו his tabernacle, fee סך. שביות, ישבה שכיות
curiously figured pictures, *Ifai.* 2. 16. משכית figured image, *Lev.* 26. 1. imagery, *Ezek.* 8. 12.
pictures of figured works, *Prov.* 25. 11. rather,
net work. שכוי *Chal.* the imagination or conceit, which figures and paints, *Job* 38. 36. משכה
the fame, *Pf.* 73. 7. שוכה a bough, *Judges* 9. 48,
49. שכים thorns, prickles, *Num.* 33. 55. שכות
barbed irons, *Job* 41. 7. משוכה a thorn hedge,
Prov. 15. 19. *Ifai.* 5. 5. מסוכה the fame, the ס being put for ש. שכך to fubfide, be appeafed entirely, *Efth.* 7. 10. to fence round, *Job* 10. 11. ----
נשך to bite; to hurt, damage; to lend upon ufury, *Deut.* 23. 19, 20, 21. biting ufury. נשכה a
chamber, *Neh.* 3. 30: 12. 44: 13. 7. for לשכה the נ
being put for ל *

שכב to lie or lay dow, to reft, die: a lying down.
משכב a lying down, a bed, the grave. †

שכח to forget, caufe to forget. השתכח to be for-
gotten, *Ecclef.* 8. 10. *Chal.* to fmd, be found. ‡

שכל the fame as שקל to weigh, ponder: to act
wifely and prudently; to inftruct, make wife, in-
telligent; to be wife, fkilful; to profper: wifdom, policy, fkill, prudence: alfo to deprive, be-
reave, be bereaved of children; to be barren,
mifcarry, fuffer abortion: deprivation, lofs of
children; barrennefs. שכול the fame. משכיל
prudent, wife, inftructive. שכלות folly, *Ecclef.*
1. 17. for סכלות. אשכול a bunch of ripe grapes,
of which the vine is deprived: fome cluftered fruit
or flower, *Cant.* 1. 14. השתכל *Chal.* to confider
attentively, *Dan.* 7. 8. שכלת underftanding, *Dan.*

* Der. Scio Check, Checker or Chequer. Choak. Sway. Affuage.
Seek. Sage. Sagax. Quiefco.　　† Cubo. Squab. W. Cyfgu.
‡ Κιχιυ.

שׁל־ה   שׁכם   217

5.11,12. שׁכלל Chal. to finish, complete for כלל *Ezra* 4.13: 5.3,11: 6.14.*

שׁכם to rise, arise early; be eminent, prominent, to be exuberant; the shoulder rising above the other limbs: a portion or rising spot of ground, *Gen.*48.22. something eminent, a butt to shoot at, *Pf.*21.13. שׁכמה towards Shechem the name of a place, *Hof.* 6. 9.   מַשְׁכִּים, מַשְׁכִּימֵי early, in the morning.†

שׁכן to dwell, inhabit, reside, remain; cause to dwell, to place: an inhabitant and neighbour.

שׁכִּין Chal. a knife, *Prov.*23.2.‡

שׁכר to satisfy thirst, drink abundantly, be drunken: strong liquor: also to satisfy, give a satisfaction for service done, to hire, reward: satisfaction, hire, reward; gain, *Ifai.*19.10. of ponds for fish. השׁתכר to be drunken, make one's self drunk, 1 *Sam.* 1.14. שׁכרון drunkennefs, *Ezek.* 23.33: 39.19. שׁכיר an hired thing, hired servant. משׁכר to earn wages, let one's felf out for hire, *Hag.*1.6. אשׁכר a satisfactory present, *Pf.*72.10. *Ezek.*27.15.‖

של as a prefix is a note of the genitive cafe, from שׁ of, אשׁר which, and ל to, for.

שׁל־ה to free, loose; to be loose, licentious; to be fecure, at ease. שׁול the hem, fringe or skirts of a garment. שׁל rashnefs, 2*Sam.*6.7. שׁלו, שׁלוה, שׁלי, שׁליו quietnefs, tranquility. שׁלו a quail, which lives in ease and plenty, *Exod.*16.13. *Num.* 13.31,32. *Pfal.*105.4. שׁילה Shiloh, a name of the Meffiah, the author of ease and tranquility, Prince of Peace. שׁלה licentious error, *Dan.* 3.

* Der. Calleo. Scaltro. Skill.   † Skim, Scum.   ‡Σκην. Σκη-νоω. Ακιναχης. Sîca, Scene. Skin. Skean, a short sword.   ‖ Σικερα Si-cera. Cyder.

C c   29.

29. שלו a crime, *Dan*.6.4. failing, error, *Ezra*
6.9. תשלו be negligent or deceived, 2 *Chron*.29.
11. תשלה deceive or difappoint, 2 *Kings* 4. 28.
שלה a petition, 1 *Sam*. 1. 27. for שאלה. שלל
to draw, pluck off, to fpoil, plunder, ftrip: a
fpoil, prey. משתולל maketh himfelf a prey,
Ifai.59.15. אשתוללו are fpoiled, *Pfa*.76.5. here
the א is written for ה after the Chaldee form.
שילל ftript, a captive, *Mic*. 1.8. --- נשל to pull,
caft, drive off; flip, fly off; to caft its fruit,
Exod.3.5. *Deut*.7. 1, 22, 19. 5: 28.40. *Joſh*.5.15.
2 *Kings* 16.6.*

שלאנן quiet, free from forrow, *Job* 21. 23. if not
put for שאנן it is derived from של free, and אנן
grieved.

שלב to be difpofed in order. משלבת anfwering,
to be parallel, fet equi-diftant, in order, *Exod*.26.
17: 36.22. שלבים parallel ledges, fteps, 1 *Kings*
7.28,29.†

שלג to be white, bright as fnow, *Pf*.68.14. fnow.‡
שלהבת flame, raging flame, *Job* 15.30. *Ezek*.20.
47. from של and להב. שלהבת יה in *Cant*.8.6.
is the flame of Jah or Jehovah, *i.e.* a moft vehement confuming flame; but if inftead of two
words שלהבתיה fhould be all one word the paffage may be rendered thus: Jealoufy is cruel as
the grave; her flafhes are flafhes of fire, her's
(are) raging flames.

שלה to fend, emit, fend forth, fend away, put
forth, ftretch out, let go, put away, difmifs; to
fend or fhoot forth: to employ, *Pfal*.5.19. שלה
שלוה a prefent fent, 1 *Kings* 9. 16. *Mic*. 1. 14. a

---

* Der. Συλω. Συλαω. Σκυλον. χολη Salus. Shell. Scale. Solvo. Abfolvo,
Abfolve, Salvus. Salve. Safe. W. Soflian.   † Slab.   ‡ Gelu.
Glacies. Sleek. Silk.

plant

plant or branch fhot forth, *Cant*.4.13. *Ifai*.16.8.
a miffile weapon, dart. משלח a fending forth ;
a difcharge, *Ecclef*.8.8. שלחן a table from which
meffes are fent.*

שלט to have power, rule, authority, delegated dominion : Chal. to have abfolute power, &c. שלטת
imperious, *Ezek*.16.30. שליט an appointed ruler or governor : Chal. an abfolute ruler. שלטן
abfolute rule: ruling power, *Eccl*.8.4,8. שלטים
fhields, arms for defence.†

שלך, השליך to caft, caft out or away, caft forth,
caft down: the cormorant, cataract, or plungeon
a fea bird, *Lev*.11.17. *Deut*.14.17. this bird darts
from on high on its prey.

שלם to complete, perfect, make up, make good a
lofs, reftore, requite, pay, recompence, reward:
to complete a work: whole, entire, perfect : to
make up a difference, make peace, be at peace :
peace, profperity; peace-offering. שלום the fame.
שלום, שלם, שלמן recompence, reward. שלמן a
fur-tout, an outer garb which covers the whole
body.

שלף to draw out as a fword; draw off a fhoe: to
fhoot forth; groweth up and is gathered, *Pfal*.
129.6.‡

שלש, שלשה three. שלשים, שלושים thirty. שלישי,
שלישת,שלישית third, third part, third time. שלישת
שלישת the fame. משלש three, *Gen*.38.24. *Ezek*.
42.6. threefold, *Eccl*.4.11. of three year old,
Gen.15.9. שלש to divide into three parts, *Deut*.
19.3. do a thing three times, 1 *Kings* 18. 34.
שלש, שליש a meafure,perhaps the third of a Bath,
about two gallons and an half, *Pf*.80.5. *Ifai*.40.

_____

* Der. Στελλω. W. Syflyd.   † Shield, Shelter. Sultan
‡ Σιλφη a little worm, Slip.

12. a captain, commander, the third in power
under the commander in chief. שלשים three
ſtringed inſtruments, 1 *Sam.*18.6. alſo rules, di-
rections, excellent things, *Prov.*22.20. likewiſe
children of the third generation.*

שלשם, שלשום the 3d day reckoning backwards;
the day before yeſterday, from שלש and יום day.

שם to place, ſet, put, ſettle, conſtitute, appoint,
lay open, ſet in array: with לב following, to attend, apply the heart or mind to: this word is
variouſly rendered but the radical idea is eaſily
applied; it ſignifies alſo, to make place for other
things, to waſte, deſolate; to be deſolate in mind,
confounded, aſtoniſhed, from ישם ſee below: a
name put upon, or ſubſtituted for a perſon or
thing; a word, a mark or note, a ſignal. שימה
a ſettlement, an appointment, 2 *Sam.*13.22. שר,
שמה a particle of place, there, thither. תשומה
a placing or putting, *Lev.* 6. 2. שמות names.
שמים the heavens, the placers or diſpoſers, in
which ſenſe it is plainly uſed, *Iſai.*5.20. *Mal.*2.2.
שומים a ſpecies of onions, ſo called from the regular diſpoſition of their involuera, ſomewhat reſembling the orbits of the planets in the heavens.
שמה, משמה deſolation, aſtoniſhment. שמם to
place or diſpoſe with great care, regularity and
order: alſo, to be exceedingly deſolate and waſte;
to be amazed, aſtoniſhed exceedingly. שממה,
שממון great deſolation, aſtoniſhment, ſtupor.
שממית the ſpider, *Prov.*30.28. which diſpoſes her
threads with wonderful exactneſs.---ישם to deſolate, be deſolate, waſte. ישימון, ישמין, a waſte,
deſert, wilderneſs. אשמנים ſee below in שמן.

   * Leaſh.

נשם---

---- נשב to breathe; נשמה breath : נשמת the
foul or fpirit of man breathed into him by God.
תנשמת the Chamœleon, a kind of lizard having
its mouth always gaping as it were for air, *Lev.*
11.30. alfo an owl, which breathes in a ftrong
audible manner, as if fnoring, *Lev.*11.18. *Deut.*
14.16.*

שמאל, שמאלית, שמיל, שמלי the left, the left hand.
השמיל, שמאיל to go or turn to the left, from שם
to place, and אל not.

שמד to fmite, deftroy, demolifh, diffipate utterly.†
שמה to move brifkly to and fro, to vibrate brifkly:
to fhine, rejoice, be glad. שמחה the throbbing
palpitation of the heart; joy, gladnefs.‡

שמט to loofe, let go, releafe, difcharge, difcontinue, be difcharged; to let fall, throw down: releafe, *Deut.*15.2,3. difcontinue, *Jer.*17.4. let her
drop, 2*Kings* 9.33. let it reft, let it alone, *Ex.*23.
11. they had difcharged, 2*Sam.*6.6. 1*Chron.*13.9.
difcharged, *Pfal.*141.16. שמטה a releafe, *Deut.*
15.1,2,9: 31.10.

שמך to lay upon. שמיכה a mantle, coverlet, rug,
blanket, *Judges* 4.18.

שמל to furround, cloathe. שמלה a cloth, cloath-
ing, raiment, apparel. שמיל for שמאל fee above.

שמן to abound, fuperabound, be plenteous, *Ifai.*
30.23. to be or become fat: oil, ointment: one
that abounds in ftrength, robuft, *Judges* 3.21.
משמן fatnefs, fat, fat place. משמני thofe that
had eaten abundantly were gorged with fat, *Pf.*
78.31. עץ שמן the pine or fome refinous tree.
שמנה, שמונה eight; the fuperabundant number,

---

* Der. Σημα, Σημαω, Σημειον Signum. Σαμιαμινθη. Shame. † Smite.
Smith. Ασμοδαιος Afmodæus. ‡ Smack; a light moving veffel.

fe

seven denoting fulness. שמנים, שמנים eighty
שמיני, שמינית eight. אשמנים fat plentiful places,
rather than desolate, *Isai.*59.10. בעל שמן prin-
ceps oleum.*

שמע to hear, perceive, hearken to, obey, under-
stand. השמיע to cause to hear, publish, proclaim,
tell, shew, make a sound or noise. שמועה, שמע
an hearing, report, rumour, tidings, fame. שמעות
causing to hear, *Ezek.*24.26. משמע hearing,|*Isai.*
11.3. משמעה bidding, 1*Sam.*22.14. guard, or at
his command, 2*Sam.*22.23. 1*Chron.*11.25. obedience, *Isai.*11.14.

שמץ to mutter, whisper: a whisper, rendered very
little, *Job* 4. 12: 26. 14. שמצה an occasion for
muttering, a thing contemptible, rendered shame,
*Exod.*32.25.

שמר to keep, keep safe, observe, watch, take heed,
beware. משמר, שמרה a watch, ward, guard,
office. משמרה a charge, watch, office. אשמורה
a night watch, the fourth part of the night.
שמרים lees or dregs preserved at the bottom of
the vessel, and preserving the wine, *Psf.*75.8. *Isai.*
25.6. *Jer.*48.11. *Zeph.*1.12. שמיר briers, used
to fence and guard corn; also, an adamant, or
some hard stone, *Jer.*17.1. *Ezek.*3.9. *Zech.*7.12.
משמרות nails, *Eccles.*12.11. for מסמרות.†

שמש the sun, the solar light. שמשתי windows to
admit the light of the sun, *Isai.*54.12. Chal. to
minister to, *Dan.*7.10.

שנאן doubled, even thousands of thousands, or
thousands doubled, *Psal.*68.17. others, angels;
perhaps it may mean whirlwinds, clouds, &c. in

---

* Der. Βαλσαμον. W. Saim. Ymenyn. † Σμις; Smiris. Σιμιρα-
Semiramis. W. Ifamer.

motion,

·motion, and is derived from שן to, repeat, and אן
impetuous motion.

שנ־ה to repeat, do a thing over again, change, alter, double: to difguife one's felf. Chal. to be
changed, *Dan.* 3.27. to change, 6.8,15. a year in
which all the feafons revolve and return. שנן to
whet, fharpen, *Deut.* 32.41. *Pf.* 64.3: 140.3. teach
diligently, whet, fharpen that they may penetrate
deep, repeat over and over again, *Deut.* 6.7. שן a
tooth, ivory: the crag or tooth of a rock, 1 *Sam.*
14.4,5. *Job* 39.28. שנון fharp, whetted. השתונן
to be pricked, *Pf.* 73.21.   שנינה a bye-word, frequently repeated; a taunt, keen cutting reflection.   השתחנית 'difguife one's felf, 1 *Kings* 14. 2.
שונים ,שנות diverfe, different.   שנים שני plu.
maf. the number two; plu. fem. שתים for שנתים
שנית the other, fecond, fecond time.   משנה
double, fecond, next: a copy, duplicate, *Deut.*
17.18. *Jofh.* 8.32. שני twice dipped, double dyed,
fcarlet, crimfon. שיני urine, fee under שה.   שנא
to change, be changed entirely, be changed in affection, to hate. Chal. to change, be different.
שנאת hatred, *Eccl.* 9.6.   שנא for שנה to change,
be changed, 2 *Kings* 25.29. *Eccl.* 8.4. *Lam.* 4.1.---
ישן to remain in the fame ftate as it were afleep,
unmolefted, *Deut.* 4.25. to fleep, be in a found
fleep. ישן, נושן old ftore, provifion : old, any
thing which has continued long in the fame fituation. שנה fleep, written שנא *Pfal.* 127.2. *
שנב, אשנב a window, cafement, *Judg.* 5.28. *Prov.*
7.6.†

שנהבים ivory, elephants teeth, 1 *Kings* 10. 22. 2
Chron. 19.21. from שן a tooth, and הב fome foreign name for the beaft, whence perhaps Ebur.

* Der. Σινω. Ενος. Annus. Sanna, Sannio, Sanno, Subfannio Zany.
Sin. Change. W. Sonio, Swn.   † Feneftra. W. Ffeneftr.

שנם to gird up. 1 *Kings* 18.46.*

שס־ה to rob, pillage, ſpoil, rifle, written שאם *Jer.*
30.16. and שוש *Iſai.*10.13. השסה ſpoil, booty.†

שסע to ſplit, cleave, rend; a cleft: ſtayed or parted them from their purpoſe, 1 *Sam.*24.7.‡

שסף to cut or hew in pieces, 1 *Sam.*15.33.‖

שע־ה to turn the eyes, to look at an object, regard, reſpect; to turn away, turn from, *Job* 7.19:
14.6. *Pſ.* 39.13. *Iſai.*22.24. turn away, *Iſai.*6.10.
not ſhut: turned to wrong objects, *Iſai.*32.3. rather than dim. למשעי to my aſpect or favourable regard, rendered to ſupple, *Ezek.* 16. 4.
השתע to turn one's ſelf, to look about in terror,
to be diſmayed, *Iſai.* 40.10, 23. ' שוע to cry out
aloud: a cry: שועה a cry, ſhout. שעה, שעתא
Chal. an hour. שעשע to turn this way and that,
to ſport and play; to delight: play, *Iſai.*11.8. to
be dandled, *Iſai.*66.12. השתעשע to delight one's
ſelf: to cry out; in the margin to take pleaſure,
*Iſai.*29.9. שעשע pleaſure, delight.---ישע to ſave
from danger, preſerve, deliver, be in ſafety. מושיע
a ſaviour. מושעה, תשועה, ישועה, שע ſalvation,
deliverance, ſafety, help, victory. שוע rich, *Job*
34.19. bountiful, *Iſai.*22.5. riches *Job* 26. 19.§

שעט to ſtamp, ruſh. שעטה ſtamping, *Jer.*47.3.¶

שעטנז cloth of linen and woollen mixed, linſy-
woolſy,*Lev.*19.19.*Deut.*22.11. ſuppoſed to be derived from ש which, עטן inweave and נז ſprinkled.

שעל to be hollow; the hollow of the hand, *Iſai.*
40.12. an handful, 1*Kings* 20.10. *Ezek.*13.19. a
fox which burrows in the earth. שועל the ſame.

משעול a hollow way, narrow path,*Num.*22.24.‖‖‖

---

* Der. Ζωννω. Ζων Zone. Cinxit, Cincture. Circingle. † Chaſe.
Fr. Chaſſer. ‡ Σχισω Scindo. Fr. Ciſeau. Ciſſeaux. Chiſſel. Sciſ-
ars. ‖ Chip. Chop. § Sound. Song, Sing. Old Eng. Stound.
¶ Shoot. ‖‖‖ The Sole or hollow of the foot.

שען to lean, rely, reſt, ſtay upon, lie near.   משען,

משענרה a ſtay or ſtaff.

שע, שעיף thought, reflection, opinion, *Job* 4.13:
20.2. written סעף 1 *Kings* 18.21. *Pſ.*119.113.

שער to ſtand erect, as the hair in fear: to fear,
dread, be horribly afraid, *Deut.*32.17. *Jer.*2.12.
*Ezek.*27.35: 32.10. the hair, hairy, it is rendered *Prov.*23.7. to think; the paſſage would be better thus, as a *hair* to a man (in his food) ſo is he:
alſo, a gate.   שער, שוער a porter.   שער a meaſure.   מאה שערים an hundred fold, *Gen.*26.12.
perhaps meaning an hundred of ſuch meaſures as
were kept at the gates of the city, where courts
and markets were formerly held.   שערה, שער,
שעורה barley, bearded as with hair.   שעיר an
hairy goat, a kid. שעירת a kid. שעיר ſome hairy
animal worſhipped in Egypt, perhaps the Ouran-
outang, rendered ſatyr, *Iſai.*13.21: 34.14. devil,
*Lev.*17.7. 2 *Chron.*11.3.   שערים vile, *viz.* figs,
*Jer.*29.17. which when corrupt are covered with
mildew and look hairy. שערה, שער a rough
horrible ſtorm, a tempeſt, *Iſai.* 28. 2. *Job* 9. 17.
*Nah.*1.3. horror, *Ezek.*27.35: 32.10. laid hold
of horror, *Job* 18.20.   שער to hurl, ſweep away
as with a ſtorm, *Job* 27.21. *Pſ.*58.9. to be horribly afraid, to fear, dread, *Deut.*22.17. *Jer.*2.12.
*Ezek.*27.35: 32.10.   נשערה tempeſtuous, *Pſal.*
50.3.   השתער come like a whirlwind, *Dan.*11.
40.   שערורה an horrible thing, *Jer.*5.30:23.14.
שערורת 18.13. and שערוריה *Hoſ.*6.10. the ſame;
perhaps in the ſenſe of horror it may be put for
סער *

שפ־ה to cruſh, break, bruiſe, *Gen.*3.15. *Job* 9.17.

* Der. Σορος. Horror. Hirpitus. Hairy. Hircus. Σισυρα to Shore.
Shower. Soar. a Shore, coaſt.

שפל שפח

to be broken, *Job* 33.21. Chal. for שאף to fwallow up, *Pfal.*139.11. שפה, שפת plu. שפתים,
שפתות a lip, fpeech, language, fentiment; margin, brim, brink, fhore, border, edge, bank, fide.
שפי high places, craggy prominencies. נשפה
high, *Ifai.*13.2. שפו ftick out, *Job* 32.21. שפות
cheefe, bruifed and crufhed in making, 2*Sam.*17.
29. שפיפן an adder, a ferpent which bruifes and
fwallows its food whole, *Gen.* 49. 17. השפות
dung, *Neh.*3.13. for האשפות fee אשף ----- ישף,
ישפה the Jafper, *Exod.*28.20: 39.13. *Ezek.*28.13.
--- נשף to blow, impel with a current of air,
Exod. 15. 10. *Ifai.* 40. 24. the twilight, the cool
breeze of evening: in *Pfal.* 119. 147. the breath
of morn. ינשוף the owl, which flies abroad in
the twilight, *Lev.* 11. 17. *Deut.* 14. 26. *Ifai.*
34. 11. אשפים conjurers from their pretend-
ed impulfes and infpirations, fee אשף *

שפה to deprefs, humble, reduce to a ftate of fubjection, *Ifai.* 3. 17. others, to fmite with a ftab.
שפחה a maid fervant or flave. משפה fubjection,
depreffion, *Ifai.* 5.7. משפחה a family fubject to
a mafter.

שפט to regulate, judge, determine, plead, execute
judgment: a judge. שופט the fame. שפט,שפוט,
משפט order, ordinance, judgment, cuftom, right,
caufe or plea.†

שפך to pour out, fhed, flip. שפכה an effufion:
a fliding or flipping of the fteps, *Pfal.* 73. 2. a
man's privy member, *Deut.* 23. 1. *quafi fuforium
dices.*

שפל to humble, be low, lay or bring low, be humble, bafe. שפלה low place, vale or low country.

---

* Der. Sheaf. Shove. Chap. W. Safn. Saffwg.   † Suffetes
magiftrates in Carthage. Old Eng. to Shift. affign.

שפלות

שפלות lownefs, rcmiffnefs; rendered idlenefs, *Eccl.* 10.18.*

שפם the upper lip, *Lev.* 13.45. *Ezek.* 24.17,22. *Mic.* 3.7. the hair growing upon it, 2 *Sam.* 19.24. from שפ־ה

שפן to hide; a large kind of moufe: the Egyptian rat which hides in rocks, *Lev.* 11.5. *Deut.* 14.7. *Pfal.* 104.8. *Prov.* 30.26. שפון hid, *Deut.* 23.19.

שפע to overflow, be abundant: abundance, afflu-ence, *Deut.* 39.19. *Job* 22.11: 38.34. *Ezek.* 26.10. a large company, 2 *Kings* 9.17. *Ifai.* 60.6. †

שפק to fuffice, 1 *Kings* 20.10. to fmite the hands in expreffion of pleafure; to be pleafed, *Ifai.* 2.6. fufficiency, *Job* 20.22. to clap, fmite, *Job* 27.23. a ftroke, 36.18. fee ספק ‡

שפר to be fplendid; Chal. and Heb. goodly, flou-rifhing, fair, agreeable, beautiful, *Gen.* 49.21. *Pfal.* 16.6. *Dan.* 3.32. or 4.2: 6.1. שפרה gar-nifhed with beautiful brightnefs, *Job* 26.13. שופר, שפר a trumpet, cornet, made of an horn. אשפר a piece of roafted bullock's flefh, from אש fire, and פר־ a bullock, 2 *Sam.* 6.19. 1 *Chron.* 16.3. שפריר a fplendid tent, royal pavilion, *Jer.* 43.10. שפרפרא the aurora, the morning light, *Dan.* 6. 19.‖

שפת to fet any thing in order, to difpofe: to fet on a pot, 2 *Kings* 4.38. *Ezek.* 24.3. to place, or-dain, *Pfal.* 22.15. *Ifai.* 26.12. שפת, שפתים pots, *Pfal.* 68.13. rather rows of ftones on which the pots were placed; lying among thefe denoted ab-ject flavery, being the place allotted for the vileft flaves: alfo, hooks, ledges, rails, *Ezek.* 50.43.

* Der. Sepelio, Sepulchre. Supplicate. Σιφλος, Σιπαλος, Σφαλλω.
† Sœpe. Sphinx; the Nile overflowed when the Sun was in Leo and Virgo, this was reprefented by the Sphinx half lion and half woman.
‡ Sufficio. Suffice.   ‖ Sparum. Spear. Spray. Sprig.

     משפתים

מִשְׁפְּתִים the divisions in a stable that divide it into distinct stalls, *Gen.* 49. 14. sheepfolds, *Judges* 5. 16. אַשְׁפְּתוּת, אַשְׁפּוֹת, שְׁפוֹת dung, ordure, a dunghill; an Hebrew word of decency like the English *stool*.

שָׁצַף little, small, short, *Isai.* 54. 8.

שָׁקָה to run, move to and fro: to water, overflow, moisten, give drink; to desire, run to eagerly. שַׂק a sack, sackcloth. שִׁיק run about, overflow, *Joel* 2. 24: 3. 13. שׁוּק a street, where people pass to and fro: the parts of the body which move, the shoulder, leg, hip, thigh. תְּשׁוּקָה attendance, eager desire, *Gen.* 3. 16: 4. 7. *Cant.* 7. 10. מֶשֶׁק a running to and fro, *Isai.* 33. 4. בֶּן מֶשֶׁק a steward, a son of moving, *Gen.* 15. 2. שֹׁקֶת a watering trough. שִׁקּוּי drink, moisture. מַשְׁקֶה, שֵׁק a butler, cupbearer. שָׁקַק to run about to and fro: to drench, water plenteously; to desire earnestly. שׁוּקָקָה, שְׁקָקָה longing, panting after, eager appetite, *Psal.* 107. 9. *Isai.* 29. 8. תַּשְׁקֵק thou waterest, *Psal.* 65. 9. הִשְׁתַּקְשֵׁק to run in great numbers, to jostle one against another, *Nah.* 2. 4.---נָשַׁק to smack, kiss; to clash with armour or weapons: to snap, crackle as fire. נְשִׁקָה a kiss, מְשִׁיקוֹת kissing, *Ezek.* 3. 13. נֶשֶׁק armour, armoury, weapons; also to kindle, *Isai.* 44. 15. be kindled, *Ps.* 78. 21. burn, *Ezek.* 39. 9. This word is formed from the sound.*

שָׁקַד to watch, wake; be ready, watchful: to lose no occasion or advantage: to hasten, *Jer.* 1. 12. watched over carefully, *Job* 21. 32. is bound or watched over, *Lam.* 1. 14. an almond tree, which blossoms early, as it were on the first opportunity. מְשֻׁקָּד made like almonds.

---

* Der. Ισχις. Σακκος. Saccus, Sacco. Sack. Aσχος. Σκιυος. Sugere. Suck. Succus. Soak. W. Cufanu.

שקט to be at reft, be quiet: quietnefs.¶

שקל to weigh; to weigh money in receiving and paying, to pay money; to eftimate: a fhekel, the ftandard weight among the Ifraelites, equal to 9*p. wt.* 2⅔ *grs.* the fhekel of filver equalled about 2*s.* 4*d.* 1*f.* of gold about 1*l.* 17*s.* 6*d.* משקל weight. משקלת a plummet or plumb line, 2 *Kings* 21.13. *Ifai.*28.17.*

שקמים, שקמים fycamore or fycamine tree or fruit.†

שקע to fubfide, fink, *Jer.*51.64. be drowned,*Amos* 8.8: 9.5. quenched, funk, *Num.*11.2. fubfided, fettled, *Ezek.*34.18. השקיע caufe to fubfide, fettle and be clear, 32.15. to let down, caufe to fink, *Job* 12.1.‡

שקערירת hollow ftreaks, *Lev.*14.37. from שקע and רר hollows.

שקף to look at an object; to look with regard at, to eye: an opening or window to look out at, 1 *Kings* 6.4: 7.4,5. משקוף the upper door poft, perhaps the window above it, *Exod.*12.7,22,23.‖

שקץ to abominate, naufeate, deteft, abhor: to pollute, make abominable: an abomination or abominable thing. שקוץ the fame.§

שקר to lie, deceive, fpeak or act falfely: falfe, deceitful: a lie, falfehood: falfely, wrongfully. משקר wanton, deceiving, *Ifai.*3.16.

שר־ה to rule, direct, regulate: to have authority, to rule, reign, *Gen.*32.28. *Judg.*9.22. *Prov.*8.16. *Ifai.*32.1. *Hof.* 12. 3. to direct the eyes, view attentively, contemplate, behold, perceive, regard; to regulate the voice in finging, to fing. Chal. to begin, *Ezra* 5. 2. שר the navel, which directs

---

¶ Der. Ασκεθης. Ησυχος. Squat. Scout.   * Scalc. Shilling. † Συκομορος Sycamore.   ‡ Sink.   ‖ Σκεπτεω. Σκεττομωι. Scope. Sceptic.   § Σκυζω, Σκυρος.

the

the nourifhment to the fœtus, *Job* 40.16. *Prov.*
3.8. *Cant.*7.2. *Ezek.*16.4. שׂר a prince, ruler,
captain. שׂרה a princefs. שׂרתי the fame, *Lam.*
1.1. שׂרותיך did fing of thee; rather, were thy
ladies of trade, or principal traders. שׂורה principal, *Ifai.*28.25. משׂרה government, *Ifai.*9.6,7.
השׂיר to make, conftitute princes, *Hofea* 8.4.
משׂורה a meafure or quantity of liquor prefcrib-
ed *Lev.* 19.35. 1 *Chron.* 23.29. *Ezek.* 4.11,16.
משׂרת liquor, fee שׂרת. שׂרית put for שׂארית
the reft, 1*Chron.*12.38. remnant, *Jer.*15.11. שׂרות
bracelets, *Ifai.*3.19. regulated to the arm. שׂור for
סור depart, *Hof.* 9.12. שׂור a watchful enemy,
an obferver. שׂור an ox or bullock, remarkably
fteady in viewing an object. תשׂרי thou refpect-
edft, *Ifai.*57.9. תשׂורה a refpectful prefent, 1 *Sam.*
9.7. שׂרין, שׂריון a coat of mail, a breaft plate or
habergeon, made of plates or fcales regularly difpofed. שׂריה a weapon, dart, directed to an object, *Job* 41.26. שׂר, שׂור a wall, from its regular ftructure, *Gen.*49.6,22. 2*Sam.*22.30. *Pf.*18.
29. *Job* 24.11. *Jer.* 5.10. שׂר a finger. שׂיר,
שׂירה a fong. שׂרר the navel. שׂרר to behold,
view repeatedly, *Job* 36.24. to fing repeatedly,
Zeph. 2.14. שׂרירות, שׂרירות imagination, luft,
obftinacy, ftubbornnefs, what the heart is ftrongly fet upon. שׂררי infidious enemies, ftrict ob-
fervers. שׂרר to bear rule, *Efth.*1.22. משׂרר a
finger. שׂרא Chal. to loofe: be loofed, *Dan.*5.6.
to dwell, remain, *Dan.*2.22. שׂרשׂר a chain which
regulates the fituation of things.---ישׂר to direct,
make ftrait, even, level, right; efteem, right, direct: to go direct, take the ftrait way, 1*Sam.*6.12.
look ftrait, *Prov.* 4.25. right, ftrait, upright,
righteous, meet. ישׂר, יושׂר equity, uprightnefs.
מישׂר,

מִישׁוֹר, מִישׁר equity, uprightnefs: a plain, an even place: ſtrait, plain. ---- נשׁר to lacerate, tear in pieces, 1 *Chron.* 20. 3. an eagle, which tears its food. מִישׁוֹר a ſaw, *Iſai.* 10. 15.*

שׁרב for שׁוּף to burn; parching heat, *Iſai.* 49. 10. parched ground, 35. 7. in Arab. to taſte, drink.†

שׁרביט a royal fceptre, *Eſth.* 4. 11: 5. 2: 8. 4. from שׂר a prince, and שׁבט a fceptre.‡

שׁרג to wreathe, be wreathed or twiſted together, *Job* 40. 17. *Lam.* 1. 14. שׁרגי, שׁרגים branches intangled one in another, *Gen.* 40. 10, 12. *Joel* 1. 17. ‖

שׁרד to remain, leave, be left after the deſtruction of others, *Joſh.* 10. 20. שׂריד one thus left. שׂרד fervice, clothes always left in the fanctuary, *Ex.* 31. 10: 35. 19: 39. 1, 41. alſo, a line which workmen make uſe of to mark how much of their materials muſt remain when the fuperfluities are chipped off, *Iſai.* 44. 13. §

שׁרט to cut, wound, fcarify: שׁרטת a cutting, *Lev.* 19. 28: 21. 5. *Zech.* 12. 3. ¶

שׁרך to twine, bend; to wind, crofs, traverfe. שׂרוך the latchet or fhoe ſtring, *Gen.* 14. 23. *Iſai.* 5. 27. מִשׂרכת traverfing, *Jer.* 2. 23.

שׁרע to ſtretch beyond the uſual fize; to have any thing fuperfluous, *Lev.* 21. 18: 22. 23. הִשְׁתָּרֵעַ that a man can ſtretch himſelf upon it, *Iſai.* 28. 20.

שׁרעף a thought diſtilling, from the heat, *Pſal.* 94. 19: 139. 23. from שׂ which, and רעף diſtil.

שׁרף to burn; a bright firy ferpent: a feraph, *Iſai.* 6. 6. משׂרפה, שׂרפה a burning.**

שׁרץ to breed abundantly as reptiles do; to move, creep: a creeping thing.

---

* Der. Sire, Sir. Meaſure.   W. Meſur.   † Syrup. Shrub.
‡ Σκηπτρον Sceptre.   ‖ Σαργανη.   § Shred.   ¶ Scratch.
** Sharp. Shrivel. Seraph.   W. Sarph.

שרק to be yellow: to hifs, whiftle: fpeckled or yellowifh, *Zech.*1.8. thought to be the proper co-lour of the vine, wine, or flax referred to: a choice noble vine, *Gen.*49.11. *Ifai.*5.2. *Jer.*2.21. שרוק principal plant, *Ifai.*16.8. שריקות fine, *viz.* flax, *Ifai.*19.9. משרוקיתא Chal. a pipe, flute, flagilet, *Dan.*3.5,7,10,15.*

שרש to root, take root, caufe to take root: to root up, eradicate: a root. שרשר wreathen chains, intwined as the roots of trees. שרשרת chains, fee in שר־ח †

שרת to minifter to, officiate, wait upon, ferve in an honourable capacity; miniftry, fervice. משרת a minifter or fervitor: liquor, a preparation of grapes, *Num.*6.3. preparation, cookery, 1 *Sam.*13.9. rendered a pan. שרית the reft, 1 *Chron.*12.38. remnant, *Jer.*15.11. for שארית †

שש to exult, leap for joy, rejoice: fine bright li-nen or cotten cloth. ששה, שש, ששת fix, יששי, ששית fixth, ששים fixty, ששה, ששא to give or take a fixth part, *Ezek.*45.13: 39.2. משוש,יששון joy, mirth, gladnefs. שוש rob, *Ifai.* 10. 13. for שום. שיש, שש fine white Parian marble, 1 *Chron.* 29.2. *Efth.*1.6. יששן, יששון, שושנה the lily, a flower of fix leaves. ---- יששי very aged perfon, 2 *Chron.*36.17. *Job* 12.12: 15.10: 29.8: 32.6.‡

יששר vermilion, *Jer.*22.14. *Ezek.*23.14.

שת־ה to place, put, lay, fet, appoint, difpofe, fet in array: to drink; be drunk, *Lev.*11.34. שית garment, attire to put on, *Pfal.*73.6. *Prov.*7.10. שית ממני let me alone, *i.e.* fet or remove thyfelf from me. *Job* 10. 20. שחת, שח the buttocks, on which men place themfelves, *Ifai.*20.4. 2 *Sam.*

---

* Der. Συριζω, Συριγξ.   † Ριζα. Radix. Root.   ‡ Εξ, Sex, Six. W. Chwech.

10.4. שתות foundations on which buildings are laid, *Pfal.*11.3. שתתים purpofes, foundations; rather refervoirs, *Ifai.*19,10. שתי drunkennefs, *Eccl.*10.17. שתיה drinking, *Efth.*1.8. משתה a feaft, banquet attended with drinking. שתי the warp,arange of threads orderly placed in the loom. שתי fem. of שנים two. שים, שתים שירת thorns. משתיא Chal. a feaft, banquet, *Dan.*5.10. שת Chal. for שש fix, plu. שתין fixty.---נשת to fail, exhauft, be exhaufted,dried,*Ifai.*19.5:41.17. *Jer.* 51.30. נשתונא, נשתון Chal. a letter, an epiftle.*

שתל to plant. שתלי plants, *Pf.*128.3.†

שתם to fhut, clofe, *Num.*20.3,15. rendered to o-pen, to fhut out, exclude, *Lam.*3.8.

שתן to urine, pifs. משתין he that piffeth.

שתק to be ftill, calm, quiet, ceafe, *Pfal.*107. 30. *Prov.*26.20. *Jonah* 1.11,12.‡

שתר to be hid, 1*Sam.*5.9. the fame as סתר

ת

תו the laft letter in the Hebrew alphabet; the anci-ent form of this letter was more like that it bears among the Englifh and modern letters. It was the terminus or crofs of the Egyptians, by which they marked the height of the inundation of the Nile, and it is ftill vifible on the mummies, and almoft on every Egyptian monument that remains. It is a dental, as a numeral it ftands for 400; it is a fervile, and when prefixed 1/t, (from את) forms nouns, as תלמיד a fcholar; 2. forms particles, as תחת under, from נחת to defcend; 3. denotes the 2d perfon future fing. and plu. mafc. and fem. of verbs; 4. poftfixed, 2d perfon fing. preter; 5. is

---

* Der. Sitis, Site. Set, Sit. Seat. Stout. Status. State. Sedeo. Sedo.
† Settle, Stool. Aλoς. Saltus.   ‡ Taceo. Stack, Stock.

put in regimine for ה; 6. forms many nouns fem.
as מלכות; 7. is paragogic and is annexed (1.)to
an infin. יבשת to be dry, יכלת to be able, שנאת
to hate; (2.)to nouns fem. תפארת *exquisite* ornament; (3.)to verbs תמותת thou shalt *entirely* slay.

תא־ה to limit, bound, point out, set bounds to: a
chamber. תאו,תוא the oryx or buffalo, rendered
wild ox, *Deut*.14.5. wild bull, *Isai*.51.20.---יתא
put for יאתא he came, *Deut*.23.21. see אתה ---
תאוה desire. תאות utmost bounds, perhaps de-
sireable production, *Gen*.49.26. from או־ה*

תאב to pine or long for, *Psal*.119.40,174. תאבה
longing, 119.20. מתאב abhor, abominate,*Amos*
6.8. perhaps for מתעב †

תאלה a curse, *Lam*.3.65. see אלה

תאם to couple together, *Exod*. 26. 24: 36. 29. to
bear twins, *Cant*.4.2: 6.6. a twin. תום, תאום
the same.‡

תאן a fig-tree: a fig, see more in אנ־ה ‖

תאר to delineate, draw, mark out: form, linea-
ment, visage.

תב Chal. to return, *Dan*.4.31. to restore, *Ezra* 5.
5: 6.5. to answer. — יתב Chal. to sit, *Dan*.7.9.
dwell, settle, *Ezra* 4.17,10. תבה an ark, chest,
see בה---תבואה income, &c. see בא---נתיב,נתב
a path, high road.§

תבל confusion: the earth, see in בל

תבן straw: מתבן place for straw, floor, *Isai*.25.10.

תבנית a model. תבונה reason, see in בן

תבוסה destruction, see in בס

תבר Chald. to break, *Dan*.2.42. brittle. Heb.שבר

תוגה forrow, see in יגה in נה

תגרה conflict, blow, see גר־ה

* Der. Θεω. Τιφημι.   † Ποθω. Opto. Tabeo. Tabes.   ‡ Διδυ
μος; Thomas. Teem. Team.   ‖ Sp. Tuna.   § Θιβτ.

תד,

תד, תודה see ידה---יתד' a pin, nail, ſtake: paddle, *Deut*.23.13.*

תדר Chal. תדירא continually, *Dan*.6.16,20.

תה־ה to be without form, order, or regularity; a waſte chaos, *Iſai*.5.6. תהו without form, vain, vanity, emptineſs, nothingworth, an idol; barren deſart. ---התיו brought, *Iſai*.21.14. come ye, *Jer*. 12.9. for התאיו from אתה

תהלה praiſe, &c. ſee הל

תהם, תהום the deep, depth, deep place, ſee הם

תו־ה to mark, make marks; limit, *Pſal*.78.41. a mark, *Ezek*.9.4,6. Chal. to tremble, be amazed, *Dan*.3.24. ---תוי for תאוי my deſire, *Job* 31.35. from או־ה

תום ſee above in תאם

תוך and תור ſee in תך and תר without the ו

תז to ſhake or cut off, *Iſai*.18.5.†

תזנות whoredoms, ſee זנ־ה

נתח---תח to cut in pieces: a piece.‡

תחלה beginning: תחלא ſickneſs: תוחלה hope, ſee theſe under חל־ה

תחנה ſupplication: camp, ſee חנ־ה

תחר־ה to ſurround, incloſe oneſelf, *Jer*.22.15. to go or run round, 12.5. תחרא an harbergeon or coat of mail ſurrounding the body, *Exod*.28.32: 39.23.‖

תחש a badger; perhaps violet coloured: blue.

תהרת under, beneath, &c. ſee נהרת

תיש an he-goat kept for breed, ſee שש

תך to be in the midſt, or between, *Deut*.33.3. תוך middle, midſt. תוך, תך deceit, fraud, *Pſal*.10.7: 55.11: 72.14. בתך, בתוך in the midſt, among, תוכי, תכיים. תיכונה, תיכון middle, middlemoſt. a

* Der. Tidy.   † to Toſs. Teaſe, Toſe wool. Fr. Toiſon, fleece. ‡ Notch.   ‖ Θωραξ Thorax.

     peacock,

peacock, perhaps from its noife, 1 *Kings* 10. 22.
2*Chron*.9.21. תכך repeated frauds, *Prov*.29.13.
--- נתך to be poured out, fufe, melt; melted:
התוך a melting, *Ezek*.22.22.*

תוכה reproof, &c. fee in כח

תכל, תכלת blue, azure.---תכלה end, &c. fee כלה
תכן to direct, adjuft, weigh, meafure: to be equal,
proportionate: have adjufted, fet firm or fure,*Ifai*.
40.13. מתכנת, תכנית, תכן. proportion, adjuft-
ment; rendered tale, fum, meafure, pattern, ftate,
compofition.---תכון place, ftation, fee כן †

תל־ה to raife on high, hang up: an heap raifed up:
ftrength; raifed, undemolifhed ftate, *Jofh*.11.13.
תלי a hanger, quiver, hung on the fhoulder,*Gen*.
27.3. תלל to elevate, heap up on high, *Ezek*.
17.22. תוללינו they that wafted us, laid us on
heaps; or, our lamentations, *i. e.* they who caufe
us to lament. תלא to be in fufpence, doubt,
Deut.28.66. bend, be inclined to, *Hof*.11.7.---
תלאה wearinefs, &c. from לא־ה ‡

תלג fnow, *Dan*.7.19. Heb. שלג

תולד generation, fee under לד

מתלהלה a madman, fee under לה

תלם a furrow, ridge in a ploughed field: to
plough.‖

תלון murmuring, fee under לן

תלע (to tear, corrode) תולעת, תולעה a worm:
worm colour, crimfon, fcarlet made from the*Ker-
mes* a fmall worm. מתלע cloathed in fcarlet,*Nah*.
2.3. the jaw teeth or grinders.

תלפיות armory, battlements,*Cant*.4.4. from תל־ה
and פי an edge.

תמ־ה to finifh, make an end of, complete, perfect:

* Der. Τοχος. Θακης. Attack. Tack. Tackle. † Τιχνη. Τεχτων. Tech-
nical: Σταχαιν ‡ Θολος. Tollo. Till. Tall. W. Tâl ‖ Τιλμα Tellus.
be

be finiſhed, compleated: to fail, faint: to ſum up, take the ſum total, 2 *Kings* 22.4. integrity. Chal. there. Heb. שמה Chal. to wonder, be aſtoniſhed. התם to make an end of. תם an end, *Jer.* 1. 3. perfect. תמה, תם integrity, uprightneſs, per-fection. תמים Thummin, perfection (ſee אורים in אר־ה) alſo perfect, whole, ſound, without ble-miſh, upright, ſincere. מתם ſoundneſs, *Pſal.* 38. 3. *Iſai.* 1. 6. תמהין Chal. wonders, miracles, aſto-niſhment. תמם to ſhew oneſelf perfect.---יתם to bereave. יתום an orphan, fatherleſs. תמים for תאמים coupled. תומם for תאמים *Gen.* 25. 24. twins, ſee תאם *

תמד, תמיד, התמיד continually, always, perpetu-ally.†

תמז Thammuz, an idol of the ſun, *Ezek.* 8. 14. from תם and מז Chal. heat.

תמך to take hold of, uphold, retain.

אתמול, תמול, תמל heretofore, yeſterday, from תם finiſh, and כל cut off.

תמונה likeneſs. תימן ſouth, ſee under מן

תמר (to ſuſtain) תמרה a palm tree. תימר, תמר high columns, pillars riſing like palm trees, *Cant.* 3. 6. *Joel* 2. 30. תמרור the-ſame, *Jer.* 31. 21. בעל תמר Baal Tamar, *Judg.* 20. 23. the lord of palms.---תמורה exchange, and תמרר bitterneſs, ſee under מר ‡

תמותה death, from מרת

תנ־ה to moan; talk of, rehearſe, lament, *Judg.* 5. 11: 11. 20. תנין a dragon, ſerpent. תנים croco-dile (from their doleful noiſe) or water ſerpent, from תן ſerpent, and ים water. תנין Chal. Heb. שני ſecond, *Dan.* 7. 5. תנינות ſecond time, 2. 7.---נתן to give, grant, beſtow, make, cauſe, permit,

---

*. Der. Themis, the goddeſs of oracles. Θαυμα. Θαυμαζω. † Θαρα.
‡ Timber.

utter, yield, fend forth; the fenfe muſt be determined by the context. נתינים Nethinims, perfons given to the prieſts for fervile offices, probably the Gibionites. מתנה, מתן, מתרת a gift,
hence תנה to comfort, hire by a premium, *Hof.*
9.10. אתנן, אתנה reward, hire.

תנובה fruit, fee under נב־ה

תנך (to be tender) תנוך tip of the ear.

תנומה flumber, fee under נם

תנופה a fhaking, wave offering, fee נף

תנור a furnace, oven, fee in נר

נתם --- תם to demolifh, mar, *Job* 30.13.

תע־ה to err, wander, ftray: caufe to err, feduce:
ftagger, caufe to ftagger, *Job* 12.25. *Ifai.* 19.4.
תועה error, *Neh.*4.8.*Ifai.*32.6. תעתע to err greatly: great error, *Jer.*10.15:51.18. a deceiver, *Gen.*
27.12. behaved wrong, towards the prophets, 2
*Chron.*36.16. --- נתעה are broken, *Job* 4.10. for
נלתעו fee לתע

תעב to loathe, abominate; be abominable, act a-
bominably. תועבה an abomination.

תעודה a teftimony, fee under ער

תעלה aqueduct; cure. תעלל infant: device, fee על

תענית heavinefs, fee under ענ־ה

תועפורת weight of filver, fee under עף

תער (to cut) fharp inftrument; a knife, razor: a
fheath or fcabbard which contains the inftrument.*

תף (to fmite) a drum, tabret, timbrel: תפרת the
fame; alfo Tophet, fee below. תפף to play with
timbrels, *Pfal.*68.25. tabring, *Nah.*2.7.†

תפוה an apple, an apple-tree.

תפל crude, undigefted: untempered cement, *Ezek.*
13.10,11,14,15:22.28. unfavory, infipid, *Job*6.

* Τιφω. Tero. Torc. Tire.   † Tympanum. Tabret. Τυππα. Τι-
πος. Tap. Tabor. Tabret. Thump. Type.

6. indigefted, foolifh, abfurd, *Lam.*2.14. תפלה
folly, *Job* 1.22: 24.12. *Jer.*22.13. ---- תתפל for
תפתל thou wilt fhew thyfelf forward, 2*Sam.*22.
27. fee פתל --- תפלה prayer, fee פל־ה
תפיני for תאפיני baken pieces, *Lev.*6.21. fee אפ־ה
תפוצה difperfion, fee under פצ־ה
תפר to few, join, *Gen.* 3. 7. *Job* 16. 5. *Eccl.* 3. 7.
*Ezek.*13.18.*
תפש to hold, catch, feize, handle; lay over with,
*Hab.*2.19.
תפרת Tophet from תף a drum ; drums were beat-
en to drown the children's cries which were offered
to Moloch. תפתיא Chal. (from the Heb. שפרת)
officers, magiftrates, *Dan.* 3.2,3.
תץ --- נתץ to break, beat, throw down, deftroy;
dafh out, *Pfal.*58.6. ---- תוצא a going out, from
יצא
תק---נתק to pull down, pluck afunder, fee in נ
תקוה a line; expeftation, fee קו־ה
תקומה power to ftand, from קמ־ה
תקן to fet in order, make ftrait, *Eccl.*1.15:7.13:12.
9. to be eftablifhed, *Dan.*4.33.
תקע to fix, infix, faften, *Exod.*10.19. to fix a tent,
*Gen.*31. to ftrike hands, *i.e.* bargain, *Job* 17. 3.
*Prov.*6.1: 11.15: 17.18: 22.26. to nail, *Judg.* 4.
14: 16.14. 1*Sam.*3.10. 1*Chron.*10.10. *Ifai.*22.23,
25. to ftab, *Judg.*3.21. 2*Sam.*18.14. to clap hands
for joy, *Pf.*47.1. *Nah.*3.19. to trumpet, found a
a trumpet, *Num.*10.3. found or blaft, *Pf.*150.3.
תקוע a trumpet, *Ezek.*7.14.†
תקף to be ftrong, *Dan.*4.17,19. prevail againft, o-
vercome, *Job* 14.20: 15.24. *Eccl.*4.12. might, pre-
vailing power, authority, *Efth.*9.29: 10.2. *Dan.*
11.17. תקיף mightier, *Eccl.*6.10.----תקופה revolution, from יקף in קף

* Der. Παπτω.   † Attack.

תר to turn, to turn about; inveſtigate, ſearch out:
a turn, ſucceſſion, *Eſth.* 2. 12, 15. תור a vow,
border, wreath, ornament, *Cant.*17.17. תר, תור
a turtle dove. תר Chal. form, diſpoſition, 1*Chro.*
17.17. (Heb. תאר) תורין Chal. oxen, *Ezra* 6.9.
*Dan.*4.22. תרי Chal. two, *Ezra* 6.17. *Dan.* 4.
26. תרתין two, ſecond, *Ezra* 4. 24. *Dan.* 5.31.
תרים chapmen, merchants, who go about to ſell
wares, 1*Kings* 10.15. 2*Chron.*9.14. תורה a law,
ſee ירה in רה. --- יתר to exceed, ſtretch beyond,
excell; to remain over and above, to be left as a
reſidue. יתר he maketh, 2*Sam.* 22. 23. perhaps
for יתן, ſee the parallel place, *Pſal.*18.32. יתר,
יתרין, מותר, יותר, יתר, יתרה reſidue; excellence, a-
bundance, profit, pre-eminence. מיתר, יותר a
cord, ſtring, or withy, which may be diſtended.
מיתר איש Mithras, *i.e.* the extenſive fire. יתרת
the caul, redundance upon the liver, the midriff.
--- נתר to looſen, ſet free: to leap, *Lev.* 11. 21.
move, be moved, *Job* 37.1. to unlooſe,6.9. *Pſal.*
146.7. *Iſai.* 58. 6. diſſolved, *Hab.*3.6. to ſhake
out of, *Dan.*4.11. Nitre, which is ſoon diſſolved,
Prov 25.20. *Jer.*2.22.*

תרגם to expound, paraphraſe, interpret, *Ezra*
4.7.†

תרבית, תרבות multitude, ſee רב

תרזה the cypreſs, Ilex or oak, *Iſai.*44.14.‡

תרומה an heave offering: deceit. תרמית the
ſame, ſee רם

תרן a long pole, maſt, beacon, *Iſai.*30.17: 33.23.
*Ezek.*27.5.

תרע Chald. a gate, door, *Dan.*2.49. mouth of a
furnace, 3.26. תרעיא porters, *Ezra* 7.24.‖

* Der. W. Hydr. † It. Turchimanno, Turchman, Turcoman,
Drogoman, Drogman, an interpreter. ‡ Δρυς, Trees, Torches.
Θυραι, Thyrſes. ‖ Door, Obturo.

תרף,

תרף, תרפים Teraphim; images. תרופה medicine, fee רפ־ה *

תרשיש Tarſhiſh, a precious ſtone; a Chryſolite, from תר and שיש vivid: alſo, the name of a place.

תירש new wine, fee under רש

תש to compreſs. תיש an he-goat kept for breed-ing.---נתש to extirpate, root out, pluck up: de-ſtroy, *Pſ.*9.6. *Jer.*12.17. forſaken, *Jer.*18.14.

---תשאורת, noiſe, fee שא־ה

תשובה a return. תושב a ſojourner, fee in שב

תושיה, תשיה reality, fee ישה in שה

תשומה a putting, fee שם

תשע, תשעה תשעים nine. תשעים ninety. תשיעי, תשיעי, תשיעת, תשיעית ninth.---תשועה ſalvation, from ישע in שע

תשוקה deſire, fee under שוק

תותח ſome weapon, dart, club, *Job* 41.29.†

ברוך יהוה אלהי ישראל מהעולם ועד העולם
אמן ואמן

---

* Der. Θειαπευω. Trepido, Tremble. Βειτας Brat. † With Mem prefixed, Mattock.

מֹשֶׁה כָּתַב אֵלֵינוּ

צֶדֶק חָטָף גֵּזַע סָר

A COMPENDIOUS

GRAMMAR of the *Hebrew* Tongue.

I.

1. The Hebrew letters are twenty-two:

Form	Finals	Sam.	Name	Sound*
א 1		⋏	Aleph	a,
ב 2		ꝺ	Beth	b,
ג 3		˥	Gimel	g,
ד 4		⸲	Daleth	d,
ה 5		ꝗ	He	e,
ו 6		⸲	Vau	u,
ז 7		⅄	Zain	z,
ח 8		Ɡ	Heth	h,
ט 9		ⱱ	Teth	th,
י 10		ꟽ	Iod	i,
כ 20	500 ך	ꝰ	Caph	k,
ל 30		ⱬ	Lamed	l,
מ 40	600 ם	ꟺ	Mem	m,
נ 50	700 ן	ꞁ	Nun	n,
ס 60		ꞷ	Shamech	ſh,
ע 70		ⱱ	Oin	o,
פ 80	800 ף	ꝯ	Pe	p,
צ 90	900 ץ	ꟹ	Tſaddi	f,
ק 100		ꝗ	Quoph	q,
ר 200		ꝗ	Reſh	r,
ש 300	¯	ꟽ	Sin	s,
ת 400		⋏	Tau	t,

2. Hebrew is read from right hand to left: when no vowel falls between two conſonants, ſupply in reading a ſhort *e*.

3. The vowels are five ו, ע, י, ה, א, all the other letters are conſonants.

4. Theſe 11 letters איתן משה וכלב are called ſervile, becauſe they ſerve all the purpoſes of grammatical inflections, by ſupplying the place of pronouns, particles, &c. See each of theſe letters in the lexicon.

* The Aleph is founded as *a* in *all*; Gimel as *g* in *go*; He as *e* in there; Vau as *oo* in *moon*; Heth as *h* in *hart*; Iod as *ee*; but before a vowel *y* as in *year*; Caph the aſpirated *k*, a ſound familiar to the Welſh; Oin as *o* in *cold*, but before a vowel *ong* as in *wrong*, or the French *on*; Tſaddi as *ſ* in *pleaſure*; Quoph as in *q* or *k* ſoft as in *kill*; Sin as *s* in *ſin*.

5. A root is a word, whence others are formed, ufually of three letters: the eleven letters that are not fervile always make part of the root, and tho' *radical* letters are never *fervile*, except ט when ufed for ת, yet fervile letters are often radical.

6. With regard to the organs of pronunciation, the letters may be confidered as

Dentals	ד, ט, ת	Liquid Dentals	נ, ר, ל
Labials	ו, ב, פ	Liquid Labial	מ
Palatines	כ, ג, ק	Liquid Palatine	ל
Sibilants	צ, ז, ס, שׁ		

Note, ר, נ, מ, ל as liquids are fometimes interchanged, as ע and צ are from their fimilitude.

II.   *Of Nouns.*

1. Nouns have two genders, mafculine and feminine; and two numbers, fingular and plural.

2. Feminine nouns are diftinguifhed from mafculine by their ending in ה or ת fervile, by the addition of which they are formed from their mafculines, thus מלך a king, מלכה a queen, מלכות a kingdom; but nouns that end in י mafculine, end in ת only, as מצרי an Egyptian man, מצרית an Egyptian woman; בן a fon, בת for בנת a daughter.

3. The plu. mafculine ends in ם or ים, as מלכם or מלכים kings: the plu. fem. ends in ות as מלכות queens; but ית or ות fing. makes יות in the plu. as מצריות Egyptian women; מלכיות kingdoms: thefe feminine plurals often drop their ו

4. Some fem. nouns in ה fingular end in תים plural; but then the plural is fuppofed to be reftrained to *two* only, as שׁנה a year, שׁנתים two years.

5. Some feminine nouns have in the plural both feminine and mafculine termination, by way of eminence,

nence, as במה an high place, במויתם exceeding
high places.

6. Nouns fem. fing. in regimine, or when connected, change ה into ת, as תורת יהוה the law of
Jehovah: nouns plural in regimine drop their ם
as מלכי ארץ kings of the earth.

6. A fimple degree of comparifon takes מ or מן
before the word compared, fee מ or מן in the Lexicon ; an higher degree takes ב or מאד fee Lexicon.

7. The Hebrews have no cafes, yet the following ferviles anfwer to the cafes of the Latins, Gen.
prefixes ה or של *of*; Dat. ל *to* or *for*; Acc. את *the*;
Voc ה O; Abl. מ *by*, or *from*.

III. *Of Pronouns.*

1. Perfonal Pronouns have three perfons, 1*ft*, אני
or אנכי *I*; plu. אנחנו, נחנו *We, Us.*　2*d*, אתה, את,
mafc. אתי fem. *Thou*; plu. אתם mafc. אתנה, אתן,
fem. *Ye, You.*　3*d*, הוא *He*, היא *She*; plu. הם,
המה mafc. הנה, הן, fem. *They.*

2. Inftead of the pronouns the following parts
are affixed to words, י or ני *Me* or *Mine*; plu. נו *Us,
Ours.* כה, ך, mafc. ך, fem. יך, כי, *Thou, Thine.*
כם mafc. כן fem. *Ye, Yours.* ני, הו, ו, *His, Him*;
נה, ה, *Her.* מו, הם, ם, mafc. הן, ן, fem. *Them,
Their.*

3. Relative pronoun, אשר *Who*, inftead of it ש
or ה is prefixed, fee ש and ה in Lexicon. Demonftrative, הלז, הלזה, הלזו, הלו, זה, זו, *This*; fem.
אלה, אל. זאת. *Thefe.* Interrogative, מי *Who?*
מן, מה *What?* מ prefixed alone afks a Queftion,
fee Lexicon.

IV. *Of Verbs.*

1. The Conjugations, as they are improperly
called, were firft named from the old example פעל
Pol, hence comes נפעל Nepol; הפעיל Epoil; הפעל
Epol;

Epol; and התפעל Etpol: or as they are termed in other Grammars, Kal, Niphal, Hiphil, Huphal or Hophal, and Hithpahel.

2. Verbs are faid to have three Conjugations, 1. Pol or Kal; 2. Epoil or Hiphil; 3. Etpol or Hithpahel: Pol denotes mere action, as פקד *he vifited*; its paffive Nepol prefixes נ in the preter tenfe, as נפקד *he was vifited:* Epoil is cafually active, it prefixes ה and inferts י after the fecond radical, to the preter, as הפקיד *he caufed another to vifit*; its paffive Epol drops the י as הפקד *he was caufed to vifit or be vifited*. Etpol the reciprocal conjugation is formed from Pol, by prefixing הת in the preter, as התפקד *he vifited himfelf*.

3. Each conjugation has 3 moods, 2 tenfes, 1 participle, Pol has two; all have 2 numbers, 3 perfons and 2 genders, as in the following example.

4. Example of a verb through mood, tenfe and perfon.   **Indicative Mood.**

Plu.   Preter Tenfe, *vifited.*   *Sing.*

Fem.	*Maf.*	*Fem.*	*Maf.*
	פקדו *they,*	She פקדה	פקד *he,*
פדקתן	פקדתם *ye,*	פקדתי*	פקדת *thou,*
	פקדנו *we,*		פקדתי *I,*

Future Tenfe, *will vifit.*

Fem.	*Maf.*	*Fem.*	*Maf.*
תפקדנה	יפקדו *they,*	She תפקד	יפקד *he,*
תפקדנה	תפקדו *ye,*	תפקדי	תפקד *thou,*
	נפקד *we,*		אפקד *I.*

Imperative.

vifit ye פקדנה   פקדו | פקרי   פקד *vifit thou*

Infinitive, *to vifit.*

פקד or פקוד

Participle Active, *Vifiting.*

פוקדות   פוקדים   פוקדה   פוקר

* The 2d perfon feminine fingular feldom ends as the firft.

Participle Paſſive, *viſited.*

פקודות   פקורים   פקודה   פקוד

5. Example of a regular verb through every conjugation in the 3d perſon ſingular.

3dConj.	2d Conjugation.		1st Conjugation.	
Etpol.	Epol.	Epoil.	Nepol.	Pol.
התקפד	הפקד	הפקיד	נפקד	פקד *Pret.*
יתפקד	יפקד	יפקיד	יפקד	יפקד *Fut.*
התקפד	*none*	הפקיד	הפקד	הפקד *Imper.*
התקפד	הפקד	הפקיד	הפקד,פקוד	פקד *or* פקוד *Infin.*
מתפקד	מפקד	מפקיד	נפקד	פוקד *Par.act.*
				פקוד *Par.paſ.*

6. Throughout all the conjugations the *perſonal* affixes are added, and the particles declined as in Pol.

7. In Nepol the נ is prefixed only to the preter and participle, but ה to the imperative & infinitive.

8. In Epoil, Epol and Etpol, the formative ה is always dropt after another ſervile, ſo throughout the future, and מ prefixed to the particles of each.

9. Epol is the ſame as Epoil, the formative י being dropt, as it is alſo often in Epoil itſelf.

10. In Etpol verbs beginning with ש or ס tranſpoſe ת as השתמר for התשמר, verbs beginning with צ tranſpoſe and change it into ט as נצטדק for נתצדק. In Chaldee verbs beginning with ז tranſpoſe ת and change it into ד *Dan.*2.9.

V. *Irregular Verbs,*

1. Are either defective, *i.e.* drop a radical letter, or reduplicate, *i.e.* double one or more radicals.

2. Defectives have either *two* radicals only, or י or נ for their *firſt*, or ה for their *laſt*, from the old example פעל, thoſe that drop the firſt radical are called defective in *pe* פ; thoſe that drop the ſecond, defective in *oin* ע; thoſe that drop the third, defective in *lamed* ל.

3. Verbs with but two radicals often take ו before the laſt, as יָשׂוּם from שָׂם ; and in Epol before the former, as הוּקָם from קָם

4. Verbs with י for their firſt radical, often drop it in the future, imperative and infinitive of Pol, to which laſt they poſtfix ת (לקח *to take*, follows this form) and in Nepol and Epoil change their י into ו

5. Verbs with נ for their firſt radical, drop it in the future, imperative and infinitive of Pol, and in the preter of Nepol, and thro' out Epoil and Epol.

6. In Etpol the two latter kind of verbs are regular.

7. Verbs with ה for their laſt radical, often drop it, or change it into י, and generally form the infinitive by changing ה into ות

8. Verbs with י or נ for their firſt radical, and ה for their laſt, ſometimes drop both firſt and laſt radical.

9. The verb נתן *to give*, often drops both its נ's.

10. In verbs א is often dropt after א ſervile, and נ and ת before נ and ת ſervile.

11. Reduplicate verbs are regular, except thoſe reſembling נלל in ſome forms uſe ו inſtead of the laſt radical, as סבותי for סבבתי ; and in Etpol, and ſometimes in other conjugations, take ו after the firſt radical.

12. Pattern of a verb defective in Pe-iod, יָשׁב *to dwell*.

Etpol.	Epol.	Epoil.	Nepol.		Pol.	
הִתִישׁב	הושׁב	הושׁיב	נושׁב		יָשׁב	*Preter*
	יושׁב	יושׁיב	יושׁב		יֵשׁב	*Future*
regular	notus'd	הושׁיב	הושׁב		שֵׁב	*Imperative*
allthro'	הושׁב	הושׁיב	הושׁב		שֶׁבֶת	*Infinitive*
	מושׁב	הושׁיב	נושׁב		יושׁב	*Part. act.*
					יָשׁוּב	*Part. paſſ.*

13. Pattern of a verb defective in Pe-nun,
נסך *to pour.*

Etpol.	Epol.	Epoil.	Nepol.	Pol.	
התנסך	הסך	הסיך	נסך	נסך	*Preter*
regular	יסך	יסיך	ינסך	יסך	*Future*
	notus'd	הסיך	הנסך	סך	*Imperative*
	הסך	הסיך	הנסך	סכת	*Infinitive*
	מסך	מסיך	נסך	נוסך	*Par. act.*
				נסוך	*Par. paſſ.*

14. Pattern of a defective verb of two radicals,
שם or שום *to place.*

Epol.	Epoil.	Nepol.	Pol.	
הושם	השים	נשום	שם	*Preter*
יושם	ישים	ישום	ישום	*Future*
notus'd	השים	השום	שום	*Imperative*
הושם	השים	השום	שום	*Infinitive*
מושם	משים	נשום	שום	*Part. act.*
			שום	*Part. paſſ.*

15. Pattern of a verb defective in Lamed-he,
גלה *to reveal.*

Etpol.	Epol.	Epoil.	Nepol.	Pol.	
התגלה	הגלה	הגלה	נגלה	גלה *Fe.* גלתה	*pre.*
יתגלה	יגלה	יגלה	יגלה	יגלהינל or יגלה	*fut.*
התגלה	notus'd הגלה	הגלה	הגלה	גלה *Fe.* גלי	*imp*
התגלות	הגלות	הגלות	הגלות	נגלו or גלות	*infi.*
תתגלה	מגלה	מגלה	נגלה	גולה *Fe.* גולה	*p.a.*
				גלוי	*p.p.*

VI. *Of Paragogic and Servile Letters.*

1. For the ferviles as well as paragogic letters,
fee them refpectively in the body of the Lexicon;
only obferve that paragogic letters are fix, א,ה,ו,י
נ ,ת and found at the end of words, where they

feem annexed only for found, but in reality fupply the place of adverbs.

VII. *The Syntax.*

RULE 1. The verb agrees with its noun, in
number, cafe and gender, as הארץ היתה *Gen.*1.2.
the earth was; and ver.3. יהי אור *let there be light.*

*Obf.*1. Sometimes a noun feminine is joined to
a verb mafculine, for the fake of dignity, as *Gen.*
1.14. יהי מארת *let there be luminaries,* i.e. *eminent
luminaries.*

Obf. 2. A noun plural, fignifying collectively
or diftributively, with a verb fingular יהי מארת.
Joel 1. 20. בהמות השרה תערוג *the beafts of the
field fhall cry,* i.e. *each of the beafts.*

Obf. 3. A verb plural with a noun fingular, as
*Prov.*28.1. נסו רשע *the wicked flee,* i.e. *each wicked man.*

*Obf.*4. The plural word expreffing the true God
has a verb fingular, as *Gen.* 1. 1. אלהים ברא *the
Aleim created.*

RULE 2. The adjective agrees with its fubftan-
tive in gender and number, as בן חכם *a wife fon.*

Obf. 1. Neverthelefs adjectives mafculine are
joined with fubftantives feminine, & *vice verfa,* as
*Gen.*1.16. המארת הגדלים *the great lights. Deut.*
1.28. ערים גדלת *great cities.* See above *Rule* 1.
Obf. 1.

*Obf.*2. Adjectives, numerals alone excepted, are
placed after their fubftantives, if otherwife, the
verb *to be* is underftood.

*Obf.*3. An adjective, having two fubftantives of
different genders, is moftly mafculine; the fame
may be faid of a verb and two nouns. See *Gen.*2.
1. and *Job* 1. 13.

Obf.

Obf. 4. An adjective or pronoun with two fub-ftantives is put in the plural number, as 1*Kings* 1. 21. and *Gen.*1.27.

Obf. 5. An adjective fingular is joined with a noun plural, fignifying diftributively, *as Gen.*27. 29. ארריך ארור *curfed are they that curfe thee*, i.e. *every one.*

RULE 3. The infinitives of verbs are ufed as fubftantives, and have מ, ל, כ, ב prefixed.

Obf. 1. An infinitive added to a verb frequently denotes fucceffion, as ברך אברכך *Gen.* 22.17. *bleffing I will blefs thee*, i.e. *continually blefs.*

RULE 4. The conjunctive ו prefixed to a verb, will fometimes fupply the want of the figns of perfon, mood and tenfe, and unite it in fignification to a preceding verb, *e. g. Gen.* 1. 28. וכבשה *and fubdue it*, **for** כבשוה *fubdue ye it.* See *Exod.*12. 23. and *Joel* 1.16.

F I N I S.

www.ingramcontent.com/pod-product-compliance
Lightning Source LLC
Chambersburg PA
CBHW020846270326
41928CB00006B/579